MUDLARKS
TREASURES FROM THE THAMES

JASON SANDY

Portraits by
TOM HARRISON

Design by
KIRSTI SCOTT

Illustrations by
CORAL PEARCE

Before going mudlarking in London, you must obtain a Thames Foreshore Permit from the Port of London Authority. You must report all objects you find that could be of archaeological interest to the Museum of London. The export of archaeological objects more than 50 years old from the United Kingdom to any destination requires a UK license.

TO MALAIKA AND JAYDEN

Millennium Bridge with St. Paul's Cathedral in background (Jason Sandy).

CONTENTS

Foreword 2

Introduction 3

Mudlarking We Will Go 4

The Art of Smoking 12

Clay Pipe Making: The Victorian Way 17

Ancient Pottery 22

Colorful Utopian Visions 34

The Mystery of Thames Garnets 44

Bellarmine Jugs and Witch Bottles 50

Pirates of the River Thames 56

Colorful Glass Beads 62

Lost and Found Toys 70

Ancient Jewelry 78

Thames Bling 86

Bottles Filled with History 94

Victorian Bottles and Glass Artwork 102

Musical Instruments and Noisemakers 110

Seal the Deal 120

Ancient Sacred River 126

Modern Sacred River 132

Fantastic Beasts of the Thames 138

Butcher, Baker, and Candlestick Maker 148

Lost, Found, and Returned 156

Buttons with Backstories 166

Weapons and Warfare 174

Death on the River 184

A Thread Through Time 192

Keep It Together! 202

Looking Good 212

At The Dinner Table 222

Coins, Tokens, and Forgeries 230

Love, Sex, and Equality 240

Buckle Up 248

Searching for Evidence of the Mayflower 256

Lost for Words 262

Working River 270

Back in Time 280

Liquid Legacy 290

Recommendations 298

Acknowledgments 299

Index 300

FOREWORD

One of the biggest thrills of mudlarking is coming across something strange and exciting along the river and identifying where it came from. Every piece helps tell a story of who and what has been there before you. Mudlarks are the history enthusiasts who discover these treasures along the Thames.

I have had the pleasure of learning about the many artifacts found by mudlarks through Jason's articles in *Beachcombing* magazine. For the past five years, he has collected photos and stories from this unique community in London and shared its finds, research, and passion in a series of articles. Each story has tackled an aspect of mudlarking, and Jason has captured the excitement of special finds in each mudlark's own words. Jason's mudlarking pieces are always a highlight for many readers, with history, discovery, and mystery woven together. As stand-alone pieces, they are a delight to read. Assembled here in book form, they paint a vivid story of the River Thames and the animals and people who have made the area their home.

The shore of the Thames has been inhabited for millions of years, first by animals and then by humans. Mammoths and rhinos walked the prehistoric shores of the Thames, and mudlarks can still find their fossilized remains today. Look carefully and you might find an ancient tool from early hunter-gatherers who settled near the site of London around 6,000 BC. An eagle eye might spot a red piece of pottery or tile from ancient Romans who arrived in the first century AD. Because of its ideal location on the Thames, London has thrived in the same location for millennia—which means that there are thousands of years of prehistorical, historical, man-made, and natural finds in this one spot, just waiting to be found.

Imagine heading out to the edge of the River Thames as the tide makes its way back out to the sea. Underfoot, the receding water reveals the foreshore, the part of the riverbed that is uncovered between high and low tides. Because this area is submerged underwater for most of the day, it's coated with mud and slick rocks. But spend a little time looking at the ground, and you start to notice the anomalies—objects whose shape, color, texture, or size make them stand out from the rest of the background items and mud.

Mudlarks in London are archaeologists, biologists, historians, explorers, hikers, and teachers. They head out to scour the foreshore, ready to find something that's either been buried in the river for eons or that was dropped in the water 50 years ago. They need to be able to visually sort through the multicolored riverbed and find interesting pieces hidden in the mud. Online research, contacting fellow mudlarks and experts, and a knowledge of local history help them identify their finds.

The best part for the rest of us is when they share their treasures with the world through articles, social media posts, online blogs, videos, television, and books. Thanks to the energy, enthusiasm, knowledge, and generosity of Thames mudlarks, we can all learn about the people and animals that have called London home throughout the ages. I thoroughly enjoyed producing this book showcasing some of the wonders these modern treasure hunters have found in *Mudlarks: Treasures from the Thames*. I hope you enjoy the stories and photographs in these beautiful pages as much as I have.

Kirsti Scott
Publisher and Editor-in-Chief, Beachcombing *Magazine*

INTRODUCTION

Mudlarking was undertaken in Victorian times by impoverished children in desperate straits. They scoured the muddy Thames foreshore for small items of value which they could resell. How times have changed! It is now a pastime for all ages, classes, and genders. Why do they get up at anti-social hours of the morning to reach the foreshore when the tide is at its lowest? Why search a cold, wet, slippery, sometimes foul-smelling river environment? The initial impetus is the thrill experienced by all treasure hunters. The seduction thereafter is in the extraordinary fragments of history that the Thames never fails to disgorge.

What I love about mudlark finds are the intimate, everyday stories they reveal about the past. A worn leather shoe of a child evokes that infant's life. The toys, coins, bottles, and sherds of pottery unlock the day-to-day experiences of past Londoners. They reveal a lived history. With every object you get the sense that these items were worn, carried, held, and used by ordinary people. People like you and me. People from a time gone by. And that connects us to their lives and to their history. It brings their stories to life.

I have worked on and around the River Thames for more than 40 years. I know many mudlarks. I have seen some of their collections, and what overwhelms me is not just the quality and variety of their objects, but the sheer volume of the material they have discovered: boxes upon boxes in a single collection.

Flick through the gorgeous illustrations in *Mudlarks: Treasures from the Thames* and you begin to understand the sheer diversity of artifacts that have been discovered on the banks of the River Thames. The river is rich in archaeology because for centuries it was the city's trash dump. What once had little, or no value, is now a joy to uncover.

In this book, Tom Harrison's portraits—with the text that accompanies them—celebrate individual mudlarks, the folk who search the foreshore and unfailingly (or so it seems) find the most remarkable objects, each with an individual story to tell. These stories must often be unraveled to be understood, and mudlarks do so by networking among themselves and sharing their findings. There is something therapeutic about the process of searching, discovery, interpretation, and then sharing freely, which I am sure is motivation for many mudlarks.

The vast majority of mudlarks are amateur archaeologists. For them, finding objects on the Thames foreshore is the beginning of a process of helping to write history, assisting us all to understand how life was actually lived by ordinary people in days gone by. It is valuable for us to record and preserve not only the mudlarks' finds, but also their motivation for persisting in their passion to scour the foreshore for hidden treasures.

Tom's portraits provide a valuable insight into the mudlarks themselves. Mudlark finds are everyday items, which are poignant windows into the past. The portraits remind us that the mudlarks themselves are not a class apart. They are representative of us, of our society today.

Mudlarks: Treasures from the Thames is a remarkable testimony—and celebration—not only of objects found on the Thames foreshore, but of the mudlarks themselves.

Adrian Evans, Esq. LVO
Pageant Master and Festival Director, Thames Festival Trust

MUDLARKING
WE WILL GO

Tobias Neto metal detecting along the Thames (Tom Harrison).

"It was a cold day in December 2015. Low tide was predicted for 2:30 PM. Despite the weather conditions, I made my way to the River Thames foreshore around noon," explains mudlark Tobias Neto. Little did he know, he was about to make the discovery of a lifetime!

"Equipped with my metal detector, I started searching the muddy banks of the Thames (facing page). I switched the machine on and was greeted by a multitude of signals which I began to investigate by scraping and digging small holes to reveal what was hidden in the bed of the river.

"After a few hours of searching, I dug up an object (above) that initially appeared to be a large brooch. I removed some of the thick mud and noticed that the cross-shaped object seemed in good condition and well preserved even though I could still not make out its inscription and details of the design. Back home in the warmth, I soaked my finds in water and soap for a few minutes. As I washed the mysterious object, I could clearly read the word 'VALOUR.' The figure of a lion above a crown was also visible.

"Some rapid online searching revealed that I may have found a Victoria Cross medal. With the help of several websites, I compared the details of my medal

with the Victoria Cross medals on my screen. I learned that the date on the reverse of the medal related to a battle. As I turned the medal over (above), I could see '5 NOV 1854.' This medal was awarded for heroic actions during the Battle of Inkerman in the Crimean War. But I asked myself, what is the chance that I found an authentic Victoria Cross medal, the highest award a British soldier can receive?

"Further research revealed that there are lists describing the current locations and ownership of all the Victoria Cross medals. There are two medals from the Battle of Inkerman whose locations are unknown. They were awarded to Private John Byrne of the 68th (Durham) Light Infantry and Private John McDermond of the 47th (The Lancashire) Regiment (shown below).

"I booked an appointment with Kate Sumnall, the Finds Liaison Officer in the Museum of London

who recorded the medal. It was carefully examined by the museum and authenticated. Almost a year later, in November 2016, the Victoria Cross medal, now known as the 'Thames VC,' was displayed in the Museum of London for a few months. I was very fortunate to

Top left: Victoria Cross medal shortly after discovery (Tobias Neto). Top right: Restored Victoria Cross medal (PAS). Bottom: Private John McDermond (1832-68) at the battle of Inkerman on 5th November 1854 (Painting by Louis William Desanges).

have the opportunity to show my discovery to the public. I am also very proud to have received a letter from the office of Her Majesty The Queen and His Royal Highness The Prince of Wales, in their capacity as patron and president of the Victoria Cross and George Cross Association, acknowledging my discovering and wishing me well in the exhibition.

"In July 2016, I visited Private John Byrnes' grave (below) in St. Woolos Cemetery, Wales, where he was buried. For me it was a moving experience as my gut feeling is that he was the recipient of the medal I found. Apparently, in a moment of despair, he threw his medal in the River Thames in London," describes Tobias.

The National Army Museum in London has acquired Tobias's Victoria Cross medal, and they hope to put in on permanent display in the near future. This is the ultimate goal and thrill of mudlarking—to find a personal object in the river, trace the person who lost it, discover their intriguing backstory, and display the artifact for the general public to see and learn from it. For Tobias, this extraordinary find was a life-changing experience and had a profound impact on him. He even had a large image of the VC medal tattooed on his arm which will serve as a lifelong reminder of his greatest find and defining moment in his life.

For millennia, the River Thames has been collecting everything left in its waters and is now a repository of lost and discarded objects like this Victoria Cross medal. The ancient river is like a glistening, silver thread, undulating and weaving slowly through the colorful, historic tapestry of London to the sea. It is a liquid history book flowing with stories waiting to be discovered and ready to reveal the city's fascinating past.

For its history, its beauty, and its vital role in the shaping of Britain's destiny, the Thames is one of the most famous rivers in the world. Without it, London would not exist. From its humble beginnings as a small trading settlement founded by the Romans in AD 43, London grew to become one of the largest and commercially successful port cities in the world. During Roman and medieval times, the port traded primarily with continental Europe. In the 16th century, Tudor explorers, merchants, and adventurers in London pursued new trade opportunities on a global scale, and the Port of London (top right) flourished and prospered.

With the "discovery" of the New World, Britain was centrally located on these new trade routes and developed a superiority in commerce, trade, and industry. As the British empire expanded to Asia and Africa, London established itself as a global capital of pivotal importance. While London's maritime trade steadily increased, luxury goods and raw materials flowed into the city from around the world. A new network of enclosed docks and warehouses were established along the river, and London became known as the "ware-

Top left: Tobias visiting Private John Byrne's gravesite (Tobias Neto).
Top right: Illustration of London in 1616 (John Vischer).

house of the world." From Asia and Africa, the main imports arriving in London were tea, coffee, spices, cocoa, silks, precious metals, gemstones, porcelain, mahogany, and teak. The trans-Atlantic trade with the British colonies in America and West Indies brought cotton, tobacco, sugar, rum, furs, and timber to London.

By the 19th century, London had become the world's wealthiest city and the financial center of a vast empire. In the period between World War I and World War II, the quantity of goods passing through London's docks reached an all-time high. By 1939, London's port had grown into one of the biggest shipping and cargo handling facilities in the world. However, the fortunes of the docks quickly changed as the newly invented container system of cargo transportation transformed the global shipping industry. The Thames in London was too

shallow to accommodate the colossal container ships, and therefore, the shipping industry moved downstream to deep-water ports such as Tilbury and London Gateway. The river now quietly flows through central London, and evidence of the "working river" is slowly disappearing as the old warehouses are converted into luxury apartments or torn down to make way for high-rise residential and commercial developments.

During more than 2,000 years of human activity along the river, millions of objects have been dropped or discarded in its waters and now lie submerged in the thick Thames mud, waiting to be discovered. "Mudlarking" is the act of searching the exposed riverbed at low tide for these historic artifacts. From the English Channel to the locks in Teddington, the River Thames is tidal for approximately 69 kilometers. There are

two tides a day, and the water level fluctuates 7-10 meters between tides. At low tide, the Thames is the longest archaeological site in Britain, with vast amounts of foreshore exposed. The dense mud is "anaerobic," which means there is no oxygen in the mud. When objects are dropped into the river, the strong currents of the incoming tide quickly bury the object in the black silt. Without oxygen, the artifacts are often preserved in pristine condition.

In Victorian times, the original mudlarks (above) scavenged for anything on the exposed riverbed which they could sell in order to survive. These impoverished mudlarks braved dangerous conditions to find practical items like coal, iron, copper nails, and ropes, which they could exchange for food and essentials for themselves and their families.

In stark contrast to the poor Victorian mudlarks, modern mudlarks are well-educated history enthusiasts and amateur archaeologists who are passionate about discovering and learning about London's past. In the 1950s and 1960s, mudlarks searched the surface for historic artifacts revealed by the ebb and flow of the tides. Their experiences are documented in British Pathé films and Ivor Noël Hume's book, *Treasure in the Thames*, published in 1956.

With the assistance of metal detectors, vast amounts of historically significant artifacts were unearthed in the 1970s and 1980s, which is considered to be

the "golden age" of mudlarking. In 1980, the exclusive Society of Thames Mudlarks was founded, and members were granted a special license from the Port of London Authority that allowed them to dig down to undisturbed archaeological layers and excavate parts of the foreshore (below).

Top: Victorian mudlarks on foreshore (Tableau by Julia Fullerton-Batten).
Middle right: Graham duHeaume holding a freshly excavated knife (Graham duHeaume).
Bottom right: Peter Elkins digging along the Thames (Graham duHeaume).

Members of the Society of Thames Mudlarks have rescued thousands of artifacts in unparalleled condition (right), which would have been lost forever. They formed a close relationship with the Museum of London who recorded the significant artifacts. Through this productive collaboration over four decades, tens of thousands of historically important artifacts were acquired by the Museum of London, which now has one of the largest collections in the world of medieval pilgrim and secular badges and post-medieval pewter toys, thanks to the mudlarks. The research of these large assemblages of finds has actually

Medieval badge of St. Cecilia playing an organ (Ian Smith).

challenged and changed historical perceptions, and new books have been written primarily based on mudlarks' finds.

In recent years, mudlarking has become a popular hobby in London that gives both adults and children a unique "hands-on history" experience and deepens their understanding of London's past. To go mudlarking in London, a mandatory Thames Foreshore Permit *must* be obtained from the Port of London Authority. All objects that are over 300 years old must be reported to the Museum of London. Mudlarks arrange regular appointments with the

Jason Sandy searching for artifacts (Jon Attenborough).

Finds Liaison Officer at the museum, who records the artifacts on the British Museum's Portable Antiquities Scheme, referred to throughout this book as "PAS."

Various methods are used by mudlarks to search the exposed riverbed at low tide. Some search "by eye" without disturbing the surface, while others use a trowel, sieve, or metal detector. Up until 1999, when the Thames Clipper ferry service began operating on the Thames, it was relatively difficult to find rare artifacts on the surface because there was little erosion. Veteran mudlarks often dug down in search of lost treasures. Nowadays, the Thames Clipper races down the river and creates large waves which pound and churn the surface of the exposed riverbed. From Putney to Woolwich, the large waves caused by fast boats

have accelerated the erosion of the riverbed at an unprecedented pace. Although it is bad for the stability of the foreshore, the erosion has made mudlarking much easier. Freshly uncovered artifacts can be found lying on the surface of the exposed riverbed at low tide. The areas which are eroding quickly are the most productive for finding objects.

The foreshore is comprised of an eclectic mix (above) of rocks, sand, gravel, mud, oyster shells, pipe stems, pottery sherds, broken glass, rusting metalwork, pins, bricks, terracotta tiles, and animal bones. Lost and discarded objects are camouflaged and hidden within this unusual terrain, and you have to look closely and intently to spot them. Mudlarks often wear waterproof boots, gloves, and knee pads to crawl on their

Above: Typical terrain of the foreshore (Jason Sandy).

hands and knees, looking for those hard-to-spot artifacts, which are often very small. They literally get "down and dirty" searching for lost treasures, and mudlarks are highly rewarded for their patience and persistence. Because the intertidal zone is only exposed for a few hours a day, mudlarking is a race against the clock. After low tide, the water level rises very quickly, and you have to be careful you don't get cut off from your exit route.

Over the years, mudlarks have found an astonishingly wide range of artifacts, dating from prehistoric to modern times. These objects give us new insights about life in London. Many museums often show only the most precious historical items owned by the monarchy, aristocracy, and wealthy upper classes, so we only see part of the story. Artifacts found in the Thames tell us about the everyday lives of ordinary people and give us a well-rounded picture of how people lived and worked throughout the centuries. Whether a fragment of an everyday item or a rare and valuable treasure, each object magically opens a window to the past. They teach us about the customs, material culture, styles, and fashions of the times, as well as social history and behavioral patterns of past Londoners.

Not only does this book illustrate and describe the artifacts recovered from the river, it also introduces you to the mudlarks who found the objects, revealing the human side of this popular

Above: Cecilia and Florrie Evans on the foreshore (Tom Harrison).

hobby. We are not able to travel back in time and meet the people who lost these objects, but you will hear directly from the people who found the artifacts and whose lives have been affected and changed by their discoveries. With their own voices, they tell their personal stories of friendship, passion, love, fear, heartbreak, and loss of loved ones. Throughout the book, they give their first-hand accounts, describing the exhilarating, adrenaline-inducing moment when they made an unexpected discovery. Many of the photos of objects featured in this book were taken on smartphones as they were found. They are not staged. By seeing these in situ photos of the objects appearing from the mud, freshly unveiled by the outgoing tide, you get a sense of the wonder and amazement of finding lost treasure in the Thames. By unearthing buried secrets and hidden history, mudlarks uncover stories that are long forgotten, or were never told.

Mudlarking is not only a hobby; it is a growing subculture in London, consisting of a friendly community of mudlarks. This book gives you an in-depth, behind-the-scenes view into the secret world of the mudlarks. It is a time capsule and a snapshot in time. London is a transient, global city. Mudlarks come and go. Those featured in this book represent a wide cross-section of the people who are actively searching the river now. Welcome to the world of the mudlarks and their extraordinary discoveries!

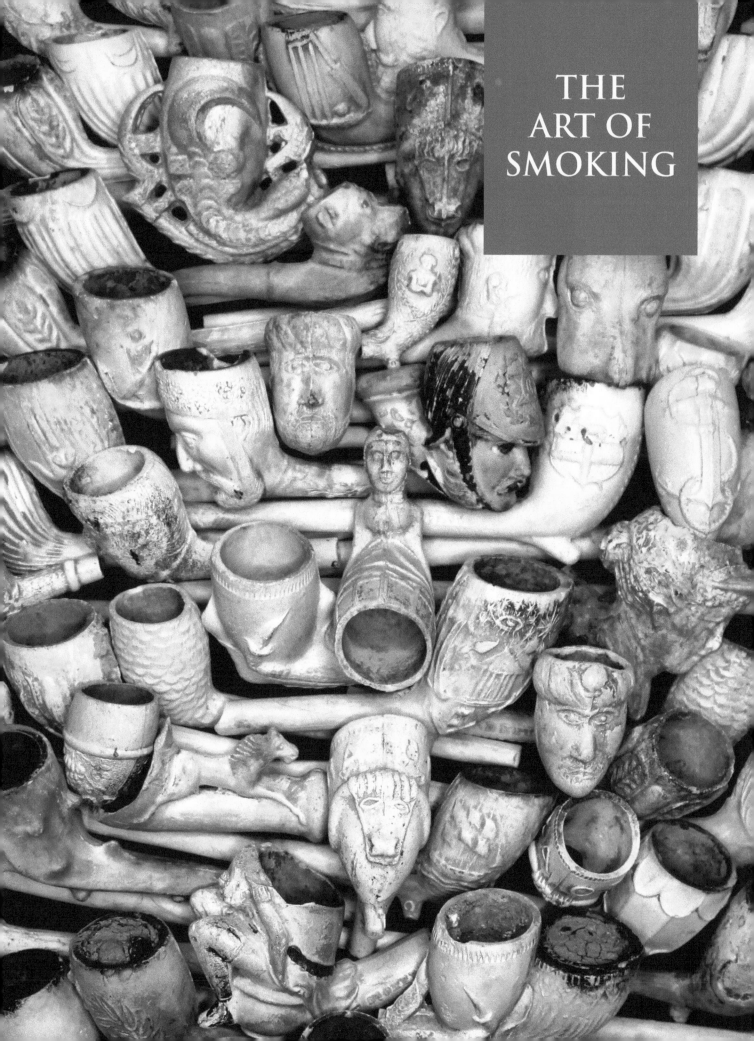

THE
ART OF
SMOKING

I magine finding an incredibly long clay pipe just lying at your feet, untouched and unbroken after 300 years! That's exactly what happened to Sara Cannizzaro as she was mudlarking on a freezing, cold February morning along the Thames foreshore in London.

"Suddenly a large boat went past, causing a huge wave and making me jump backward to avoid wet feet. As the wave retreated, I quickly checked whether it had left anything behind. It was then that I saw it, trapped by a rock—the longest clay pipe I had ever found on the River Thames!" explains Sara.

It truly is a miracle that it survived intact despite the turbulent and rough conditions at the bottom of the river. The longest clay pipes ever produced were 12–26 inches long and are often referred to as "churchwarden" clay pipes. In the 18th century, church buildings were open all night, and churchwardens were responsible for watching the church premises. To pass the long hours, they would smoke their clay pipes. The exceptionally long stems of the "churchwarden" clay pipes would keep the heat and smoke away from the face so the line of sight was not obstructed as they kept watch.

Clay pipes are some of the most common and interesting objects found on the Thames foreshore in London. Although the pipes are made of thin, fragile clay, the soft Thames mud has protected many of them for centuries. The famous Elizabethan explorer, Sir Walter Raleigh, is credited with introducing tobacco to Tudor England, and he supposedly tempted Queen Elizabeth I to start smoking.

I n the late 16th century, the price of tobacco in London was very expensive as only small quantities of tobacco were imported into the country at that time. Only wealthy individuals could afford to smoke, and the clay pipe bowls were therefore very small. As the imports increased, the price of tobacco dropped, and common people could afford to smoke. The size of the pipe bowls increased steadily through the 17th and 18th centuries as the price of tobacco continued to sink due to the well-established and bountiful trade routes with the American colonies.

Considered to be the cigarettes of their day, clay pipes were often pre-filled with tobacco and sold by shops for a single use before they were discarded. It is no wonder that thousands of clay pipes are still found along the Thames foreshore where workers would smoke as they went about their business. The locations of the busiest ports in Georgian and Victorian London can still easily be identified by the amount of clay pipe stems and bowls that litter the Thames foreshore to this day.

Facing page: Nicole White's collection of clay pipes (Jason Sandy).
Above left: Churchwarden clay pipe (Sara Cannizzaro).
Above right: Clay pipe evolution over the centuries (Jason Sandy).

In the 16th and 17th centuries, clay pipes were mostly undecorated, but in the mid-18th century clay pipe makers began to use molds with decorative designs. Based on the Royal Coat of Arms of the British monarchy, an English lion and Scottish unicorn were often depicted on opposite sides of the clay pipe bowls made in London between 1730–1770 (above). As it was considered a dangerous beast, the mythical unicorn is chained and restrained. The traditional legend of hostility between the two heraldic animals is recorded in a children's nursery rhyme which goes like this:

> *The lion and the unicorn*
> *Were fighting for the crown*
> *The lion beat the unicorn*
> *All around the town.*
> *Some gave them white bread,*
> *And some gave them brown;*
> *Some gave them plum cake*
> *and drummed them out of town.*

The Prince of Wales feathers were also a common design on 18th-century clay pipe bowls (above). In the 19th century, clay pipes developed into miniature works of art. Victorian pipe makers demonstrated their creativity and imagination by decorating their pipe bowls and stems with unique designs. They explored natural themes such as vegetative patterns, tree bark, branches, acorns, oak-leaf patterns, grape vines, fruit, flowers, thistles, shamrocks, roses, and thorns. Pipe makers even shaped the clay pipe bowls to represent monarchs, military heroes, famous

personalities, and cartoon characters. Other designs included sporting activities (like soccer and cricket), nautical themes (such as sailing ships and anchors), mythological scenes, Masonic symbols, military crests, regimental badges, and livery company arms. The possibilities were endless! It's hard to imagine why people discarded the beautiful pipes in the Thames. Nicola White has found a large amount of clay pipes (page 12) that illustrate the wide variety of creative designs.

Many clay pipe bowls were also decorated with animal themes. Julian Farge found an incredibly detailed clay pipe in the shape of a chicken's foot holding the pipe bowl (below left). A clay pipe bowl in the shape of an egg clutched by sharp eagle's talons was found by Monika Buttling-Smith (below right).

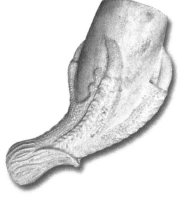

Top left: Clay pipe bowl with lion and unicorn (Jason Sandy).
Top right: Clay pipe bowl with Prince of Wales feathers (Jason Sandy).
Bottom left: Chicken foot clay pipe bowl (Julian Farge).
Bottom right: Eagle talon clay pipe bowl (Monika Buttling-Smith).

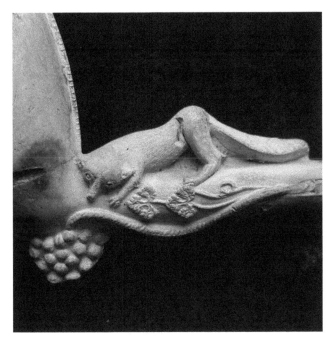

Left: Clay pipe with a fox and grapes (Alessio Checconi).
Above: Clay pipe bowls in the shape of a dog's head (David Hodgson).

Some pipe bowls were formed in the shape of cockerels' heads, foxes, dogs, and other animals. Alessio Checconi found a complete clay pipe decorated with a fox and grapes (above left). Clay pipe bowls in the shape of cute dogs' faces (above right) were found by David Hodgson.

Long before Starbucks arrived in Europe, the first coffee shop opened in London in 1652. In the 18th century, drinking coffee and smoking clay pipes quickly became a popular combination. The coffee was imported from Turkey, and the image of a Turk's head (with a beard and turban) was used on signs to advertise the coffee houses. Even clay pipe bowls were made in the shape of Turk's heads as illustrated by the clay pipes (below) found by Nicola White.

Character or portrait clay pipes were often produced to commemorate famous personalities, military dragoons, and members of the royal family in the 19th and early 20th centuries. David Hodgson has found many figural clay pipes (above) including one which looks like the popular Victorian author, Charles Dickens, and the famous British general, Field Marshal Wolseley.

Charles Dickens and Field Marshal Wolseley clay pipes (David Hodgson).

In 1887, Queen Victoria celebrated her Golden Jubilee (50-year reign), and many clay pipes (below) depicting the Queen were produced to commemorate this momentous occasion.

Bottom left: Turk's head clay pipe bowls (Nicola White). Bottom right: Queen Victoria Golden Jubilee clay pipe (David Hodgson).

Sadly, tobacco played a major role in fueling the African slave trade. Professional photographer Hannah Smiles has beautifully captured thought-provoking images of these sombre clay pipe bowls which were formed in the shape of slave heads (below). These figural clay pipes are a poignant reminder of the African slaves who were shipped to the British colonies in America and the Caribbean to toil in the tobacco fields. While these slaves suffered under horrendous conditions, British gentlemen were leisurely smoking tobacco from pipes that looked like the plantation slaves.

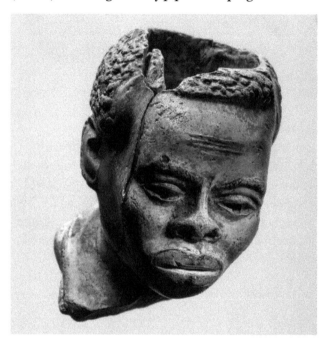

When filling the clay pipe bowl with tobacco, a tamper was often used to compress the tobacco at the bottom of the bowl. In 2015, a mudlark found a complete, post-medieval pipe tamper made from a dark hard wood. The top is decorated with the head of a stylized horse or lion, and the shaft has been carved with alter-nating, concave facets. Diagonal, incised lines on the head and collar depict hair and a mane. Pipe tampers were both decorative and functional.

Perfectly preserved by the soft, dense mud of the River Thames, mudlarks have discovered a huge variety of clay pipes which give us a unique glimpse into the social history and popularity of smoking in London. The numerous styles and designs of clay pipes display the creativity and craftsman-ship of the pipe makers and the "art" of smoking. Through the wide variety of motifs depicted on the pipe bowls and stems, we can also learn about the popular culture and interests of Londoners throughout the centuries.

Top left: Slave clay pipe bowl (Hannah Smiles).
Bottom left: Tobacco plantation slave pipe bowl (Hannah Smiles).
Above right: Post-medieval wooden pipe tamper (PAS)

Rex Key in his clay pipe workshop (Jason Sandy).

CLAY PIPE MAKING:
THE VICTORIAN WAY

Beginning in the late 16th century, clay pipe making has been a long tradition in England, passed on from generation to generation. From the 17th century onwards, pipe makers used iron molds in order to produce their clay pipes. Historians were not exactly sure how the earliest clay pipes were produced in the late 16th century until mudlark Alan Place miraculously found the earliest known clay pipe mold (below) in the River Thames in 2011. Based on the size and shape of the pipe carved into the mold, the Museum of London has dated it to AD 1580–1610. Surviving over 400 years in the waterlogged conditions of the Thames foreshore, this wooden mold is the only known example in Britain that still exists.

To regulate the manufacture of clay tobacco pipes, the Worshipful Company of Tobacco Pipe Makers and Tobacco Blenders was granted a charter by King James I in 1619. Because of the rising popularity of smoking, there were over 1,000 clay pipe makers in London by the end of the 17th century. While searching along the River Thames, Tony Thira found a beautiful 17th-century token with three clay pipes depicted on it (below). The brass token is possibly from a clay pipe making business located south of the River Thames in London. The pipe making industry flourished until the beginning of the 20th century when cigarettes became more popular than pipe smoking. As a result, the commercial production of clay pipes dwindled and ceased in the 1960s.

Left: 16th century clay pipe mold (PAS).
Above: 17th-century clay pipe token (Tony Thira).

In Broseley, England, where clay pipe production began in 1590, there is the only man who still produces clay pipes using the traditional Victorian methods with original pipe molds from the 19th century. Rex Key has been making clay pipes for over 50 years, and he has a collection of over 14,000 clay pipes which he has acquired over the many decades. I had the fortunate privilege of interviewing Rex in his clay pipe workshop. During my four-hour visit, Rex kindly demonstrated the traditional Victorian method of producing clay tobacco pipes, illustrated and described in the following photos and text.

STEP 1: Originating in Cornwall, the fine grey clay was shipped to Rex's production facility in large sacks. Rex took a handful of soft, moist clay out of the bag and beat it repeatedly on the work surface in order to release the tiny air bubbles caught in the clay.

STEP 2: Next Rex set the ball of soft clay on his work bench and gently rolled it into a long tube using both hands. At one end, he left a lump of clay which would eventually become the pipe bowl. At the other end, Rex carefully inserted a long, straight piercing rod through the center of the pipe stem.

STEP 3: In his workshop, Rex has several shelves full of beautiful clay pipe molds to choose from, so I asked him to make an eagle's claw clay pipe because of the intricate, detailed design. After retrieving the iron mold from the shelf, Rex used a small paintbrush to gently apply paraffin (a type of oil) to both sides of the iron mold to ensure that the clay didn't stick to the sides of the mold.

Photos by Jason Sandy.

STEP 4: Then Rex took the long clay roll and bent it to fit in the shape of the mold. He gently pressed the clay into one side of the mold and put the other half of the mold on top.

STEP 5: After securing the two sides of the mold together, Rex set them in a table-mounted clamp which he slowly and firmly tightened. Using a traditional "gin press," he pulled down the lever arm which extended a rounded stopper into the open hole at the top of the mold. When the steel tip entered the hole, it created the hollow in the pipe bowl. During the process, the soft clay was pushed firmly against the sides of the mold, impressing the intricate design into the soft clay. After releasing the lever handle, Rex carefully pushed the piercing rod into the newly formed pipe bowl to ensure there was a continuous air path from the tip of the pipe stem to the bowl.

During his 50 years of pipe making, Rex has produced clay pipes for a wide variety of clients including Pinewood Studios, Warner Brothers, and even Princeton University. His pipes have appeared in several Hollywood movies including "The Pirates of the Caribbean" and many period dramas on British television. Now in his seventies, Rex is retired and is looking for an apprentice whom he can teach in order to keep this long tradition going for future generations. In the summertime and for special occasions, Rex still demonstrates pipe making at the Broseley Clay Tobacco Pipe Works. If you want to find out more about clay pipe making and see a large variety of clay pipe designs, I would highly recommend a visit to the museum in Broseley located west of Birmingham, England.
www.ironbridge.org.uk/explore/broseley-pipeworks

STEP 6: After releasing the clamp and trimming the excess clay from the top of the bowl, Rex laid the mold on its side and opened it, revealing the beautiful design of the clay pipe. He took his custom-made steel stamp and pressed his maker's mark (REX M KEY—BROSELEY) into the clay pipe stem.

STEP 7: After removing the long wire from the stem, he extracted the soft clay pipe from the mold and laid the pipe on a tray to air dry. Several days later, Rex used a small trimming knife and carefully removed the burrs along the seam of the clay pipe. Most of the moisture had evaporated, and the pipe was ready to be fired.

STEP 8: Traditionally, Victorian pipe makers used a wood-fired kiln made of bricks to fire the clay pipes at 900° C (1,650° F). To expedite and regulate the process, Rex uses a modern electric kiln which can fire over 1,000 pipes at one time. After the firing process, the pipes are complete and ready for use.

NICOLA WHITE

I grew up in Cornwall, and beachcombing played a large part in my childhood. In my spare time and after school, I could often be found scouring the wild Cornish beaches for driftwood, sea glass, and shells among other things. When I moved to London in the late 1990s, I lived very close to Greenwich. One weekend I discovered the steps down to the Thames foreshore. As I wandered along the foreshore at low tide, I was thrilled to discover worn, colorful gems of river glass, and faded pieces of pottery scattered at my feet. I returned time after time to collect these fragments. It was the perfect way to escape from my busy job in a large French bank and to enjoy some peace and solitude.

During one such outing, when the tide was lower than usual, I was excited to find a coin lying in the mud. When I picked it up, I could just make out the ghostly, faded face of Queen Victoria. I went on to find buttons, military cap badges, clay pipes, and jewelry. Each time my imagination was inspired by the secret stories behind these lost and discarded treasures.

Mudlarking for me is a magical pastime which is accompanied by a sense of excitement and anticipation each time I take a trip to the foreshore at low tide. I love everything about it. From the sound of the river as it washes onto the shore each time a boat goes by, to the fading light of an evening lark and the vibrant array of colors shimmering on the river. Time stands still as I walk along looking for treasures thrown out by the tide.

Undoubtedly, it is my desire to find out as much as I can about the artifacts that has fueled my interest in history, social history, and archaeology. There is something hugely motivating about researching an object that you have found yourself. I have learned a lot of miscellaneous and yet fascinating information that I would never have learned had it not been for this pastime.

What thrills me the most is to find something that is linked to a specific person or a place from the past. It fascinates me and moves me when these reminders of people who lived and worked in London centuries ago are washed up on the foreshore. I have realized that people never really disappear. There is always something left to remind us of their presence. One of my favorite finds is a simple, small, brass luggage tag inscribed with a name and an address. From this, a story unraveled before my eyes of a man who fought in World War I and married his landlady. I tracked down his final resting place which is a pauper's grave in Greenwich. Because of this tag, his story was discovered, and a life was remembered. Finding all these fragments of lives from the past makes me wonder what my own story is. I am determined to make it a good one.

Portraits by Tom Harrison.

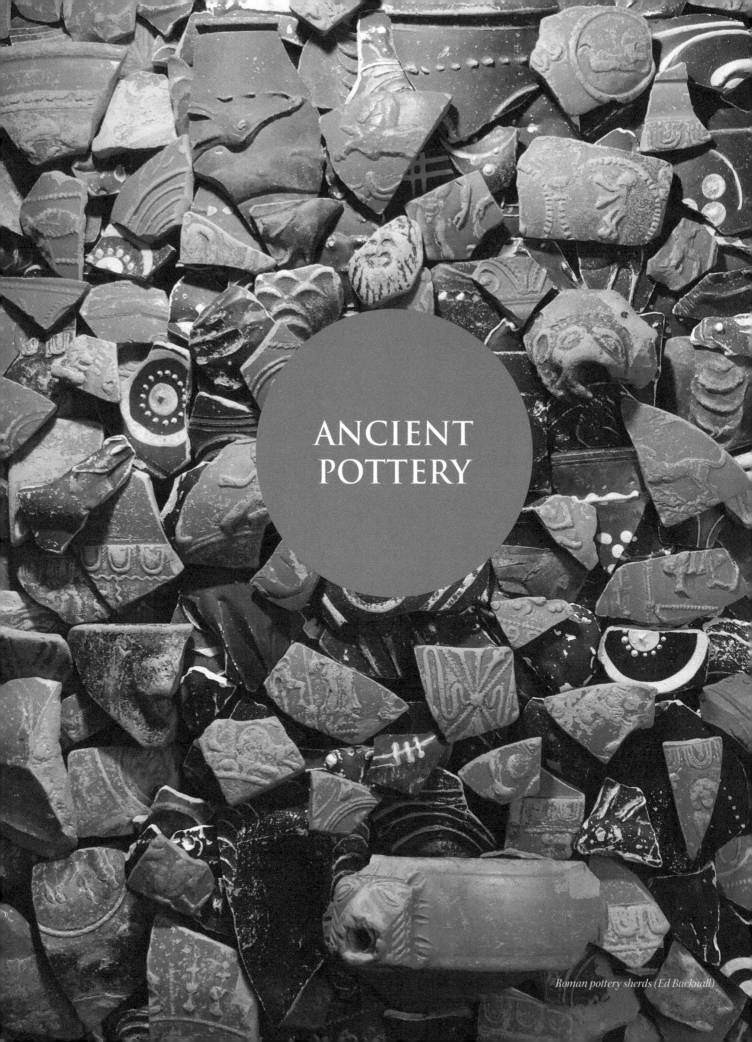

ANCIENT
POTTERY

Roman pottery sherds (Ed Bucknall)

Around 4,400 years ago, the Beaker people began migrating to Britain from mainland Europe, bringing with them a new type of pottery vessel called a "Bell Beaker" because of its characteristic bulb-shaped bowl and upward flared rim. In the Beaker culture, pottery was one of their most treasured possessions, and it is often found in their graves. One of the earliest finger-pinched, rusticated beakers found in the River Thames (below) dates to the early Bronze Age and is on permanent display in the Museum of London.

After the Romans established a colony in Britain in the 1st century AD, they began producing pottery using local clays. Most of the pottery produced in Britain was made for basic utilitarian uses while

high-quality Roman tableware, such as Samian ware, was manufactured in Gaul (France) and imported into Britain. Along the River Thames and River Medway in southeast England, Roman pottery production was prevalent. Mudlarks Simon Bourne and Steve Trim have found several complete Roman vessels as well as hundreds of pottery sherds. In August 2020, Simon discovered an incredible, complete black-burnished ware vessel (above).

"When I saw the black turtle-like object about 20 feet from me, my heart skipped a beat," Simon explains. "I was so excited, but also apprehensive. A complete pot is super rare. Could this be my lucky day? I scraped off the mud with my finger-tips, realizing I was the first person to touch this pot since the potter made it nearly 2,000 years ago! I felt like I'd won a competition. We believe the vessel to be a 1st to 2nd century AD flask, which most likely held wine." To watch the full video about the discovery of this extraordinary, wheel-turned flask, check out Simon's YouTube channel (Si-finds Thames Mudlarking) and see his other mudlarking adventures, too.

Top right: Complete Roman black-burnished ware flask (Simon Bourne).
Bottom left: Illustration of early Bronze Age beaker (Coral Pearce).

With a great passion for finding Roman artifacts, Ed Bucknall has discovered an extraordinary array of Roman pottery sherds along the River Thames (page 22). Many of these sherds are Samian ware, a type of fine red-gloss ceramic used primarily to serve food. It was reserved for special occasions and was intended to impress the guests at the dinner table. Samian ware was often decorated with molded figures in relief such as mythological gods and goddesses, animals and beasts, hunting scenes, flowers, and foliage. Richard Hemery found a beautiful sherd of Roman Gaulish terra sigillata depicting an archer with his bow and arrow drawn taut, ready to fire at a wild animal while hunting (right). Decorated with a palm tree and band of ovolo (egg-and-tongue) pattern along the top, this sherd has been dated to the 1st–3rd centuries AD.

Monika Buttling-Smith and Ed Bucknall have discovered ultra-rare Samian ware sherds illustrating gladiators in battle. Monika's sherd of Gaulish Samian ware (below) was probably produced in Lezoux (France) between AD 65–90. "The molded decoration depicts Mars, the God of War, standing on a plinth with his spear arm raised and holding a small

Top: Samian ware sherd with archer and palm tree (Richard Hemery). Bottom: Gladiators on pottery sherd within the Roman amphitheater in London (Monika Buttling-Smith).

Roman oil lamp found by
Monika Buttling-Smith
(Hannah Smiles).

circular shield in his left hand. To his right, a gladiator is seen mid-battle in a circular medallion. Both are topped by a band of ovolo decoration," explains Monika, who took her sherd to the Roman amphitheater where gladiators once fought in Roman Londinium over 1,800 years ago. What a thrilling, spine-tingling experience!

From AD 200 to 300 in the Nene Valley (England), Roman Britons produced expensive and fashionable tablewares made of a thin, pale fabric with a dark brown color coat. In the River Thames, mudlarks have found many sherds of Roman hunt beakers and cups decorated with barbotine and painted decoration. They often depict hunting scenes, mostly dogs chasing wild animals. Hunting was a popular sport in Roman times. Duncan John found a beautiful sherd of a Roman hunt cup depicting a cute rabbit with raised ears (top left).

I n the medieval period, clay continued to be used as an inexpensive material to make essential household items such as jugs, cooking pots, pipkins, pitchers, jars, dishes, bowls, plates, and chafing dishes. To meet the large demand for pottery, there were many kilns in and around London in the Middle Ages. Surrey border ware is one of the most prevalent types of medieval pottery found in the River Thames. It is made of a slightly sandy, whitish clay fabric which was wheel-thrown by hand and shaped into the desired form before it was fired in a kiln. To decorate the vessels, a "bib" of lead-based, green glaze was often applied to their surface in localized areas.

Several years ago, Mark Paros spotted the base of a medieval jug protruding from the mud. He carefully extracted the base and four other pieces. Fortunately, Mark was able to carefully restore the 15th-century greenish-brown glazed jug (middle left). Known as Cheam border ware from Surrey, the jug has a carinated shape and would have been used in a medieval household for storing and pouring liquids.

Mark also found a large medieval jug that was unfortunately smashed into 87 sherds. After hours and hours of sorting and cleaning the individual pieces, he painstakingly reassembled the medieval jug like a three-dimensional jigsaw puzzle. To his utter amazement, the large vessel was mostly complete with only a few pieces missing (bottom left). It is nothing short of a miracle that Mark was able to reconstruct the 14th-century bung-hole pitcher which is 13 ½ inches tall.

This page, top to bottom: Roman hunting beaker sherd with rabbit (Duncan John). Medieval Cheam border ware jug (Jason Sandy). Medieval bung-hole pitcher (Jason Sandy). Facing page, top to bottom: Medieval dragon figurine (Tom Bland). 16th-century Flemish figurine (Mark Paros).

Medieval pottery was sometimes decorated with small figurines of people and animals. Tom Bland discovered a 14th-century zoomorphic form in the shape of a dragon (above). The animal has a snout with two circular nostrils, wide mouth, and long neck. It is made of coarse border ware with a green glaze. The dragon could have been attached to a medieval lobed cup which was used as a communal drinking cup for ceremonial purposes.

While mudlarking along the River Thames in London, Mark Paros found a Flemish figurine dating to the 16th century (right). Made of fine white pipeclay, it is probably a representation of an angel or saint, possibly St. Michael.

Finding a bearded face from a Bellarmine jug is one of the most exhilarating mudlarking experiences! Brown stoneware sherds are a common find, but it is rare to find a face. I have been very lucky to find a few of these wonderful pieces of history over the years (above). Each face is uniquely different, and the facial expressions range from friendly smiles in the 16th century to grotesque scowls in the 17th century. For more information about these fascinating jugs, refer to the chapter called "Bellarmine Jugs and Witch Bottles" on page 50.

Mudlark Jo Cook found a beautiful sherd of 16th-century stoneware depicting two gentlemen (right). In the foreground, a man is depicted with a well-trimmed beard and curly hair under his flat hat. He is wearing traditional 16th-century clothes with a tall collar decorated with a crosshatch pattern and radiating folds below. According to historians, the two German men could be from the Schmalkaldic League, which was a military alliance of Lutheran princes within the Holy Roman Empire during the mid-16th century.

One of my personal favorite pottery sherds is from a 16th-century German stoneware vessel (facing page). A stylish gentleman is shown wearing an undu-

lating "ruff" collar, which was popular at this time. He almost looks like William Shakespeare! The stoneware fragment is decorated with German inscriptions above a series of architectural arches. The column supporting the two arches resembles a bunch of bananas. Above the column is a female face with flowing hair descending to her circular breasts.

Westerwald stoneware is another type of salt-glazed pottery which was produced in German towns such as Höhr-Grenzhausen in the area known as the Westerwald. In the River Thames, I have found many broken sherds of beautiful, bluish gray tankards and jugs decorated with vivid cobalt blue and manganese colored glaze in the 16th–17th centuries (page 30). The raised decoration is exceptionally detailed with undulating floral patterns, circular shapes, curvaceous hearts, cherubs, lions, and other mythical creatures.

In the 17th century, tin-glazed earthenware became very popular in Britain. Delftware production started in Holland and was exported throughout Europe. As demand for Delftware in London increased, several potteries employing Dutch workers were established along the south bank of the River Thames in Montague Close, Pickleherring, Rotherhithe, Norfolk House, and Glasshouse Street. They produced plates, chargers, jugs, tankards, tiles, vases, and apothecary ware. Ornate decoration was painstakingly hand-painted onto the surface of the pottery before it was fired.

Over the years, mudlarks have found hundreds of Delftware sherds painted with vivid blue, green, orange-yellow, red, and purple colors. Mudlark Owen Ooievaar discovered an exceptionally large

Facing page, top to bottom: 16th–17th-century Bellarmine jug sherds (Jason Sandy). 16th-century German stoneware sherd (Jo Cook). This page: Tudor stoneware sherd (Jason Sandy).

Facing page: Westerwald stoneware sherds (Jason Sandy). This page, bottom left: 17th-century Delftware dish sherd (Florrie Evans). This page, top right: Hand-painted Delftware wall tile sherd (Jason Sandy). This page, middle right: 17th-century Italian costrel (PAS).

piece of hand-painted Delftware. In the center of the dish, a cute blue bird is depicted among abstract flowers painted with radiating blue lines (below). A few years ago, I found a fragment of tin-glazed wall tile with a gorgeous flower created with only a few masterful brushstrokes. I like how the edges of the tile have been worn smooth by time and tide (top right).

One of the most unusual and stunning pieces of pottery found in the Thames in recent years is a colorful, lion-headed costrel (right) found by Gryff Rees. It is 11 inches tall and was produced in northern Italy around AD 1600–1650. The vessel has a tapered neck which swells into a spherical body and a circular base. The handles on either side of the costrel are formed as lions' heads with open mouths. The costrel has been glazed with a unique red and white bichrome slip, which creates an eye-catching, marbleized effect.

Throughout the ages, pottery has been enormously popular, particularly for its utilitarian uses. Even now, we use different types of fired clay every day in our homes. Stop to think about it: From your morning cup of coffee, to eating a bowl of soup for lunch, to serving dinner on your finest china, we often use various types of pottery without even thinking about it. Even your bathroom sink and toilet are probably made of porcelain (vitreous china) and were shaped in a mold before being fired in a kiln. We also use beautiful ceramic flower vases, pots for plants, sculptural artwork, commemorative plates, and other objects made of pottery to decorate our homes. Glazed ceramic and porcelain tiles are often used on the walls and floors in our kitchens and bathrooms. Earthenware, stoneware, ceramic, and porcelain still play a very important role in our modern lives.

SIMON BOURNE

I've always had a curiosity for old objects and collecting. I remember picking out attractive stones from the playground tarmac when I was a kid thinking it was treasure. I also remember collecting trinkets from around the house and putting them in a Kinder Surprise case and burying it in the garden, hoping someone would dig it up one day. I wasn't keen on the subject in secondary school, and I chose geography over history because I kinda fancied the teacher. I thought history was "boring"— at least the way they taught it. When I was 30, I decided to buy a metal detector and see if I could find objects myself. That's when the passion really kicked in.

When I was looking for places to metal detect, I used the internet to see if the Thames foreshore was an option. I stumbled across the crazy website made by Steve Brooker called "Thames and Field." What I saw on the website made my jaw drop. It's changed now, but back then, there were thousands of pictures of amazing coins and artifacts. I couldn't believe what I was seeing. Not knowing anyone, I plucked up the courage to go to the club meeting to see what mudlarking was all about. I met some great people who showed me the ropes, some of whom I am still friends with. Despite many people leaving the hobby, the die-hards stick around.

Ever since I started in 2011, the thrill of mudlarking has been the anticipation of not knowing what I'll find next. It's the reward of getting up early, not always in nice weather, and transporting yourself back to when the Thames was a completely different world. As my collection grows, I look forward to finding something I haven't found before. Even if I have one already, I still get excited because I have learned through this hobby what the objects are, and I can usually identify them. We get to handle these objects, which I think is what was missing at school. These artifacts are a tangible link to our past. It's challenging too. As mudlarking is becoming more popular, it is increasingly difficult to make as many finds as a few years ago. So, when you do find something, it's a real achievement. Since I started sharing my "mudventures"

on YouTube, I am motivated to make better videos. That encourages me to go out and try harder, so I can share cooler stories.

I have many favorite finds, but one of them would have to be the World War I dog tag that was worn by Nathan Posener—a tailor's son from Limehouse and a member of the Royal Flying Corps. It was a privilege to successfully return it to his grandson. I recently found a tobacco tin dating to 1714, and I'm currently researching it and hope to find out more, with the help of the National Maritime Museum in Greenwich. Being the first person to touch a complete Roman pot (wine vessel) in over 1,700 years was a truly heart-warming moment when I plucked it from the mud. I doubt I will be able to repeat it.

Portraits by Tom Harrison.

COLORFUL
UTOPIAN
VISIONS

Unlike the scenic, picturesque beaches and golden sandy shores where people often go beachcombing, the exposed riverbed of the River Thames in London is a dark and often unwelcoming terrain. At low tide, the surface of the foreshore is littered with broken shards of sharp glass, rusty nails, bent pins and needles, animal bones, dead rats, and other unsavory surprises. The color of the foreshore in most places is a dull mix of sombre grey, brown, and black tones. In stark contrast to this dark background, delightfully colorful pottery sherds lie waiting to be discovered.

Florrie Evans has been mudlarking along the Thames for several decades. She and her young daughter, Cecilia, have found some lovely, colorful pottery sherds.

"Pottery was the first thing I ever collected from the river as a child. When my daughter was old enough to toddle along with me on my larks, she was drawn to colorful pieces (left) just as I had been," exclaims Florrie. "Although today I'm more interested in uncovering hidden treasures, I still get to live out my first pottery passions with my daughter! When she's not with me, I find myself picking up pretty pieces especially for her. There's instant eye-pleasing satisfaction to be had from a colorful or patterned design, peeping up at you from the mud, begging to be loved again—the Thames' answer to seashells and sea glass! We love fragments of 'story' best—little people, birds, or animals, tiny cityscapes, and pieces which take us on an imaginative journey."

Over the past few years, Jacqui Wise has discovered some extraordinary sherds of broken pottery (facing page) along the Thames foreshore. One of her most colorful pieces is a Victorian Prattware pot lid (below) made in Staffordshire, England, in the 19th century. Victorian manufacturers often sold their popular fish and meat pastes in ceramic pots. To make the products more attractive and

Facing page: Collection of colorful pottery sherds (Jacqui Wise). Above: Collection of Thames pottery sherds (Florrie Evans). Top right: Colorful oriental sherd on the Thames foreshore (Anna Borzello). Bottom right: Victorian pot lid (Jacqui Wise).

increase sales, Felix Pratt (1813–1894) introduced multi-colored printing on his Prattware ceramics inspired by historic paintings. This colorful image of a battle scene is from an old oil painting by Dutch painter Philips Wouwerman entitled "Cavalry Battle in Front of a Burning Mill" from circa 1660.

Jacqui has also found a stunning 1930s Art Deco fragment manufactured by Rubian Art Pottery in Staffordshire (above left). It depicts two Japanese geishas in traditional dress engaged in conversation under a colorful parasol decorated with a bold floral pattern. One of the geishas is gently fanning herself as birds fly through the sky above the landscaped garden in the distance.

England is often associated with tea drinking. That's why one of my favorite pottery sherds

from the Thames (above right) is a broken Victorian teacup which is decorated with an idyllic, utopian scene in the British countryside. An elegant English woman wearing an elaborate dress and broad hat is depicted within a beautifully landscaped garden. She is carrying a cornucopia bursting with fruit and vegetables, and her cute dog stares at her, awaiting a treat. In the distance, a tall Japanese pavilion is surrounded by weeping willow trees on the other side of a serene pond in this picturesque scene.

A few years ago, Anna Borzello found a beautiful porcelain egg cup decorated with a painting of Tower Bridge in London (left). It's a wonderful connection to this iconic bridge and feat of Victorian engineering. Tower Bridge was completed in 1894 and is still one of the most famous bridges in the world.

Top left: Art Deco sherd of Japanese geishas (Jacqui Wise). Top right: Picturesque scene on Victorian teacup (Jason Sandy). Left: Egg cup depicting Tower Bridge (Anna Borzello). Facing page, top right: Various birds illustrated on pottery sherds (Anna Borzello). Facing page, bottom: Three peacocks on Victorian chamber pot (Anna Borzello).

Animals are a common theme depicted on Victorian pottery. Anna has collected some extraordinary pieces of porcelain depicting birds of all different species. One of Anna's largest pottery sherds is a broken Victorian chamber pot decorated with three beautiful peacocks. The transferware pattern is highly ornate and was created by taking a black monochrome print on paper and pressing it onto the surface of the chamber pot before it was fired in the kiln. This technique for transferring the design was developed in England in the late 18th century. It became hugely popular in the 19th century to mass-produce and decorate ceramics, as it was infinitely cheaper and easier than laboriously hand painting each item.

One of the most common types of transferware pottery found along the Thames foreshore is the famous blue and white transferware called the Willow Pattern. Over the years, Anna has collected a lot of sherds with the iconic pattern which was created in Shropshire, England, towards

the end of the 18th century. The pattern was used to decorate ceramic serving dishes, plates, bowls, cups, and saucers, which were mass-produced and affordable for most households. Although the pattern looks Asian, it was created by English artists combining and adapting motifs inspired by hand-painted patterns imported from China.

To boost the sales of the Willow Pattern pottery, a fictional story was invented based on the imagery depicted in the chinoiserie pattern. It tells the plight of the daughter of a wealthy mandarin who had fallen in love with her father's accounting assistant. After the mandarin fired his assistant and arranged for his daughter to be married to a powerful duke, the young accountant returned to rescue the mandarin's daughter. They escaped by boat to a secluded island were they happily lived for years, but they were later discovered and killed by soldiers in revenge. The lovers were magically transformed into a pair of doves (facing page) who flew away together.

The most bizarre pottery sherd found by Anna portrays three giraffes galloping away from a hunter riding a horse with his rifle aimed at the exotic animals (below). Anna says, "It is one of my favorite sherds. I didn't even know giraffe hunting was a thing, but here it is—colonialists treating Africa as a playground and then carrying the image back to the dinner table of the Imperial heartland."

Several mudlarks are artists and keen collectors of these colorful pieces of pottery. Their artwork has been influenced by the diverse pottery sherds they have discovered themselves. "Color inspires me as an artist, and it's exciting to group colorful, decorative pieces of pottery together to paint, especially those with traces of gilding," explains Jacqui. Describing her favorite pottery sherds, Jacqui proclaims: "I love the colors, the beautiful flow of the brushstrokes, and the network of cracks on the surface of the glaze, all of which make it a more interesting piece for me to paint as a watercolorist. The beauty and history of the River Thames and the objects I find mudlarking provide a constant source of inspiration for my artwork."

Jacqui's personal favorite piece of art (above) is an assemblage of various colorful pottery sherds from the 19th and early 20th centuries, which she has collected while mudlarking along the Thames. The colors are bold and vibrant, and the ornate floral patterns complement each other, creating a beautiful collage of historic pieces.

Facing page: Sherds of Willow Pattern (Anna Borzello). Left: Giraffe hunting scene in Africa (Anna Borzello). Top: Colorful painting of Thames pottery sherds (Jacqui Wise).

Bee created with pink pottery sherds and music scores for wings (Lynne Pew).

Lynne Pew is another British mudlark and artist who creates extraordinary artwork with the tantalizing sherds of pottery she has collected over the past 20 years. When Lynne first started mudlarking along the River Irwell in Lancashire, she "started to notice beautiful bits of pottery in and around the river's edge and would pick them up and take them home to display. I was fascinated and intrigued by their beauty and had absolutely no idea why they were there or where they had come from. Each piece was beautiful in its own way: colors faded and cracked, edges worn smooth, snippets of designs reminiscent of my grandparents' best china."

I asked Lynne what inspired her artwork, and she explained: "I just really wanted to put these broken little pieces back together as something beautiful. It seemed like they'd been on such a journey. Discarded into the river then tumbled about for over 100 years at the mercy of time and tide."

When Lynne found her first striped piece of pottery, she knew immediately that she wanted to make little bees as a nod to Lancashire's history. "The River Irwell runs right through Manchester, and the 'Worker Bee' was first adopted as a motif for Manchester in the 18th century. The bee reflected a time when the city became a leader in the Industrial Revolution, symbolizing it being a hive of activity and enterprise for its hard-working citizens. I incorporated music scores for wings to represent Manchester's rich musical heritage," explains Lynne.

Incorporating her colorful pottery sherds, Lynne has created many bees and other motifs such as dragonflies, butterflies, hearts, and angels. Her favorite creation is a bee formed with pink pottery.

Discovering a piece of colorful pottery in the river is a magical experience! These colorful sherds give us a tantalizing glimpse into the past.

SHERD:
a broken pottery fragment, especially one of historic or archaeological value.

SHARD:
a piece or fragment of a brittle substance, including pottery, glass, rock, and metal.

When speaking of broken pottery, the words shard and sherd are interchangeable, though the term sherd is preferred by archaeologists.

The illustrations of people show us what life was like back then. Images of scenic landscapes demonstrate the highly romanticized and utopian visions of the Victorians. Bold, creative patterns and vivid colors attest to the popular tastes of the 19th and early 20th centuries. These stunning, colorful pieces of history have inspired many artists, such as Jacqui and Lynne, to create beautiful, imaginative works of art. The broken pieces once discarded in the river are now cherished again for generations to come.

If you want to see more artwork by Jacqui Wise, visit her Instagram account @jacquiwise or her online Etsy shop at JacquiWiseArt. Lynne Pew regularly posts photos of her artwork on Instagram @alice_and_the_mudlark and her Facebook page: @TheMudlark. Check out her website at www.themudlark.co.uk for custom-made works of art with colorful pottery sherds found in England.

Jason Sandy

JO COOK

I moved close to the Thames in 2008 and would often wonder what was down there as I walked along the towpath. I've always had an interest in archaeology. As a child, I used to find money and loved going fossil hunting on UK beaches. In 2019, my dad got a metal detector. He kindly lent it to me, and I went on some organized digs on farmlands. After many hours spent not finding anything other than rusty nails, I thought about checking out the Thames foreshore instead. I got my permit and headed down to a local spot with the metal detector. I found a George V penny and a tiny, fossilized sea urchin. I was immediately hooked! I soon got fed up with lugging the detector around, so I carried on with just my trusty trowel and two eyes.

I started off locally, and after researching access to the foreshore, I ventured into Central London. Although I find some excellent things locally, I prefer to go into London. Over time I have found "hot spots" for treasures, such as a secret spot I call "Bellarmine Beach" where I've found hundreds of pieces of 16th–17th-century Bellarmine jugs, including some nearly complete faces.

I also go out to the Thames Estuary where I know a spot that turns up the most beautiful glass buttons, beads, and perfume bottle stoppers. To be honest, I get as much of a thrill finding a beautiful, glass Art Deco button as I do finding a hammered coin. It's hard to choose favorite finds. I was thrilled to bits to find my first Roman coin. It was in such good condition

that I wasn't even sure if it was real. Another one of my favorite finds is a Tudor dress hook which would have been used to hitch up a woman's skirt to keep it out of the filth on the streets.

I'd say my best find is a Roman glass intaglio dating from the 3rd or 4th century AD. Measuring 1 cm (0.4 inches) in length, it would have been set in a ring which was perhaps worn by a Roman centurion. It features a goddess, possibly Diana. It really is an amazing artifact! I also love finding small personal items like Georgian wig curlers, Tudor knit combs, and clay and glass marbles. I even have a collection of dolls' eyes. I've learned so much about our ancestors' history and everyday lives. The objects I find would have been important to their owners in a time when people didn't have so much "stuff."

Mudlarking isn't just about finding long lost treasures though. There is a fantastic community of like-minded people, and I love bumping into friends and seeing what they've found. After larking, we sometimes meet up for a drink, swap tips, and gossip about who found what.

For me, the thrill of mudlarking is rescuing historical items that would have otherwise been lost forever. I like daydreaming about who they once belonged to and how they ended up in the river. It's so peaceful down on the foreshore, even in Central London. I clear my brain of stress, wondering what surprises are waiting for me. I'm rarely disappointed and count myself lucky to have found some wonderful treasures.

Portraits by Tom Harrison.

THE MYSTERY OF THAMES GARNETS

Garnets on the Thames foreshore (Jason Sandy)

Why are semi-precious gemstones lying on the bottom of the River Thames in London? Has a jewelry heist gone terribly wrong? No one knows, but each year mudlarks find hundreds of red garnets in several locations along the exposed riverbed at low tide.

For millennia, garnets have been used in jewelry and to decorate precious objects. The Anglo-Saxons, who lived in England from the 5th–11th centuries AD, especially loved garnets. They inlaid the semi-precious gemstones in a wide variety of prestige objects, from sword pommels to fine jewelry as illustrated in the incredible artifacts recovered from the Sutton Hoo ship burial and Staffordshire Hoard. The garnets have been cut into transparent, wafer-thin sheets and fitted into individual cells using the cloisonné technique, backed with gold foil containing patterns of lines and indentations to enhance the brilliance of the stones.

In London, a 7th-century Anglo-Saxon brooch (below) was discovered in a woman's grave in Covent Garden and is now on display in the Museum of London. It is decorated with twisted gold filigree on gold plates and inlaid with a mosaic of polished, red garnets. According to the Museum of London, this rare type of brooch was "fashionable among aristocratic Anglo-Saxon ladies," and the woman who wore it could have been "of noble, possibly even royal, birth."

When the tide recedes along the Thames, vibrant red garnets glisten like pomegranate seeds (from which their name originates) in the sunlight as they lie clustered on the surface of the exposed riverbed (facing page).

"There is something magical about picking garnets from the riverside grit," explains Anna Borzello. "They are tiny, red, and satisfyingly faceted. Best of all, they are such an unlikely find in Central London."

Florrie Evans describes the thrill of gem hunting, saying, "Garnets make me think of India, exotic trade, and treasure; finding them in the Thames seems so incongruous—magical in fact. Mudlarking for me is very much a treasure hunt and garnets are gems after all!"

We are uncertain where the garnets are from or how they ended up in the River Thames. Robin Hansen, curator at the Natural History Museum in London, confirmed that garnets are not native to the Thames; they were deposited there by people. But why? There are many theories, but there is still no conclusive evidence to solve the mystery. Alan Murphy, who has been mudlarking for over 30 years and has collected hundreds of garnets, believes that "they are Almandine garnets from India or South Asia, brought to London via the trade routes of the British East India Company." Alan explains that possibly "while hessian (burlap) sacks of garnets were being unloaded from ships, unscrupulous characters could have thrown some overboard to return at low tide to retrieve them to sell in the many inns along the Thames."

Hazel Forsyth, a senior curator at the Museum of London who has extensively researched gemstones and has written a book about the Cheapside Hoard jewels, believes that "the garnets' presence on the foreshore is probably due to accidental loss of a shipboard consignment." She thinks that some of the Thames garnets could have been intended for jewelry making before they were lost in the river.

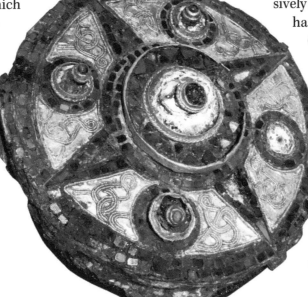

Anglo-Saxon brooch from Covent Garden, London (Jason Sandy).

Gold ring with red garnet by Hannah Upritchard (Anna Borzello).

Silver garnet-set rings on top of the large garnet (Florrie Evans).

Victorian ring with red garnets found in the Thames (Jason Sandy).

To assess whether the Thames garnets are jewelry-grade gemstones, I sent some of them to Kit Casati, a jewelry designer in the United States. He has kindly conducted several tests and cut some of the Thames garnets in a "cabochon" style with a diamond saw and diamond-plated wheels. Kit confirmed that some of the garnets from the Thames are large enough and of sufficient quality to be cut and set in jewelry.

With a hardness of 7.5 on the Mohs Scale, garnets are also used as an abrasive agent in industrial applications. Once the garnets have been crushed into finer grains, they can be used for sand blasting, water jet cutting, polishing, lapping, and even for cutting steel. For centuries, many industries and their workshops were located along the River Thames. Based on the industrial locations along the Thames where garnets are found, it is possible that they are a by-product or waste from industrial use. But, many of the larger, uncrushed garnets could not have been used for these abrasive purposes.

Shrouded in mystery and intrigue, the garnets are a highly desirable mudlarking find on the Thames foreshore. "I like the fact that no one knows for certain how they ended up on the foreshore, and that the most likely theories link them to London's ship-building past," explains Anna Borzello. "I mudlark all the time, and I love wearing something that I've found that links me to the river." Many mudlarks have commissioned jewelry designers to set the rough, uncut garnets into rings and jewelry. Hannah Upritchard, Nicolette Parker, and Wendy Meister have created a wide variety of beautiful jewelry set with Thames garnets.

Several years ago, three-year-old Cecilia discovered one of the largest red garnets (her birthstone) while mudlarking with her mother, Florrie Evans. It's a whopping 1 ¼ inch in length. Florrie says, "It's currently on display in my daughter's bedroom. We enjoy holding and turning it in our hands. When my daughter is older, perhaps she will want to set it. Whatever she chooses, I hope she will always treasure it as she does now!" Florrie commissioned Nicolette Parker, a London-based jewelry designer, to make rings (middle left) from some of the smaller garnets she has found in the Thames.

In 2017, I posted a photo (bottom left) on Instagram of some Thames garnets and a 19th-century Victo-

rian garnet-set ring I had found on the Thames foreshore. Kit Casati saw my post and contacted me. "I was fascinated with the history and journey that these raw garnets must have made to end up where they did, before Jason discovered them," explains Kit. "I am always amazed at the natural growth patterns of minerals as they form in their various crystalline structures. To me, they are the Earth's sacred geometry that has been frozen in time. Garnets are one of my favorite gemstones."

Kit, who has designed and produced jewelry for numerous Hollywood actors, kindly offered to make a pendant for my daughter if I sent him some of the Thames garnets. I was very touched by his kind gesture and sent him (a complete stranger) a packet of 25 garnets that my daughter had found in the Thames. I wasn't sure what to expect, but I received a package in the mail nine months later. My daughter was delighted to see her returned garnets set in a stunning silver pendant (top left). To enhance the appearance of the garnets, Kit cleverly placed them in silver loops so that light can pass through the gemstones from both directions.

Garnets are considered by many people to have special powers. Alan Murphy explains that a garnet is "intimately tied to the Earth, and is a talisman of protection and unyielding strength, both physically and intellectually. Its energy helps alleviate worry, panic, fear, and assists in maintaining a calm connection to the present. It allows one to perceive the absolute support of the universe." Because his wife suffers from Lupus SLE, Alan says that he "decided to help her by using a garnet she could wear as a talisman to help heal her pain and help protect her both physically and intel-

lectually while I'm not with her." The biggest garnet Alan has found is now mounted in a medieval-style silver ring (right), which was designed and produced by Hannah Upritchard.

Although their origins and use remain unknown, red garnets are an intriguing and magical find from the River Thames. Their raw, deep red appearance and intrinsic beauty have inspired jewelry designers in the United States and UK to create stunning rings, pendants, and other items using the historic garnets retrieved from the muddy river bed. The powerful garnets are also being used as talismans by people suffering from illness who call upon the healing powers of the garnets. But for now, the red garnets in the River Thames will remain an unsolved mystery.

Top: Glowing effect of red garnets (Kit Casati). Above right: Silver ring with red garnet (Alan Murphy). Bottom: Thames garnet jewelry (Wendy Meister).

CECILIA AND FLORRIE EVANS

I was lucky enough to grow up near the river, and in my first memory of mudlarking, around four years old, I was drawn to the foreshore in pursuit of a swan's feather. There, nestling under the grubby quill, was a small sherd of blue and white china. I didn't know until years later that it was a piece of Willow Pattern—the first of many. I've been in pursuit of river treasure on and off ever since. On a school trip to the newly restored Hampton Court Palace after a fire in 1986, I saw a display of Tudor clay pipes unearthed during the renovation, and so was thrilled to find them for myself on the foreshore.

After that, I became more focused in my searching, realizing that there was more to the river than pottery and pipes. Ancient beads and buttons were my Holy Grail, for the personal stories they tell, the associations with the wearer, and the social history too. This interest in historical costume has never left me and feeds into my job today as an art historian and gallerist. The river is my happy place, my headspace, and my passion. When I had my daughter in 2014, it was inevitable that she would come with me to the river, from a baby in the sling, until today, always my best mudlarking companion. Her eyes are close to the ground, and she sees what I miss! For now, she loves it too, and hopefully we are making memories to treasure together. Perhaps I am recapturing my own childhood by the Thames—happy memories of mudlarking with my own mum.

Portraits by Tom Harrison.

It's hard to pinpoint our favorite finds, or our most significant, because every piece we bring home has the added special memory of the moment we found it. However, my daughter's giant garnet which she picked up as a three-year-old has definitely gone down in mudlarking lore as the biggest yet to be retrieved from the river. My string of beads dating from the Iron Age to the 20th century is pretty epic! We love all glass finds, and our miniature 17th-century apothecary bottles give me as much of a thrill as if they were the rarest of onion bottles! I'm also very partial to my Tudor chatelaine hook. As I hold it in my hand, I wonder who the woman was that lost it, what sort of things she hung from it, and what sort of life she led.

More recently, there has been a cross-over with my working life too. After curating a small exhibition of mudlarked finds alongside exquisite still life photographs of Thames-found objects by photographer Hannah Smiles—a passion project for us both—we were invited by the Totally Thames Festival to create an even bigger mudlarking exhibition called "Foragers of the Foreshore" for their festival in 2019. It took place at the Bargehouse, a massive warehouse space with three floors of exhibits near the OXO Tower on the Southbank. It drew in more visitors than the festival had ever seen before and felt like mudlarking had at last entered the everyday vernacular.

BELLARMINE JUGS AND WITCH BOTTLES

17th-century Bellarmine jug (Dean Buddin).

While nightlarking along the exposed riverbed of the River Thames in London, Dean Buddin made a once-in-a-lifetime discovery. He spotted the handle of a German stoneware jug sticking out of the mud. This is a common sight on the foreshore, but normally, it's only a broken fragment.

"I could just see a little bit of a handle sticking out of the mud, so I had a little scrape around it," explains Dean. "To my surprise, it seemed to have more attached to it. The more I scraped around the handle, the more I could see, and the bigger my smile got. Out popped a nearly complete Bellarmine jug. I was over the moon!" The jug was completely intact except for a small piece missing at the top (right). It is truly a miracle that this 17th-century German stoneware jug survived for over 400 years in the River Thames.

Manufactured in various towns along the Rhine River from the 16th–18th centuries, these vessels are commonly called "Bartmann" (bearded man) or "Greybeard" jugs. The bearded face on the neck of the jugs is thought to represent a "wild man" found in popular European myths of the period. The stoneware vessels are also known as "Bellarmine" jugs because of their association with the Catholic cardinal, Roberto Bellarmino (AD 1542–1621), a strong opponent of Protestantism who wanted to ban alcohol. To mock the unpopular Catholic cardinal who was greatly disliked, Protestant Germans drank ale and wine from stoneware jugs which they nicknamed "Bellarmines" because the bearded faces on the jugs had an uncanny resemblance to Roberto Bellarmino who had a flowing beard.

Above, left to right: 16th-century Bellarmine face, 17th-century Bellarmine jug top with handle, 17th-century Bellarmine face (Jason Sandy).

Each Bellarmine face is unique, and I have found many types of bearded faces in the River Thames (above). In the 16th century, the exquisite faces were created with great skill and detail. As the production and exportation of the jugs increased, the faces became more grotesque and crude in the 17th century. Bellarmine jugs were made with a dense, grey clay and fired to create an iron-rich, brown surface and salt-glazed appearance. The bellies of the bulbous jugs were decorated with medallions (left), which often contained figures, geometric patterns, symbols, heraldic devices, crests, or coats-of-arms of affluent patrons, European cities, royal houses, and ecclesiastical organizations.

Medallion from a Bellarmine jug (Jason Sandy).

Bellarmines were made in various sizes as drinking jugs and for decanting wine in taverns (right). They were also used for a multitude of other purposes including the storage of ale, cider, and wine and for transporting goods such as acids, oils, vinegar, and mercury. Because of its variety of uses, the non-porous stoneware was a key export from Germany in the 16th and 17th centuries and was shipped around Europe, the British Isles,

and colonies in North America, South America, Africa, India, and Australia. Bellarmine jugs were used in many households in England in that time period.

I had the privilege of interviewing Alex Wright, the founder and owner of the Bellarmine Museum in Swaffham, England. When Alex found his first Bellarmine jug in Kings Lynn, England, in 1976, his life-long passion and fascination with the German stoneware jugs began. "I found my first Bellarmine embedded in the side of a large pit on a building site. I carefully pulled it out only to discover that a large piece of the back was missing. This did not dampen my enthusiasm. It had a face mask and a medallion, and I was the first to see it for over 300 years. Most importantly, it was mine," describes Alex.

After collecting a vast array of Bellarmine jugs and other German stoneware over the past 40 years, he founded the Bellarmine Museum in

Collection of Bellarmine jugs (Alex Wright).

Bellarmine Museum in Swaffham (Alex Wright).

Swaffham. "I created the Bellarmine Museum to give interested enthusiasts an opportunity to view all the items in my three books (*The Bellarmine and other German Stoneware I, II and III*). The collection has continued to grow, and the museum has now been open for several years," explains Alex. "Most of the Bellarmines in the museum come from old collections or recent finds I have purchased. None were donations. In my collection, there are over 150 Bellarmines and hundreds of fragments including face masks and medallions. There are also over 200 other German stoneware pots (c. AD 1200–1770)," describes Alex.

Alex has even acquired several Bellarmine jugs discovered by mudlarks in the River Thames in London. It is now the largest private collection of publicly displayed Bellarmine jugs in the world. The museum collection contains examples of the pottery which can also be found in the United States, in such places as Jamestown, Virginia, where many Bellarmine jugs were discovered during archaeological excavations of the former British colony established in 1607.

In the 17th century, there was a great fear of witchcraft, and superstitious people blamed witches for their illnesses and misfortunes. In Europe and America, witches were actively hunted down and brought to trial. There were several witch trials in Britain in the 17th century, but the Pendle Hill witch trials of 1612 are probably the most famous in British history. In Lancashire, 12 people were accused and charged with the deaths of ten people by the use of witchcraft. Following a series of trials, ten "witches" were found guilty and executed by hanging. During the deadliest witch hunt in the history of colonial America, 200 people were accused of being "witches." After a series of hearings and prosecutions of the people accused of witchcraft in colonial Massachusetts, 19 "witches" (14 women and 5 men) were found guilty and executed by hanging following the infamous Salem Witch Trials between February 1692 and May 1693. The fear of witches led to many more executions, and people sought to protect themselves against the witches and their evil spells.

Bellarmine jugs were sometimes used as so-called "witch bottles" in the 17th century. The grotesque faces and human-like shape of the bottles represented the body of a witch. To torture the witches and repel them, the bottles were filled with harmful or repulsive substances such as menstrual blood, urine, rusty iron nails, bent needles, hair and nail clippings, pins, cloth hearts,

Historical illustration of Salem witch trials.

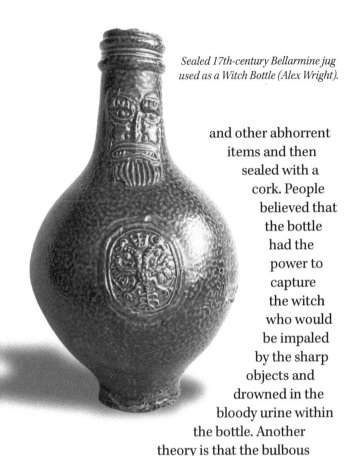

Sealed 17th-century Bellarmine jug used as a Witch Bottle (Alex Wright).

and other abhorrent items and then sealed with a cork. People believed that the bottle had the power to capture the witch who would be impaled by the sharp objects and drowned in the bloody urine within the bottle. Another theory is that the bulbous shape of the Bellarmine jug represented the witch's bladder. "The nails and the bent pins would supposedly aggravate the witch when she urinated and torment her so badly that she would take the spell back off you," explains Alan Massey from the University of Loughborough.

The powerful witch bottle was believed to be effective against evil spirits as long as the bottle remained hidden and unbroken. To guard the entrances to the home, the witch bottles were strategically concealed beneath the fireplace hearth or buried under the doorsteps or threshold into the house to prevent witches and evil spirits from entering.

In 2004, a complete witch bottle was found during excavations in Greenwich. It provided a rare opportunity for archaeologists to analyze its contents from the 17th century. When they opened the bottle, they found bent nails and pins, a nail-pierced leather "heart," fingernail clippings, navel fluff, and hair. The bottle and its contents are currently on display at the Discover Greenwich Visitor Centre in southeast London.

The Bellarmine Museum also has a rare, sealed witch bottle from 1620–1675 AD that was found in Swardeston, England (left). Alex Wright explains that "this Bellarmine was made in Germany, transported to England by Dutch traders (probably to a merchant in Norwich) and ended up in Swardeston." The witch bottle was found under a doorstep in a public house (pub) during renovations several years ago. Alex has not opened the bottle, so it still retains its nearly 400-year-old contents. "From an X-ray of the bottle, you can see many brass pins, an iron pin, and a silver pin. The organic material does not show up in the X-rays," describes Alex (below). This sealed witch bottle is an amazing time capsule which is evidence of the superstitions and fear of witchcraft in the 17th century.

If you would like to find out more about German stoneware and witch bottles, I would highly recommend a visit to the Bellarmine Museum in Swaffham. For more information, check out the museum's website: www.bellarminemuseum.co.uk.

X-ray of Witch Bottle contents (Alex Wright).

MALCOLM DUFF

When I was seven years old, I used to go to the Thames looking for horses' teeth and wondered how they got there. I first started mudlarking because I got bored with finding modern to Victorian copper coins in fields and woods. When I saw an advertisement in the local news about detecting on the Thames, I went down to the river and was immediately surprised at the amount of debris and lead there was. It was so exciting to think that I was the first person to handle objects that hadn't been seen for 500–1,000 years. There was no going back from there. I am obsessed with mudlarking, and I have gone on average two or three times a week for the past 25 years.

It is sometimes dangerous. I used to wade out to my waist with chest waders and a long scoop. One day I was so engrossed that I didn't notice a Thames Clipper boat going past, and I was hit in the back by a large wave which almost knocked me off my feet. I was very lucky that the wave pushed me towards the bank instead of dragging me out. With chest waders on, it could have been a very different outcome. My friend, Sami, who witnessed the event, presented me with a brand-new life vest.

I have had some lovely finds while wading in the Thames, including a beautiful, bronze, poor man's memorial ring with a complete skeleton on it, plus numerous coins. Being a fisherman as well, I go mudlarking no matter what the weather throws my way. One day I was in the Queenhithe area when a chap approached me. He said, "Excuse me. I'm not being rude, but aren't you a little bit mad detecting in this snow?" I replied, "Yes, but you must be every bit as mad because you are down here taking pictures of me." We both started to laugh like hyenas, warming us up somewhat. He then asked if he could film and interview me, to which I agreed as we seemed to have struck up a friendship.

My favorite finds are a 17th-century William III tankard from The Anchor pub with the owner's name inscribed on it. I also discovered a pewter flask of the same type as was found on the *Mary Rose* ship. It has a hole pierced through it, which was likely made by a musket ball and may be evidence that the wearer was killed, as flasks were worn around the neck.

I love to share my knowledge with the many friends I have made on the riverbank. I like listening to their experiences and identifying what they have found if they don't know what it is. I was privileged to be in the first series of the TV show *Mud Men*, where I had the pleasure of meeting and laughing with the late, great Geoff Egan. He was a wonderful man who with all his knowledge, was still interested in what you had to say even though I had far less experience than him.

Portraits by Tom Harrison.

As you look across the quiet, serene river today, it's hard to imagine the vast sea of ships that once clogged the Thames. By the 18th century, London had become the largest and most important port in the world. Thousands of ships entered the port each year, carrying goods and produce from around the globe.

The long process of paying custom taxes and unloading the cargo into warehouses meant that ships sometimes waited up to three months on the river, causing a gridlock and preventing the free movement of other ships. Statistician Patrick Colquhoun estimated that at the end of the 18th century there were 8,000 vessels on a six-mile stretch of river around London Bridge. He calculated that the amount of property floating on the river at any one time was worth approximately $96 million in today's dollars. The valuable cargo attracted pilferers and river pirates who targeted and plundered the vulnerable ships. Colquhoun estimated that over

PIRATES OF THE RIVER THAMES

$640,000 of goods (a staggering $58.7 million at today's rates) were stolen in 1797. Because of the great financial losses caused by piracy, the Thames River Police was established in 1798 in Wapping (London) as the first organized police force in the world.

Once river pirates were captured, they were tried and imprisoned in Marshalsea or Newgate prisons. Pirates who were captured abroad were also brought back to London and tried by the High Court of the Admiralty. If the pirates were condemned to death, they were transported in a cart and paraded across London Bridge

The Rhinebeck Panorama of London's Docks, c. 1807.

so everyone could see them as they traveled to Execution Dock in East London, which was used for over 400 years to execute pirates, smugglers, and mutineers.

Shortly before an execution, crowds would gather along the riverbank or watch from boats on the Thames to get a better view of the hanging. To prolong the agony, pirates would be hanged from a shortened rope (so it didn't break their necks) over the tidal river at low tide. If the pirates didn't die by slow asphyxiation, they would drown as the incoming tide submerged them. The corpses were customarily left for three tides before they were cut down. Captain Kidd was probably the most infamous pirate to be hanged at Execution Dock. As a warning to incoming ships and pirates sailing up the Thames, some of the corpses were tarred and hanged at the entrance into London from the sea. It must have been a pretty gruesome sight!

Although river pirates disappeared centuries ago, still today we find traces of their former existence. Mudlark Mike Walker has discovered numerous "pirate cob" coins of various shapes and sizes while mudlarking at low tide along the exposed riverbed of the Thames (right). To expedite the transport of precious metals from the South American colonies back to Spain, mints produced irregular coinage called "cobs." Rough chunks of gold, silver, and copper were cut to the appropriate weight and struck with crude dies. The coins varied greatly in size, shape, and impression, and were often disfigured with large cracks and imperfections. In the 16th and 17th centuries, pirates ransacked many Spanish galleon ships on their way from the Caribbean to Spain, seizing their cargo of coins. Some of the Spanish cobs made their way back to London as illustrated by this copper Spanish 8 Maravedis cob coin dated 1652 (below) that was found by Mike Walker.

Top: Illustration of the overcrowded docks in London (Gustave Doré). Bottom: Pirate cob coins (Mike Walker).

Pirate cob dated 1652 (Mike Walker).

Spanish ½ Reale coin dated 1781 (Oliver Muranyi-Clark).

Execution Dock token (Philly Gumbo).

Other coins from various Spanish American colonies have also been found in the River Thames. Oliver Muranyi-Clark found a Spanish 1/2 Reale coin minted in Mexico and dated 1781 (top left). Often referred to in pirate folklore as "Pieces of Eight," a silver Spanish 8 Reales coin was found by Nick Stevens. Possibly plundered from a Spanish ship and brought back to London, this large 8 Reales coin is very unusual because it has been re-milled and re-circulated as a King George III Bank of England dollar (five shillings) coin dated 1804.

The last hangings at Execution Dock took place in 1830, but evidence of the infamous dock can still be found on the riverbed at low tide. While mudlarking in April 2019, Philly Gumbo found a rare 17th-century trade token (top right) stamped with the words "Execution Dock." Worth a farthing, this trade token was issued by John Shaw for his business located at Execution Dock in the 17th century. As one can imagine, shops took advantage of their prime location when crowds gathered to watch the gruesome events.

Several years ago, Steve Brooker also found a copper coin (facing page, top) dated 1677, which was purposely rubbed smooth and hand-carved with an illustration of the gallows. I wonder if a condemned pirate created this token as he awaited his certain demise at the gallows?

If the river pirates were not condemned to death, they were thrown into prison with other criminals. In the 18th century, London's prisons were massively overcrowded. As a result, the government began converting decommissioned warships into floating prisons (below) called "hulks" on the River Thames. Some prisoners were locked up on the ships until space could be found on a convict ship bound for Australia, but many prisoners served their entire sentence on the hulks floating on the Thames. While on the boat and at work, the prisoners were shackled to prevent escape.

The Discovery *Convict Ship along the Thames, 1829 (Royal Museums Greenwich).*

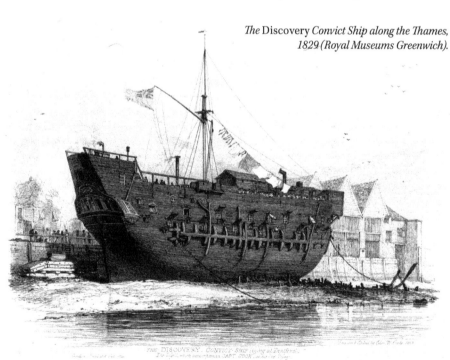

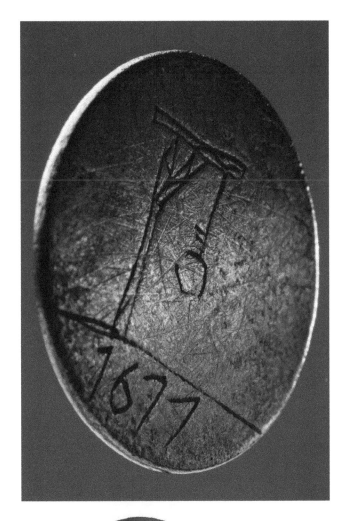

In 2009, mudlarks Rick Jones and Steve Brooker thought they had found a large cannon ball until they picked it up and a chain slithered out of the Thames mud, still attached to an iron ball (below) dating from the 1700s or early 1800s. Kate Sumnall, a curator at the Museum of London, says: "The river is the repository for so many of London's stories, and this extraordinary find gives us a tantalizing glimpse of the human trials and tribulations of past Londoners. Whether a would-be Houdini freed himself from the great iron on his leg, or perished in shackles, or whether this ball and chain was simply discarded, we can never know."

These intriguing artifacts discovered on the exposed riverbed of the Thames provide an interesting insight into the lives, imprisonment, and execution of pirates when London was the largest port in the world. To commemorate Execution Dock, a replica of the gallows has been built on the riverbank in front of the Prospect of Whitby pub in East London. As a result of river pirates on the Thames, the first police force in the world was established, and the maritime police unit is still located on the same spot along the River Thames. Today they continue patrolling the river as they did back in the 18th century.

Top: Gallows token dated 1677 found by Steve Brooker (Hannah Smiles). Bottom: 18th-century ball and chain (Rick Jones).

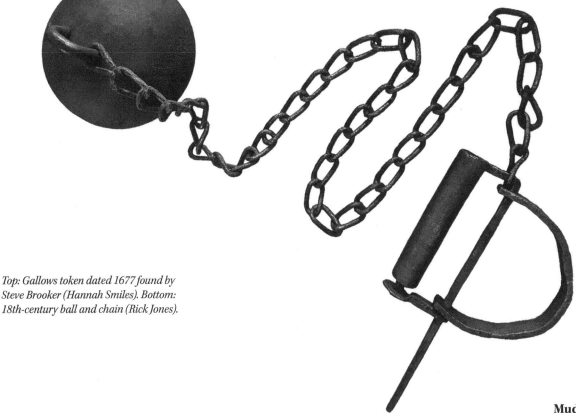

MIKE WALKER

My interest in the River Thames started at a very young age. During a family trip to the Sea Life aquarium in London when I was around seven years old, I remember being fascinated by a display showcasing mostly modern objects which had been pulled from the Thames. I wondered to myself what else could be lying under the murky waters of the river.

I soon forgot about it until I came across an article about mudlarking on Facebook many years later when I was 17 years old. Unlike the display, the article focused solely on the historic artifacts that had been plucked from the mud. This re-ignited my interest, and I was drawn into searching online for other articles, videos, or whatever I could find relating to mudlarking. Now at an age where I could travel of my own accord, I was determined to give mudlarking a go myself. After some research into licenses required, access points, and carefully studying the PLA maps, I finally made my first trip down onto the sandy foreshore at Bankside during one afternoon of study-leave during my A-levels.

Like most people, I did not find much on my first trip other than some broken ceramics and pipe stems. Of course, at the time, I was fascinated by these. But, I was determined to find an old coin and continued to make trips to the foreshore. After my 6th or 7th trip, I finally found my first old coin—a Richmond farthing of Charles I.

From this point, I was hooked. Mudlarking is similar to a gambling addiction. If you have a poor day for finds, you are determined to invest more time and keep coming back in the hope of finding something on the next trip. If you have a good day for finds, it spurs you on to keep going back again and again. The thrill of finding something which has not been touched by human hands for hundreds or even thousands of years is just so great. That is what draws me back time and time again.

I regularly get asked two questions by passing dog walkers and tourists: "what is the best thing you have found?" and "what is the most valuable thing you have found?" The second question I have no interest in answering because, unlike the original mudlarks of the Victorian age, modern mudlarks are not interested in the value of their finds. However, everyone still has a gold coin or artifact at the top of their wish list, and I'm one of the lucky (and very grateful) few to have found one! Therefore, my best coin, without any doubt in my mind, is a 4 Escudos of Josephus I of Portugal dated 1759.

One of my favorite and rarer finds is my 17th–18th-century latten spoon with a strawberry knop which I plucked from the river mud back in 2015. This may seem like an unusual thing to class as a "favorite artifact," but these spoons are extremely rare to find complete. It is in such good condition that part of the polished, silver surface of the bowl is still visible.

Portraits by Tom Harrison.

COLORFUL
GLASS BEADS

Full of mystery and beauty, beads embody history and humanity. These tiny objects reveal intriguing stories of social and economic circumstances, popular fashions, political history, and religious beliefs. Beads have always been popular in almost every culture around the world. In ancient grave sites, the deceased were often buried with their beads, demonstrating the religious importance and cultural symbolism of beads. When Christopher Columbus first landed in America in 1492, he gave the Arawak Indians strings of colorful, glass beads to impress them and win their friendship. In the 17th and 18th centuries, beads were a valuable "currency," which Europeans produced and exchanged for furs in North America, spices in the Far East, and gold, ivory, and slaves in Africa. Even today, colorful beads can be found in many types of fashion accessories around the world.

Over the past four decades, mudlarks have discovered thousands of beads in the River Thames in London. Ranging from the Iron Age to Modern times, these beads are a tangible connection to Londoners who wore them around their necks and wrists as status symbols and colorful, fashionable accessories to complement their attire and enhance their beauty.

A few years ago, John Higginbotham discovered a large, translucent blue Celtic bead from 800 to 100 BC. The surface of the bead has raised protrusions with decorative, white spirals which look like eyes. Considered to have amuletic properties, this "eye bead" is classified as an Oldbury Type 1407 bead. Surprisingly, a metal ring is still attached to the bead which could have been used to suspend the large bead as a pendant. Just imagine a whole necklace made from these blue beads which would have glistened in the sunlight. They would have been worn as an impressive symbol of status and power.

In AD 43, the Romans arrived in Britain and successfully established a settlement called Londinium that thrived for nearly 400 years before they abandoned the city around AD 426. Although the Romans left around 1,600 years ago, mudlarks still find traces of Roman life. Florrie Evans has discovered several glass beads, which would have adorned an elegant Roman woman's neck or wrist. These colorful glass beads (right) were made in different shapes and sizes. They now have a frosty appearance after a thousand years rolling around at the bottom of the river.

As I was mudlarking along the Thames in Central London, I discovered a Roman bead (top right) made from orange glass. The Museum of London has dated it to AD 50–410,

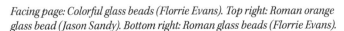

Facing page: Colorful glass beads (Florrie Evans). Top right: Roman orange glass bead (Jason Sandy). Bottom right: Roman glass beads (Florrie Evans).

and it is in perfect condition. The bead is slightly sub-spherical and is decorated with a central band running around the circumference with undulating ridges above and below. It was probably part of a necklace comprised of many similar beads.

The Romans also loved wearing necklaces with large glass beads. They were experts in glass-making and produced beautiful glass "melon" beads, which have convex ribs around the circumference to catch the light. A few years ago, I found a large Roman melon bead (left). According to the Museum of London, it is from AD 43–300. The bead now has a frosted greenish-grey color, but it would likely have been a transparent bluish-green glass bead when originally made.

In 2018, two mudlarks coincidentally discovered two halves of the same Roman bead at different times. Guy Phillips explains, "While searching the foreshore, I spotted the fragment of a Roman melon bead. Picking it up, its shape and muted, yellow color immediately reminded me of an Instagram post from Florrie a few months earlier." At a mudlarking exhibition in 2019, Guy and Florrie brought the bead pieces together (bottom left) "to discover whether the two halves were indeed from the same bead. Remarkably they were—what an extraordinary reunion! The iridescent color on the break line may indicate that the two halves were separated for a considerable period of time, making their

coupling all the more improbable!" It is truly a miracle that the nearly 2,000-year-old Roman bead is now complete again.

Medieval beads are a rare find from the River Thames, but mudlark Oliver Muranyi-Clark has found a few unusual beads made of bone (right) that have been dated to the late medieval or early post-medieval period. One of them is a spherical bone bead decorated with a cross hatch pattern of incised lines. The other bead is a beautiful work of art. A piece of bone has been hand-carved and faceted into a square, truncated trapezohedron shape with raised circles.

In the 17th century, a dark chapter in Britain's history began when merchants started trading with West African tribes and transporting slaves to the Caribbean and American colonies. By 1660, the Royal African Company was granted a monopoly over the English slave trade after it was founded by wealthy London merchants and the British royal family. Dating to 1660–1675, two lead seals (right) from the Company of Royal Adventurers Trading to Africa were found by Malcolm Duff and Tom Bland. In the center of the seal, a shield is shown with an elephant carrying a castle on its back, flanked by two native Africans. As part of the slave trade, European glassmakers mass-produced huge quantities of glass beads, which

Top left: Roman glass melon bead (Jason Sandy). Bottom left: Roman glass melon bead (Hannah Smiles). Top right: Medieval and post-medieval carved bone beads (Oliver Muranyi-Clark). Bottom right: Lead seal from the Company of Royal Adventurers Trading to Africa (Tom Bland).

were used as a valuable commodity and "currency" for buying slaves in West Africa who were then transported to the New World and traded for sugar, tobacco, rum, and cotton, which were taken back to Europe.

Oliver has also found a wide variety of colorful, glass trade beads (top) on the Thames foreshore. According to the Victoria and Albert Museum, "These beads are known as trade, aggry, or slave beads. They formed an important element in early trade networks between Europe and Africa. At that time, glass beads were a major part of the currency exchanged for people and products. The beads proved to be a cheap and efficient means of exploiting African resources, especially as glassmaking technologies developed in Europe." It's hard to believe that these stunning, seemingly innocent glass beads were used for such a horrible, evil, and inhumane purpose.

One of the nicest trade beads that Oliver has found is a chevron bead (below) produced by

Venetian glassmakers in Murano, Italy, between 1500 and the early 1600s. It was formed by forcing or blowing molten glass into a mold with striated edges which created the ridges on the outer surface. Additional layers of alternating blue, white, and red glass were added before it was quickly drawn into a six-foot-long cane. It was then cooled, cut into short pieces, and chamfered at both ends to create a unique, star-shaped pattern.

A few years ago, Fran Sibthorpe and I discovered two glass trade beads that are almost identical, although we found them in two different areas along the river in London. Fran was born and raised in Britain, but she is of African Caribbean descent from Trinidad in the West Indies. Her ancestors were slaves transported from West Africa to the Caribbean. Therefore, Fran feels a special connection to this trade bead (left). "I found this large 17th-century Dutch chevron bead partially submerged in the Thames foreshore 'gloop' just waiting for me as I was about to leave the foreshore," explains Fran.

Top: Colorful trade beads (Oliver Muranyi-Clark). Middle: 17th-century Dutch glass trade bead (Fran Sibthorpe). Bottom: Venetian glass chevron bead (Oliver Muranyi-Clark).

In the 19th and 20th centuries, colorful beads in necklaces, bracelets, rosaries, and other accessories continued to be a popular. One of the largest assemblages of Victorian and 20th-century beads from the River Thames was passionately collected by a mudlark named Denver. As Florrie was mudlarking with her daughter along the Thames Estuary in 2017, they met Denver for the first time on a bright, spring day. Florrie describes Denver as a "big, burly man, ginger, topless, sweating and burned in the sunshine. He'd been collecting beads and gave my thrilled daughter his pocketful. Seeing her excitement, he offered on the spot to send her his 'life's collection,' if we gave him our address. I was a bit embarrassed and overwhelmed by this spontaneous act of kindness.

I didn't expect anything further from the encounter, but my daughter clearly hadn't forgotten his promise. When the postman delivered a compact, heavy package a few months later, she immediately said 'it's from Denver the Bead Man'. She was right!" Florrie and Cecilia were delighted when they opened the package and discovered a "joyous riot of rainbow beads (below) from the Thames estuary which were a special gift to my daughter, who was three-years-old. If beads could talk, these little beauties would have a cacophony of stories to tell," explains Florrie. One of her most-special beads (facing page, bottom) is an early 20th-century Czech bead made from clear yellow glass with an intricate applied glass rose.

"When I picked up this bead, it immediately triggered my senses and emotions as I knew what it represented. Momentarily, I just looked at it with poignant, wide eyes and was immediately transported to my ancestors—it evoked my heritage. Sadly, I knew that this particular trade bead had been part of the slave trade. The association with colonialism (red, white, and blue colors) took this find to another dimension. I wondered who had handled this trade bead, from manufacturer to its arrival on the foreshore. A testimonial find never to be forgotten."

Along with other trade beads, Florrie has found two extraordinary "Millefiori" beads (above) from around the 18th century. The name originates from the Italian words "mille" (thousand) and "fiori" (flowers) which describes a glassmaking technique most frequently associated with Venetian glassware.

Top: Venetian Millefiori and trade beads (Florrie Evans).
Bottom: Bead collection from Mudlark Denver (Florrie Evans).

In one location along the River Thames, I have found two turquoise-colored beads in the shape of a skull (top left). They are "memento mori" beads, which serve as a reminder of death and one's mortality. Although these beads are modern, memento mori beads have been produced for many centuries.

As I was mudlarking on a sunny morning, I spotted two colorful beads (top right) nestled together on the exposed riverbed. The surface of the beads is decorated with turquoise and coral, inlaid between brass wire. The handmade beads were produced in the mountains of Tibet or Nepal. It is believed that the color combination of orange and turquoise can release the healing energies of passion, creativity, and peace.

Beads are still an important part of society today. Walk into any department store, and you will find beaded necklaces, bracelets, and many more fashion accessories. Rosary beads and prayer beads are still used by devout Catholics, Muslims, and Buddhists in their daily prayer rituals. During Mardi Gras in New Orleans, necklaces made of colorful, plastic beads are thrown and used as a "currency" during the festivities. Regardless of their use, beads are captivatingly beautiful pieces of history.

Top left: Skull-shaped "memento mori" bead (Jason Sandy).
Top right: Handmade beads from Tibet or Nepal (Jason Sandy).
Center: 20th-century Czech bead with rose (Florrie Evans).

FRAN SIBTHORPE

From an early age, I have been interested in history and archaeology. Happy, annual, childhood, summer holidays were spent along the Jurassic coast in Dorset, providing hours of beachcombing opportunities. I enjoyed the fresh air and the freedom to wander and explore while collecting my favorite tiny ammonites. Beachcombing along the Essex coast also fascinated me, especially finding shark's teeth! I would take my finds home and research them using an encyclopedia.

My childhood experiences of building tree-branched dens across a stream in the Epping Forest and making mud pies were perhaps my introduction to the word "mudlarking!" Years later, I moved to London. One evening a group of friends and I ventured down to the Thames foreshore. I found and collected some small blue and white transfer-ware sherds. A few years later I rediscovered them, and I wondered what else might be down on the foreshore. So, I applied and received my foreshore permit from the Port of London Authority.

In 2016, I had a unique opportunity to go mudlarking (eyes only) on the Tower of London foreshore as part of the Totally Thames Festival and another time with the Thames Discovery Programme. Both events were amazing and increased my searching skills. Mudlarking has enabled me to discover historical knowledge specific to each artifact. I'm particularly interested in finding tiny objects. All my finds are "eyes only" without any mechanical devices.

No two mudlarking sessions are the same for me. They differ depending on personal and environmental situations. There are times for solitude and times for meeting other mudlarks which gives me an opportunity to share, identify, and learn about artifacts. Even though a find is not always guaranteed, I still enjoy the moment and a splosh at the water's edge. Discovering a historic artifact is like a personal gift from the past. I tend to immediately photograph or video in situ and record any significant finds in my notebook. I enjoy researching the artifacts—there are usually interesting stories to be revealed.

I encourage others, especially from the Black community and other ethnic minority groups, to participate in mudlarking, as it has really opened my eyes to the hidden past and journey through the finds as stepping stones. I'm grateful and fortunate to be able to have some of my finds assessed and recorded by the Finds Liaison Officer (FLO) at the Museum of London. My favorite finds include a small glass Roman Nicolo intaglio engraved with a solitary figure; an unusual, conjoined 17th-century trade token from the Salter's and Brewer's Arms; a post-medieval ceramic "china" marble dating to 1840-1880 and decorated with a pinwheel flower motif; and a large, chevron-patterned, glass trade/slave bead from the 17th to 19th centuries. This bead transports me back to my ancestors and my Caribbean heritage.

Portraits by Tom Harrison.

LOST AND
FOUND
TOYS

Two 17th–18th-century hand-carved bone dice, Roman hand-carved bone gaming piece engraved with the number XIIII, 17th–18th-century hand-carved bone domino, and medieval gaming piece inscribed with clusters of rings and dots from the collection of Jason Sandy (Hannah Smiles).

I t was very dark as I was mudlarking late at night along the River Thames in London in October 2018. After hours of searching with little success, I spotted something unusual in the pool of light formed by my head lamp on the dark riverbank. It was a folded piece of pewter which seemed to have some decoration.

I couldn't see much in the dark, so I waited until I got home to inspect it closer. To my surprise, the decoration was formed by numbers along the curved rim of the mystery object. I spent hours carefully unfolding and straightening the soft pewter disc in order to see the full image. My patient work paid off as an 18th-century toy pocket watch appeared (right).

I'm sure the kid who lost this extraordinary toy was devastated. Produced between 1700 and 1750, this toy pocket watch is a close imita-

tion of a real pocket watch of that time period. It's one of my favorite finds in my collection!

More medieval and post-medieval toys have been discovered in London than any other place in the British Isles. This is primarily due to the anaerobic (no oxygen) mud of the Thames foreshore which has perfectly preserved the toys. For centuries, children have been attracted to the Thames because of the large number of ships and other boats constantly moving along the river. When the

Top: Victorian toy horse with red and green enamel (Jason Sandy).
Bottom: 18th-century toy pocket watch (Jason Sandy).

tide was out, the exposed riverbed was a great place to explore, full of curiosities. Children inevitably lost some of their toys as they played along the river.

Over the years, mudlarks have found a wide variety of toys including miniature figurines, guns, cannons, watches, animals, soldiers, domestic utensils, and dolls. Before I wrote this book, I was given a private tour of the Museum of London's archive, and senior curator Hazel Forsyth showed me cabinets filled with hundreds of pewter toys acquired from Thames mudlarks over the last four decades. The Museum of London's collection of early base-metal toys is one of the largest and most important of its kind in the world.

The vast variety and quantity of pewter toys discovered in the Thames have actually changed the way historians view the medieval period. Hazel Forsyth, co-author of the book *Toys, Trifles & Trinkets*, stated that, "these medieval toys are exceptionally rare and have helped transform perceptions of childhood during the Middle Ages." In light of the new archaeological evidence,

Forsyth states that we now know that, "some parents [in the Middle Ages] were very devoted to their children and gave them every luxury and pleasure they could afford."

Several years ago, a mudlark found an exquisite medieval toy knight (bottom left), perfectly preserved by the soft mud of the River Thames. Wearing a coat of chain mail and carrying a sword in his right hand, the knight is riding a horse. "This knight on horseback is the earliest hollow-cast pewter figure known in England, and it is one of the earliest examples of a mass-produced medieval metal toy," according to the Museum of London. Based on the stylistic features of the toy knight, the museum has dated it to the early 14th century.

A mudlark also unearthed the hollow head of a medieval pewter puppet (bottom right) from the 14th or 15th centuries. The puppet head has long flowing hair with a short fringe, and the hat is missing. Within the hollow neck, a finger or stick would have been placed to animate the puppet. You can just imagine a young child gleefully playing with the puppet, entertaining friends in the Middle Ages.

Left: Illustration of medieval toy knight in the Museum of London (Coral Pearce). Above: Illustration of medieval toy stick puppet in the Museum of London (Coral Pearce).

In the 16th century, small figurines wearing traditional Tudor dress were produced as children's toys. One of the most delicate and extraordinary toys found by a Thames mudlark is a pewter, hollow-cast, full-length female figure (right). Her hair is covered by a heart-shaped French hood decorated with lines and dots which could depict jewels. She wears a buttoned partlet with a standing collar and large, slashed puffs on both shoulders. Her bell-shaped, heavily pleated skirt opens at the front to reveal an ornately patterned kirtle decorated with embroidered panels. The exquisite details of the dress reveal the popular fashions of that time period.

In the 17th century, the toy industry in London was very productive and manufactured a wide variety of toys made of pewter. The toys were often miniature versions of everyday household items such as dishes, plates, saucers, bowls, spoons, pitchers, clocks, etc. A few years ago, I found a toy "dripping pan" decorated with a sexfoil rose within a pelleted, concentric circle (bottom left). With this toy, children would pretend to cook and imitate their parents who would place a rectangular pan across the hearth to collect the hot juices dripping from a roast on a spit. Alan Murphy found an elaborately

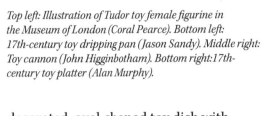

Top left: Illustration of Tudor toy female figurine in the Museum of London (Coral Pearce). Bottom left: 17th-century toy dripping pan (Jason Sandy). Middle right: Toy cannon (John Higginbotham). Bottom right:17th-century toy platter (Alan Murphy).

decorated, oval-shaped toy dish with a vine and floral motif around the edge including the maker's initials, *AF* (bottom right). Sometimes fish, suckling pigs, or other animals would be depicted in the center of the dish or frying pan.

Miniature weapons like toy guns and cannons were also produced that could actually fire (below). Some of the 17th-century toy cannons found on the foreshore are damaged after exploding during use. Children probably had access to gun powder from their father's musket. Some toy cannons were as powerful as adult pocket pistols, and a misfiring or explosion could have resulted in serious or even fatal injury.

Along the River Thames in West London where I live, I have found many Victorian toys. Because of the solidity and durability of the lead toys, they often survive intact in the harsh Thames environment. The wide variety of toys provides an insight into children's play-time activities and toy production in Victorian times. Lead was used to make the toys as it was a cheap and widely available metal.

Victorian children loved playing with many types of figurines. The style of clothes depicted on the toy figures (left) demonstrates the fashions of the working classes in the 19th century. Toy soldiers, painted red (bottom left) to imitate the "redcoat" uniforms of British soldiers, were used by children to recreate epic battles which they had heard about at school or from their relatives. Military figures of all types have been found in the River Thames, such as cavalrymen riding on horses (bottom center).

Toy animals made of lead were also popular in Victorian times (bottom right). Numerous toy horses and cockerels have been found on the Thames foreshore, which seems to indicate that they were some of the most popular animals that Victorian children enjoyed playing with.

In Victorian times, small "Frozen Charlotte" dolls were very popular in Britain, and I have

Top left: Victorian toy figurine (Jason Sandy). Bottom left: British "redcoat" toy soldier (Jason Sandy). Bottom center: 19th-century toy cavalryman (Jason Sandy). Bottom right: Victorian toy duck (Jason Sandy).

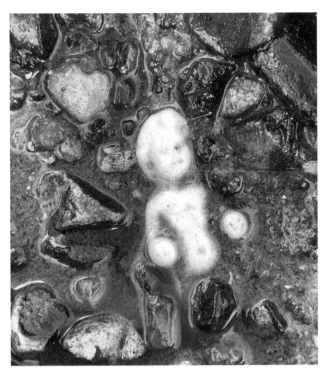

found a few of them in the river (top left). The dolls were made from white bisque porcelain in the shape of little girls (top right). Their name originates from macabre poem "Fair Charlotte," a folk ballad based on a poem by American author Seba Smith, published in 1843.

The story is about a young girl named Charlotte who rode on a sleigh to a New Year's ball but refused to dress warmly because when she arrived, she wanted everyone to see her pretty dress. During the journey through the cold, wintry conditions, she unfortunately froze to death. Victorians liked this macabre story so much, it became a tradition to bake the little dolls in their Christmas "pudding." Children enjoyed finding the hidden treat as they ate their dessert.

Small figurines of Saint Nicholas were also baked into Christmas puddings. Nick Stevens found a

nice example on the foreshore. A few years ago, Sarah Newton discovered a cute "snow baby" (bottom) with outstretched arms. The adorable, little figurine is wearing snow suit and gloves covered in snowflakes made of crushed bisque.

By researching the toys found on the exposed riverbed of the Thames, we gain a rare insight into childhood playtime activities throughout the ages. The various types of toys help us understand what fascinated children and captured their imagination centuries ago. The abundant number of toys found in the Thames proves that children have lived and played along the river for millennia. Even today, the intertidal zone still has a magnetic appeal which attracts children to this magical place when the tide recedes.

Top left: Frozen Charlotte doll on the foreshore (Jason Sandy).
Top right: Frozen Charlotte made of bisque porcelain (Jason Sandy).
Center: Porcelain snow baby (Sarah Newton).

CORAL PEARCE

When I was learning about history at school in the 1960s and 1970s, the most important date, and one which was remembered by all schoolchildren, was 1066—the year of the Norman invasion and the Battle of Hastings. Years later, when we came to live just a few miles from the town called "Battle" in East Sussex, it was hard to believe that this was the very place where such a historic event took place. Inspired by this knowledge, I bought myself a metal detector and searched our garden, just in case! So far, nothing of significance has surfaced, but I shall persevere.

During frequent trips to London, I had often noticed people walking on the foreshore of the River Thames. Not only did I wonder what they were doing, but I wanted to do it myself! It was not until sometime after, while watching a program called *Mud Men* on television, that I realized what the people on the foreshore were doing. They were mudlarking. The presenters of the program—Steve Brooker, Johnny Vaughan, and Nick Stevens—were not only knowledgeable, but highly entertaining and were so enthusiastic about what they were doing that I, too, wanted to mudlark like them.

I applied for my Port of London Authority license in order to go mudlarking. I am not always able to get to the Thames as often as I would like, and this was exacerbated by the Covid pandemic, which prevented me from going to the Thames for two years. It was around this time that I began to produce paintings of mudlarks holding artifacts in their hands. For me, one of the thrills of discovering an artifact is the fact that your hand is the first hand to touch it since it was lost centuries ago. It's as if the hand of the loser has reached out, pressed a personal gift into your palm, and said "Here, this is for you." I try to paint the hands without any reference to an era to raise the question: have I painted the hand that lost it, or the hand that found it?

As a podiatrist, I am drawn to the innersole of an 16th-century shoe. It is narrow and pointed, with no obvious bias. However, it is possible to see the indentations of the foot that wore it. There are stitch holes around the edge, which had once been pierced by a needle held in the hands of a Tudor cobbler. The sole is very small. It's hardly any larger than my eldest child's first shoes. I am tempted to believe it belonged to a child or young person. I wonder if those toes were pinched by its shape, or if the wearer felt every cobble, every little piece of grit on the crudely made streets of Georgian London? Little did those Londoners of old know that their belongings would one day be held in the hands of the future with such reverence.

I was honored to be asked by Jason Sandy if I would create some paintings of several artifacts for this book. It's a thrill to see my work in print alongside the wonderful finds made by so many dedicated mudlarks.

Portraits by Tom Harrison.

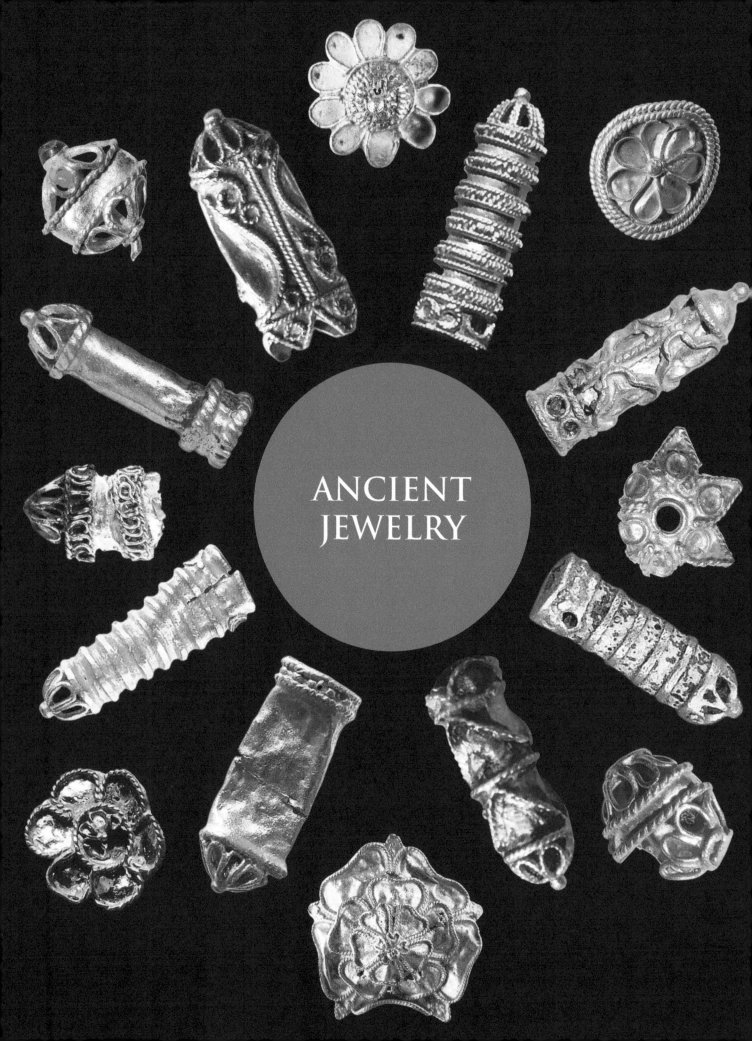

ANCIENT
JEWELRY

Since prehistoric times, people have adorned themselves with jewelry. These precious objects were worn, not only to enhance personal appearance, but to display social status, wealth, power, or authority. For instance, large gold torcs—solid neck rings—were worn by great Celtic warriors during battle and various rituals in the Iron Age. Anglo-Saxon rulers were often ceremoniously buried with invaluable pieces of their jewelry made of gold and precious gemstones, as illustrated by the Sutton Hoo burial in England. In the River Thames in London, mudlarks have found some exquisite pieces of jewelry, from the Iron Age to Modern times, which reveal fascinating insights about the people who once wore them.

Over the years, wonderful examples of Celtic brooches, decorative pins, and beads have been recovered from the river. Dating to 400–200 BC, a beautiful brooch (top right) was formed in a deep C-shaped bow and decorated in the La Tène I style with incised lines. It looks like a mythical beast with a coiled spring forming the head and tapering tail curled back onto the body. Using a pin and catch plate, it would have been used to secure an outer garment over an undergarment. The decorated brooch would have been located in a prominent position to be highly visible and attract attention.

Personal appearance was very important to the Romans living in Londinium. From archaeological evidence, we know that women wore make-up and beautiful jewelry such as necklaces, brooches, bracelets, and finger rings. One of the nicest Roman zoomorphic brooches found by a mudlark is in the shape of a lion (second from top), dating to the 2nd century AD. The lion's mane is formed with engraved, wavy lines, and its tail is curled as it walks with all four legs on the ground. Astonishingly, the brooch is complete and still "fit for purpose."

Mudlark Jason Davey found a unique Roman brooch (third from top), which is the only one of its type found in the United Kingdom. It is a bronze plate brooch from AD 43–410. Cast in the form of a stylized boat, it has a curving prow and representation of oars or an anchor. On the reverse, the pin is fixed between twin lugs and a catch plate.

A complete Roman "Hod Hill" brooch (bottom) was also found by a mudlark on the Thames foreshore. Dating to AD 43–70, the brooch is curved with decorative fluted ridges, and two lugs projecting from the middle of the bow. The delicate, hinged pin is still intact, and the brooch can still be worn as originally intended nearly 2,000 years ago.

Facing page: Tudor gold ornaments from the PAS/Caroline Nunneley (Collage by Jason Sandy).
This page, top to bottom: Celtic La Tène I style brooch (PAS). Roman lion brooch (PAS).
Roman boat brooch (PAS). Roman Hod Hill brooch (PAS).

In January 2020, mudlark Judy Hazell discovered a stunning Roman dolphin fibula (brooch) nestled between some rocks on the riverbed. It's simply amazing that ancient Roman artifacts are still being unearthed by mudlarks! Dating to the 1st century AD, this brooch has been shaped into a beautiful arch, like a dolphin jumping out of the sea. The spine of the brooch is decorated with two parallel lines, which accentuate the graceful form, and wings project from the top of the brooch where the pin would have been attached.

In the early medieval period, Anglo-Saxons wore eye-catching pieces of jewelry to display their wealth and social status. One of the most beautiful examples (above center) was recovered from the Thames in 1856. Called the "Chelsea ring," the zoomorphic decoration illustrates a mythical dragon within a central circle, surrounded by the heads of four monsters at the top and bottom of the ring. The dragon's tongue and tail are intertwined in an elaborate design. Made in England around 775–850 AD, the silver ring is now on permanent display in the Victoria and Albert Museum in London.

Brooches were also a popular fashion accessory in medieval England.

Mudlarks have found a wide variety of decorated medieval brooches, but circular brooches are the most common. One of the most extraordinary annular brooches found by a mudlark is made of pure silver and dates to the 13th–14th centuries. The circular frame is decoratively cast with a double twisted pattern comprised of a solid strand and a pelleted strand, which repeat around one side of the brooch. Where the pin is fixed to the frame, pellets within stamped circles adorn the pin.

In the Middle Ages, religion played an important part of everyday life. A 15th-century brooch found by a mudlark has been engraved with the opening verse from Psalm 6 and Psalm 38. The scripture written in Latin says, "O Lord, do not rebuke me in thine anger." This annular brooch would have been fixed to a garment so that the message was clearly visible to the onlooker.

Above left to right, top to bottom: Roman dolphin brooch (Judy Hazell). Anglo-Saxon zoomorphic ring (Ethan Doyle White). Medieval annular brooch (PAS). 15th-century annular brooch with scripture verse (PAS).

Near the site where the former Tudor Palace of Placentia once stood along the River Thames in Greenwich (London), numerous highly decorated, gold artifacts have been found by several mudlarks including Tony Thira, Mike Walker, Oliver Muranyi-Clark, and Steve Brooker. Dating to the 16th century, many of the tiny gold pieces are decorated with filigree and twisted wire to form creative designs, as seen on page 78.

In the 16th century, gold ornamental pieces were sewn onto expensive fabrics. Portraits painted in the 16th century illustrate Tudor aristocracy with gold aglets, beads, flowers, stars, and studs fixed to their sleeves, hats, and gowns to showcase their wealth and social status. When I visited Arundel Castle in England, I saw a 16th-century painting (top right) of Thomas Howard, the 4th Duke of Norfolk (1536–1572), with pairs of gold aglets fixed to his luxurious garment. The decorative aglets look similar to those found by mudlarks in the Thames (bottom right).

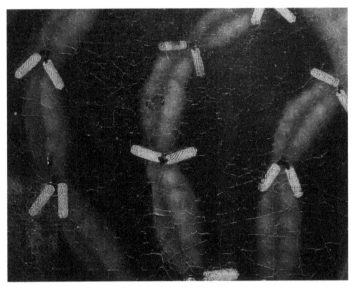

Built in 1443, the Palace of Placentia was the birthplace of King Henry VIII and his famous daughters, Queen Elizabeth I and Queen Mary I, nicknamed "Bloody Mary." The gold pieces found in the Thames could have been accidentally lost in the river as wealthy royals and aristocrats were getting in and out of boats on their way to the palace. Maybe a hat or other garment fell into the river and disintegrated over time, leaving the gold accessories behind. Since many different types and styles of Tudor gold artifacts have been found, it is highly likely that the objects had been fixed to various articles of clothing. The dense river mud has perfectly preserved these artifacts which exemplify the extraordinary craftsmanship and creativity of the skilled goldsmiths in the 16th century.

Top to bottom: 16th-century painting of Thomas Howard, 4th Duke of Norfolk, with detail of pairs of gold aglets sewn into fabric of Tudor garment (Jason Sandy). Tudor gold aglet on the Thames foreshore (Tony Thira).

As its international trade network expanded during the 16th century, the export of British products and raw materials steadily increased, and Britain imported more and more goods from around the globe. Powerful merchants based in London controlled the flourishing trade industry. A few mudlarks have recovered 16th-century personalized rings (above left) from these wealthy merchants, which they had used to authorize and seal trade documents. Malcolm Russell discovered a brass ring (above right) from AD 1450–1550 engraved with the letters "R D." The ring has a rectangular bezel, faceted corners, and a crown above the letters. Through his research, Malcolm was able to track down six merchants with the same initials who lived near the location where he found the ring.

A similar 16th-century merchant's ring (below left) was discovered by Alan Suttie. The faceted bezel is engraved with interwoven letters "I S." In a nautical theme, the band of the ring has been formed with a twisted rope design.

One of the most extraordinary rings ever found in the Thames (bottom right) was discovered by Steve Camp. It is a 16th–17th-century gold signet ring which would have been worn by a wealthy merchant or businessman. The engraving depicts two hounds chasing a rabbit within a square-topped shield surmounted by the initials "T G." It was made by a gold-smith in London.

Top left: 16th-century merchant's ring found by John Higginbotham (PAS). Top right: Merchant ring engraved with "R D" (PAS). Bottom left: Brass merchant's ring (PAS). Bottom right: Gold signet ring with rabbit and dogs (PAS).

The Tudors were hopeless romantics—just look at Henry VIII and his six wives! One of the greatest love stories of all time, *Romeo and Juliet*, was written by William Shakespeare between 1591–1595. Several heart-shaped brooches from the 16th century have been found in the River Thames. One of the brooches (above) has been cast with molded decoration across the surface of the heart. A patriotic rose or flaming sacred heart is depicted at the top of the brooch. The original pin must have broken off and was replaced with a piece of crude wire so that the brooch could still be worn.

Centuries ago, "love tokens" were made by bending silver sixpence coins into an "S" shape. In 2019, I found a silver hammered Elizabeth I sixpence coin (right) dated 1580, which was bent into a love token. Coincidentally, I discovered this Tudor love token near Shakespeare's Globe Theatre. This love token was made around the same time Shakespeare wrote *Romeo and Juliet* in the late 16th century. If a man was interested in starting a relationship with a woman, he could

make a love token and give it to her to demonstrate his love and admiration. If the woman accepted his proposal, she would keep and cherish the love token. Some of the love tokens were pierced with a hole, suspended from a necklace, and worn as evidence of their relationship. If the woman did not reciprocate his love, the token would be returned or discarded. The valuable silver love token I discovered was probably thrown in the river on purpose.

From the Iron Age to Tudor period, jewelry was worn as a status symbol and a display of one's wealth. The fabulous brooches, finger rings, aglets, and ornate pieces made of gold reveal the styles and fashions of each time period. The beautiful, delicate works of art illustrate the skillful craftsmanship and creative imagination of the jewelry makers over the centuries.

Top left: Tudor heart-shaped brooch (PAS). Above: Tudor love token from a Elizabeth I sixpence dated 1580 (Jason Sandy).

JUDY HAZELL AND PHILLY GUMBO

We have both been interested in history and archaeology for many years after going on a trip up the Nile to visit many ancient Egyptian sites. We also enjoy fossil hunting in Lyme Regis, Dorset. Living in London, there is so much history from prehistory, Roman, Anglo-Saxon, medieval, and many eras after and in between.

In August 2015, we visited Sir John Soane's Museum and Hunterian Museum in Central London. Afterwards, we were on our way to visit the Tate Modern when we came to the Trig Lane stairs along the river. We wondered what all the people on the foreshore were doing. We went down and were amazed by the amount of clay pipe stems and beautiful bones lying on the exposed riverbed. We spent some time there and were hooked! After returning home, we started looking at maps to see where else we could visit.

We first heard about mudlarking after we had been to the foreshore quite a few times. It was a lovely chap who was a member of the Society of Thames Mudlarks called Alan Murphy who explained that we would need a license and told us where we could dig and scrape. Alan also told us about off-limit areas. We applied for our licenses that evening. Since then, not a week has gone by when one or both of us have not been to foreshore (apart from lockdowns during the pandemic). We have met some very knowledgeable and helpful people since we started mudlarking. This hobby has such a lovely community of people, each with their own different areas of expertise.

We both enjoy the thrill of mudlarking and the thought of finding something rare or so unusual that we have to spend time researching and discovering its history. We are always amazed to know that we are the first people to see and hold these artifacts in hundreds of years. We love to tick items off our ever-growing list of things we would like to find. Not knowing what you will uncover from one trip to the next keeps us going back to the foreshore.

Some of our favorite finds have been a Roman dolphin fibula (brooch) from AD 50–150, a silver skull mourning ring, a Tudor money box slit dating AD 1550–1650 (which is quite rare as most people find finials), and a Mallorca Dinero of Carlos II showing the Habsburg family chin. Some of our most coveted finds are 17th-century trade tokens, as you can tell a lot from them even though they are very small. We also like the elusive and mysterious three-holed buttons.

Portraits by Tom Harrison.

THAMES
BLING

On a beautiful, summer evening in July 2018, I went mudlarking to take advantage of the super-low, night tide. As it started to get dark, I switched on my trusty headlamp to illuminate the gravel riverbed along the water line. Wearing knee pads and rubber gloves, I crawled along the foreshore, carefully examining the surface, searching for historic artifacts exposed by the receding tide. Suddenly, a large red gemstone appeared among the gravel, illuminated in the darkness by my headlamp!

My heart was beating out of my chest as I carefully picked it up. It didn't feel like plastic or glass, so I hoped it could possibly be a cut garnet or even a ruby! Days later, Joanna Whalley, a gemologist at the Victoria and Albert Museum in London, confirmed that it is a whopping 8.2 carat Hessonite garnet from Sri Lanka. One of my Instagram followers in Scotland saw my post and offered to set it for me as a present for my wife to celebrate our 13th wedding anniversary. Professional jewelry designer Ruth Patterson created a beautiful gold necklace with several uncut Thames garnets fixed to the chain and the Sri Lankan garnet suspended as a stunning pendant. The red garnet glows in the sunlight. Rescued from the depths of the river, the gemstone has been given new life and will be cherished as a family heirloom by generations to come.

Facing page: Modern rings found by Lukasz Orlinski (Collage by Jason Sandy).

This page, top to bottom: Hessonite garnet on the Thames foreshore (Jason Sandy). Hessonite garnet pendant designed by Ruth Patterson (Jason Sandy). Thames garnet necklace (Jason Sandy).

The 17th century was a tumultuous time in London. The city endured the English Civil War, overthrow of the British monarchy, the Great Plague of 1665, and the Great Fire of London in 1666. During these horrific events, many people lost their lives. In memory of their loved ones, family members wore gold mourning rings. Rae Love found one of these 17th-century rings (top left) engraved with a skull and inscribed with the name, Alex Cheeke, and the date of his death on February 15, 1668. While recording this ring, the Museum of London located Cheeke's will which provided fascinating insights into his life. Several years ago, Malcolm Duff unearthed an unusual memento mori ring (second from top left). Around the circumference of the ring, a full skeleton is depicted.

Mudlarks have also discovered unique rings which reveal stories of love in the 17th century. As a symbol of love and affection, posy and fede rings were made of gold or silver and were given as gifts. Inside the band, a short, personalized poem was engraved. On a sunny afternoon, Mark Beverlo spotted a valuable gold fede ring (third from top left) lying on the exposed riverbed. Two clasped hands holding a heart are illustrated on the front of the ring dating to 1640–1680. "No heart more true than myne" has been inscribed on the inside of the band. After the relationship ended, maybe this gold ring was deliberately discarded in the river.

One of the most interesting 17th-century heart-shaped buckles found in the Thames is decorated with the portraits of King William and Queen Mary surmounted by a crown (bottom left). Dating to 1689–1694, "the buckle was worn on the front of the shirt, where the neck cloth joined the opening in the front of their shirt," according to the Museum of London.

Top to bottom: 17th-century gold mourning ring (PAS). 17th-century skeleton ring (PAS). 17th-century gold fede ring (Jason Sandy). 17th-century William and Mary buckle (PAS).

In the 19th century, Victorian jewelry makers created wonderful brooches using colored glass to imitate precious gemstones. While mudlarking along the River Thames, Christine Fernbank found an extraordinary Victorian brooch (right). A beautiful, faux amethyst gemstone is set in the center of ornate, geometric patterns of decoration. It's a spectacular work of art! A few years ago, mudlark John Higginbotham discovered a gorgeous 19th-century brooch. To imitate a blue sapphire, a cut glass gemstone was set in an elaborate, baroque setting made of pewter.

Graham duHeaume also found a lovely Victorian brooch (left). Two flowers are formed with several pink glass stones surrounding white pearls. The flowers are fixed to a circular, silver frame with incised decoration, accompanied by natural leaf patterns.

A beautiful gold locket engraved with an elaborate baroque pattern and flowers (bottom left) was found by Simon Bourne. When he opened it, Simon found a heart-shaped piece of glass and piece of fabric. Maybe a precious keepsake had been placed inside before the locket was lost?

A few years ago, I found a modern, heart-shaped locket (bottom center) made of red glass set in a brass surround. The back is unfortunately missing, but the locket could have contained the picture of a loved one. Shortly after Christmas in 2019, I discovered a heart-shaped pendant, carved from a sodalite stone, believed to have natural healing powers (bottom right). An elegant, heart-shaped pendant made of silver

Top right: Victorian brooch with cut glass (Christine Fernbank).
Middle left: Victorian brooch with cut glass flowers (Graham duHeaume). Bottom left: Gold, heart-shaped locket (Simon Bourne). Bottom center: Red glass, heart-shaped locket (Jason Sandy). Bottom right: Sodalite, heart-shaped pendant (Jason Sandy).

was found by John Higginbotham. The pendant was formed with an openwork pattern of interwoven circular shapes. Glistening like diamonds, cut glass stones are set within the complex, geometric pattern.

Sadly, many mudlarks have found engagement and wedding rings, which may have been discarded in the River Thames in frustration after a failed relationship. I can only imagine the heartache and disappointment a person felt as they threw the ring into the river. Florrie Evans discovered a beautiful, gold engagement ring set with five large diamonds (below left). It is very valuable, so it could have easily been sold rather than discarded in the river.

As I was mudlarking under a bridge, I spotted an engagement ring lying on the surface of the riverbed. As I picked it up, I was pleasantly surprised to see a large, heart-shaped aquamarine gemstone set in the ring. Sailors believe that aquamarine has supernatural powers to protect them at sea, so I wonder if a sailor had given this precious ring to his fiancée or wife before embarking on a long journey.

In the 20th century, costume jewelry became very popular because it was inexpensive to buy and looked real. Using new techniques, gold and silver were imitated by metal alloys, and colored glass and crystals were cut to appear like valuable gemstones. Mass-production made the jewelry affordable and accessible to everyone. Over the years, Lukasz Orlinski has found a wide array (page 86) of stunning, modern rings with elaborate designs.

While searching near a busy bridge in West London, mudlark Tobias Neto discovered some fantastic modern rings which probably fell or were dropped into the river as people crossed the bridge (facing page, top). The gem-encrusted lizard ring is a wonderful example of a jeweller's creativity. One of the most interesting rings Tobias has found is a gold ring set with a red gemstone engraved with Islamic symbols (facing page, inset). People wear these "Sharaf-e Shams" rings to banish sorrow, depression, bad luck, and negativity.

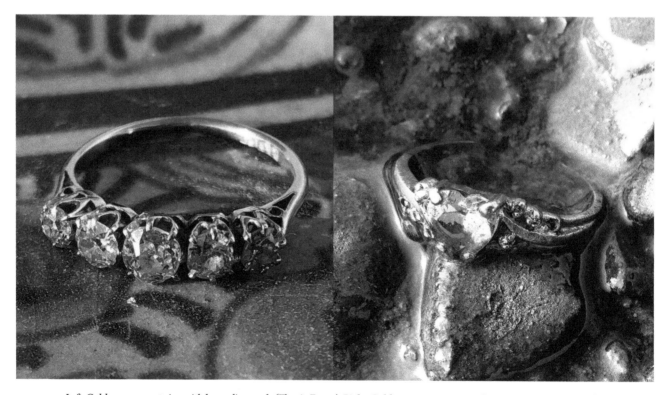

Left: Gold engagement ring with large diamonds (Florrie Evans). Right: Gold engagement ring with aquamarine gemstone (Jason Sandy).

Pieces of jewelry are some of the most exciting finds from the River Thames. These beautiful works of art demonstrate the jewelry makers' creativity and imagination. The combination of precious metals and valuable gemstones make a stunning combination, even though colorful, cut glass and inexpensive metals were often used as substitutes. They are personal items that were once highly treasured by their owners. Some jewelry was accidentally lost, but many of the expensive engagement rings and wedding bands were purposely discarded in the Thames because of heartache or anger. Rescued from the turbulent currents of the River Thames, these lost personal items are now treasured once again by the lucky mudlarks who find them.

Top: Modern rings found in the Thames (Tobias Neto). Bottom: Sharaf-e Shams ring (Tobias Neto).

RAE LOVE

Up until the age of eleven, I lived near the site of an old manor house, totally overgrown and in ruins, surrounded by a moat and trees. My brother and I would frequently go down to the River Thames and sit on a wooden jetty, watching the boats go by. When the tide was out, we would trudge through the thick black mud, picking up small finds on the way. When we arrived home, we would empty our bags of goodies and use them to decorate our play den (shed). We found lots of old coins, but because they could not be spent, we used them as play money.

As an adult with six children of my own, there was little to no time to pursue my interests, although I would watch any related programs on TV. I started collecting antique pottery and porcelain when our children were still fairly young. I bought books and magazines for research purposes and read an ad in one magazine for a new metal detecting/ mudlarking club. This piqued my interest in metal detecting and mudlarking. I joined the club, got a foreshore permit from the Port of London Authority, and duly purchased my first metal detector. I only ever used a detector on the Thames foreshore twice. I prefer to search by eye or scraping. However, this didn't stop me from purchasing a further three detectors, just in case. All of my finds from the foreshore have been found without the use of a detector. After a few years of recording my finds with on the Portable Antiquities Scheme, I progressed to become a member of the Society of Thames Mudlarks in January 2009.

Over the years on my mudlarking journey, I have been privileged to have met some amazing

fellow mudlarks who are always happy to divulge any info they can help you with. I have learned so much about history from researching my finds that I never would have known otherwise. When I'm on the foreshore, it often takes me back to the times when my younger brother and I were having fun along the river. We loved to be there. It channels a connection to my brother that is very precious to me. Sadly, he passed away at age 21.

I have been very fortunate to have had some amazing finds over the years, but I can no longer pinpoint an outright favorite anymore. I had a few at one time, but to be honest, the list got ridiculously long as I liked them all. At the top of the list was a gold memoriam ring dated 1668, followed by a beautiful large, oval aquamarine stone. I do have a love of pins, buckles, lead tokens, and jetons. Each one is more personal and different from the last. They say that beauty is in the eye of the beholder, and that rings true for me.

Through my love of mudlarking, I was very privileged to have met a mudlarker/detectorist by the name of John Mills who introduced me to his lovely mudlarking wife, Steph. We all became really good friends over the years and would meet up on the foreshore, getting a few nightlarks in now and again too. John knew his stuff and was happy to help anyone. Sadly, John passed away a few years ago, but Steph and I have remained good friends and mudlarking buddies. I know John would be so proud smiling down on her and saying, "Cor blimey Steph," as she picks up yet another good find.

Portraits by Tom Harrison.

BOTTLES
FILLED
WITH
HISTORY

18th-century apothecary bottles (Jason Sandy).

C ollecting the city's rubbish for nearly 2,000 years, the River Thames is a great repository of discarded objects, especially glass. The dense, soft mud of the Thames encapsulates the bottles and protects many of them from breakage. As the foreshore is slowly being eroded away by the waves of passing boats, historic glass bottles are revealed as the tide recedes. During very low tides, I have fortunately found and rescued several complete bottles before the strong river currents swept them away or smashed them on the rocks.

In London, some of the lowest tides of the year occur late at night from July until October. Hoping to find older artifacts on stretches of the riverbed which are only accessible a few times a year, I strap on my high-powered headlamp and go mudlarking in the dark (top left). At night, the empty foreshore is a magical place surrounded by wonderfully illuminated bridges and buildings whose reflections shimmer on the calm surface of the river (top right). As I was night-larking with two friends in October 2018, I discovered a delicate 18th-century apothecary bottle (below). Remarkably, this complete bottle is still corked, and the original contents still remain inside.

On February 9th, 2020, a freak storm coincided with an extremely low Spring tide. Classified as an "extratropical cyclone," Storm Ciara brought torrential rain and high winds from the west, which blew the tide out much further than predicted. There were only a few brave souls on the Thames foreshore that morning, and we were highly rewarded for our mudlarking efforts despite the horrendous weather conditions. As the tide

receded lower than I had ever seen before, I spotted the beautiful, flared rim of an 18th-century apothecary bottle (page 97, top left). As I extracted it from the mud, I couldn't believe it was complete. It's truly a miracle that these fragile glass vessels survived for 300 years in the turbulent River Thames.

Top left: Central London illuminated at night (Jason Sandy). Top right: Jason Sandy nightlarking with London Bridge and Tower Bridge in the background (Neil Hall). Bottom right: Corked apothecary bottle containing its original contents (Jason Sandy).

Since I found these bottles on the riverbed below a historic dock, I can imagine that they could have been dropped from a ship, before or after a long journey on the open sea. In the 18th century, glass bottles were often used to store medicines until they were needed during a long voyage. These bottles I discovered could possibly have been a vital part of a sea surgeon's medical supplies to treat ill sailors or those wounded in battles at sea. According to the inventory of a sea surgeon's medical chest, glass bottles were used to store oils, balsams, juices, dried seeds, powders, smelling salts, minerals, preserves, distilled waters, syrups, decoctions, cinnamon, cloves, maces, nutmegs, whole and parts of animals, extract of colo-quintida, essence of cantharidin, spirit of nitre, camphor, and turpentine. I wonder what medicine or apothecary's concoction is still contained in the corked bottle I found?

I n the 17th century, bottles were developed with a unique, wide bottom and low center of gravity to prevent the bottle from tipping over and spilling its fine wine or spirits on ships sailing across stormy seas. These elegantly shaped, glass bottles (top right) became known as onion bottles. It is very rare to find an unbroken bottle of this type in the turbulent Thames.

While nightlarking in July 2021, Michal Knap discovered a complete onion bottle (bottom right),

which was cushioned for centuries in the soft, dense mud. "When I first spotted the bottom of the bottle, I thought it was broken. As I slowly scraped and pulled the complete bottle out of the mud, I turned it around and saw the seal on the front of the 17th-century onion bottle. I was shocked and very excited! On the way home, I was very nervous, because I thought I might break it. I have never seen an onion bottle with a seal, and it's amazing it has survived intact," explains Michal.

Facing page: 17th-century apothecary bottle (Jason Sandy). Top left: 18th-century apothecary bottle (Jason Sandy). Top right: Onion bottle from c. 1700 found by Steve Camp (Jason Sandy). Middle right: 17th-century onion bottle fresh from the mud (Michal Knap).

Top left: Illustration of onion bottle (Coral Pearce). Top right: Nicola White holding an onion bottle on the foreshore (Alessio Checconi). Bottom: 17th and 18th-century onion bottles (Nicola White).

A glob of molten glass was used to create the bottle seal which has been stamped with two initials, "I D." Although Michal has not yet been able to decipher whose initials they are, he says it is "a sealed wine bottle from around 1675–1680 and possibly belonged to a notable gentleman with those initials." Mudlark and artist Coral Pearce created a beautiful painting (above) of Michal's onion bottle.

During the extremely low Spring tides in February 2022, Nicola White bent down to pick up a clay pipe when she spotted a small dome of glass protruding from the surface of the mud. As she began digging, more and more of the bottle appeared. To her surprise, the bottle (top right) was miraculously complete. This is the second onion bottle which Nicola has found in the Thames. Not only

are these bottles (below) beautifully shaped, but their surface also has a vivid rainbow of colors that have developed over the centuries in the river. The iridescent appearance is caused by alkali (soluble salt) being leached from the glass by the slightly acidic water of the Thames. As light passes through the multiple layers of thin, flaking glass, a prism effect is created.

Top left: All Souls College bottle seal (Jason Sandy). Bottom left: All Souls College in Oxford (Ozeye). Bottom right: 18th-century bottle from All Souls College (Anthony Bagshaw).

In July 2018, I found a glass seal from an 18th-century bottle as I was mudlarking. The mysterious bottle seal took me on an adventure to a medieval college at Oxford University. Stamped on the surface of the seal (left) is "All Souls Coll: C:R." As very little information about the bottle is available online, I drove to Oxford University to find out more. After looking around the beautiful campus of All Souls College (below left), Professor Ian Maclean kindly gave me great information about the seal and said it "is from a pint port bottle. They were filled with port wine purchased in barrels by the College. The bottles were for College use only. 'C R' refers to the Common Room, which at that time was the owner of all the wine in the College." The bottle seal which I found is from the very first All Souls bottles (below right) which were produced by Dennis Glasshouse in Stourbridge in 1750.

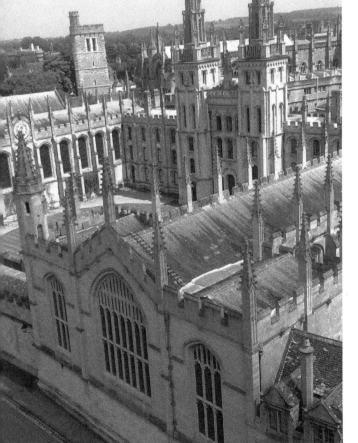

When Lawrence of Arabia was a Fellow at All Souls College in 1920, he personally conducted an inventory of the wine bottles by candlelight in the college cellars. The All Souls College students drank approximately 3,000–3,600 bottles of port wine per year. That's a lot of wine! Did some students take a boozy trip down the Thames from Oxford to London and drop the bottle in the river? We'll never know for sure, but it's fun to imagine how the bottle seal ended up on the bottom of the Thames in London.

Old bottles recovered from the Thames are truly filled with so much history. Whether complete or broken, the bottles reveal intriguing backstories about the people who once used them.

MICHAL KNAP

I was born and raised in Poland and moved to London in 2016. As a child, I became interested in history, treasures, shipwrecks, and archaeology. I remember watching a show on TV about an expedition and excavations from the 16th century, and I liked it very much. My mom had some National Geographic magazines at home, and I loved looking through them—although we didn't have many of them because they were a bit expensive to buy. When I discovered that our school library had many different National Geographic magazines, I was very excited. I have fond memories of looking at the photos rather than reading the articles because some English words were difficult for me to understand.

I am 29 years old, and I started mudlarking in June of 2020. Mudlarking gives me a thrill because I like to find treasures. I enjoy researching and learning about the history of each object I find. I like to go mudlarking along the river at night because it is peaceful and calm, and no one will know my treasure spots.

I am deaf so it is easier to focus on searching for treasures as I can't hear any noise around me. I don't wear my hearing aids when I go mudlarking because I don't want to lose them. The weather can change into rain or wind, and that can damage them.

When I communicate with other mudlarks on the foreshore, they have to speak slowly because I read lips. If they can't understand me, I write a message on my phone so they can read it. Some mudlarks don't want to talk to me because they have no patience, or they don't have time because the tide is coming in quickly.

I have made some good friends while mudlarking, and we keep in touch. We help each other to solve the mysteries of some treasures we find. I enjoyed participating in the mudlarking exhibitions in 2021 and 2022. There was a good atmosphere, and it was great to meet new people who are mudlarks I hadn't met before. They were impressed by my finds.

My favorite finds are a 17th-century long-necked sealed "shaft and globe" wine bottle, 17th-century trade token with the inscription "AT YE GRASHOPER IN NEW FISH STREET," 17th-century glass apothecary bottle, marbled slipware costrel from the 16th–17th centuries, and clay pipes decorated with faces and other nice designs.

Portraits by Tom Harrison.

VICTORIAN BOTTLES AND GLASS ARTWORK

Mosaic of river glass (Christine Fernbank).

During the 19th century, new types of drinks were developed and became very popular. Victorians especially liked carbonated drinks such as ginger beer, lemonade, cream soda, lemon squash, soda water, and koala. To prevent the carbonation from escaping, a British soft drink maker named Hiram Codd designed and patented a uniquely shaped bottle in London in 1872. Known as a "Codd" bottle, it contained a glass marble and rubber washer within the hollow chamber of the pinched bottle neck. At the top of the bottle, an air-tight seal was created when the marble was pushed tight against the washer by the pressure of the drink's carbonation.

Although they are relatively rare, several of these bottles have been recovered from the Thames. Ed Bucknall found a stunning example from T. COCKERTON with colorful blue and green iridescence (right). Over the years, Nicola White has ollected several beautiful Codd bottles with frosted, aqua tones (below right). The names of shops and bottle makers are molded into the surface of the glass which allows us to research and discover their interesting backstories.

After drinking the refreshing beverages, children would often smash the bottles to retrieve the glass marble so they could play with them. The British term "codswallop" is possibly derived from the act of walloping a Codd bottle to release the marble. Over the years, I have found numerous Codd marbles in the river. They have a beautiful aqua color and frosted appearance after tumbling around in the river for over 100 years.

In 1809, William Hamilton came up with another ingenious solution to keep carbonated drinks fizzy. It

Top: 19th-century Codd bottle from T. Cockerton (Ed Bucknall).
Bottom: Nicola's Codd bottle collection (Nicola White).

Left: 19th-century torpedo bottle from H. D. Rawlings (Jason Sandy).
Below: Torpedo bottle from Harrods Stores (Nicola White).
Bottom: Victorian poison bottle (Jason Sandy).

seems strange now, but he invented an unusual bottle designed to lay on its side. This kept the cork wet so the carbonation couldn't escape from the bottle. Because of their oblong shape, they were aptly nicknamed "torpedo" bottles. Over the years, I have found many broken pieces of torpedo bottles, but it took six years before I discovered my first complete one (above left). Molded on the surface of the glass, it has an image of a spread eagle and the inscription: H. D. RAWLINGS, NASSAU STREET, LONDON. Lemonade, soda, and ginger beer are some of the carbonated drinks produced by Henry Doo Rawlings.

A few years ago, Nicola White found a complete torpedo bottle with the name, HARRODS STORES, molded into the surface of the glass (above right). Established by Charles Henry Harrod in 1824, the business started from humble beginnings. Now Harrods is one of the largest and most famous department stores in the world. Located on a prominent 5.5-acre site in West London, the store boasts 330 separate departments with 1.1 million square feet (100,000 square meters) of retail space. In 1832, Charles's first grocery store business called Harrod & Co. Grocers opened in Central London. Perhaps this bottle containing a carbonated drink was sold at his grocery store before it was discarded in the Thames.

In the 19th century, poisons were sold in uniquely shaped, glass bottles for use at home. The words, NOT TO BE TAKEN, were often embossed on the bottles to indicate its poisonous contents (below). However, not everyone was literate and could read the warning labels or embossed lettering. To prevent accidental consumption of the poison, the bottles were produced with a bold color (emerald green or cobalt blue) and easily recognizable, distinctive shape (usually hexagonal) so their contents were unmistakable.

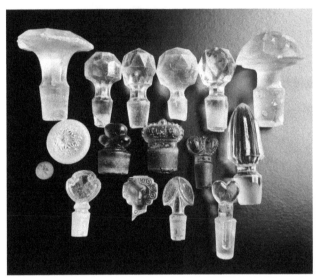

Sarah Newton has recovered many of these poison bottles which had been discarded in the Thames. In her collection, she has numerous emerald green (above left) and cobalt blue bottles (above right) in all different shapes and sizes. Unfortunately, the colorful and unusually shaped bottles sometimes attracted children's attention rather than repelling them, which tragically led to several deaths.

Over the years, Sarah Newton has also found a wide range of beautiful glass bottle stoppers (right), which are wonderfully ornate and decorative. Some of the smaller glass stoppers are from delicate perfume bottles dating to the late 19th and early 20th centuries. The faceted, globular stoppers are from cut glass decanters which were used for storing wine and spirits. My favorite stopper found by Sarah is an emerald green bottle stopper in the shape of a British crown (bottom right). It is from a small, emerald green bottle which contained smelling salts produced by The Crown Perfumery Company established in London in 1872.

Since 2013, mudlark and artist Christine Fernbank has been collecting beautiful pieces of colorful shards of glass along the Thames foreshore. You would never know that she is 84 years old because of her youthful enthusiasm and

Top left: Emerald green poison bottles (Sarah Newton). Top right: Blue poison bottles (Sarah Newton). Middle right: Decorated, glass bottle stoppers (Sarah Newton). Bottom right: Crown-shaped, glass bottle stopper (Sarah Newton).

boundless energy. After purchasing and repairing a damaged, vintage Tiffany lamp several years ago, Christine was inspired to start producing her own mosaics with patterned and textured glass found in the river.

On her first trip to the Thames Estuary, she discovered "a treasure trove of old broken glass from an old tip (dump). Many pieces were from old poison and wine bottles. There were also chunks of cut glass bowls and tumblers, some with star cut bases. I knew these would look beautiful against the light, and I started a massive collection."

Christine carefully arranges the shards of river glass with complementary colors before fixing them in place. "The technique I use is to surround each piece with copper foil, paint with liquid flux, solder it, and join it to the next piece," explains Christine. "I don't plan anything, but assemble panels like a jigsaw puzzle, finding colors and shapes that look good together. Bottle bottoms and colored wine glass bases are the main components, but I also use large chips of glass, glass pebbles, and construct borders from plain cut glass."

Over the past few years, Christine has made a wide variety of colorful mosaics (above). The works of art are intended to be backlit so that natural daylight brings the ancient glass to life. Illuminated from behind, the individual shards glow, and the sun passes through the patterned

Above: Glass mosaic made by Christine Fernbank from Thames glass shards (Vicky Annand). Top right: Lamp shade made from multi-colored Czech glass (Christine Fernbank).

glass, casting vivid colors and playful shadows on the surrounding surfaces.

Inspired by the vintage Tiffany lamp she repaired years ago, Christine is currently working on a lampshade (above) "constructed from 1930s Czech glass from the Thames Estuary, which is quite difficult to find. The multi-colored shards from old vases are very beautiful. The glass is lined on the back with either yellow, red, or blue, so when it is lit, it will have a golden glow." Christine enthusiastically proclaims, "my obsession with glass will continue, and each trip to the Thames Estuary gives me new ideas!"

Nicola White has been mudlarking for many years along the River Thames, Thames Estuary, and River Medway in South East England. Nicola is especially attracted to broken shards of river glass which she collects for her artwork she calls "Tideline Art." Nicola explains, "I am greatly inspired by the fact that each shard of glass I pick up has had a previous life and a history all of its own. I love to put these forgotten, once loved, or discarded fragments back together, and give them a new purpose in a piece of art." Her inspirations include Alfred Wallis, Guy Taplin, Margaret Mellis, and "all those who see beauty in something used and thrown away and can breathe new life into it!"

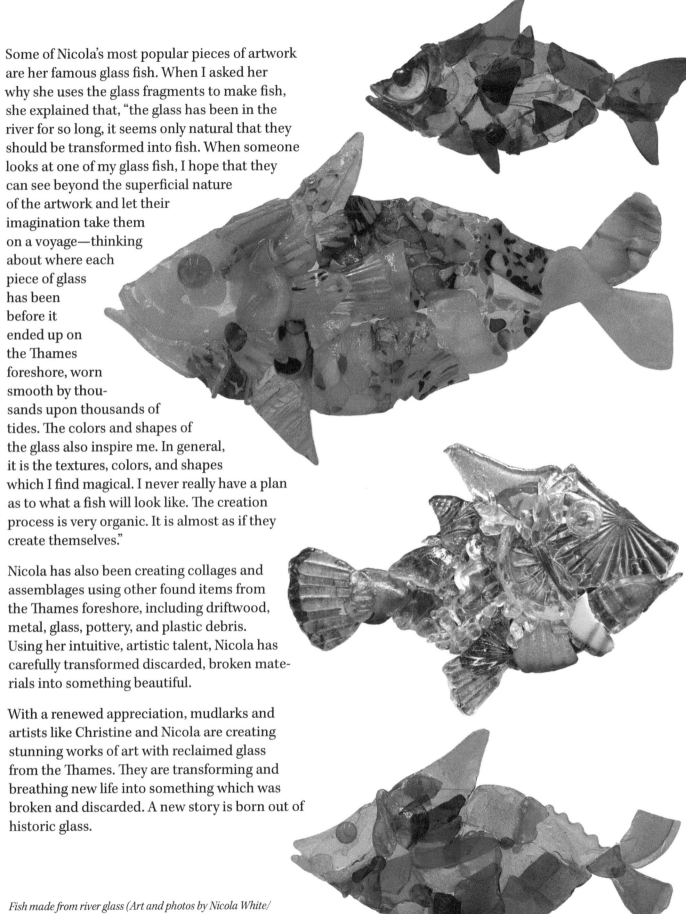

Some of Nicola's most popular pieces of artwork are her famous glass fish. When I asked her why she uses the glass fragments to make fish, she explained that, "the glass has been in the river for so long, it seems only natural that they should be transformed into fish. When someone looks at one of my glass fish, I hope that they can see beyond the superficial nature of the artwork and let their imagination take them on a voyage—thinking about where each piece of glass has been before it ended up on the Thames foreshore, worn smooth by thousands upon thousands of tides. The colors and shapes of the glass also inspire me. In general, it is the textures, colors, and shapes which I find magical. I never really have a plan as to what a fish will look like. The creation process is very organic. It is almost as if they create themselves."

Nicola has also been creating collages and assemblages using other found items from the Thames foreshore, including driftwood, metal, glass, pottery, and plastic debris. Using her intuitive, artistic talent, Nicola has carefully transformed discarded, broken materials into something beautiful.

With a renewed appreciation, mudlarks and artists like Christine and Nicola are creating stunning works of art with reclaimed glass from the Thames. They are transforming and breathing new life into something which was broken and discarded. A new story is born out of historic glass.

Fish made from river glass (Art and photos by Nicola White/ www.tidelineart.com).

CHRISTINE FERNBANK

I have always been interested in the past. When I was young and living in the countryside, I read an article about mudlarking in the Daily Telegraph, and I longed to do it. I first started mudlarking in the 1980s when I was taken as a guest by the secretary of the Society of Thames Mudlarks. They were excavating the 17th-century layer of the North Bank of the Thames. I was fascinated by what they were finding and collected a box of items from the foreshore. At that time, it was covered with shards of glass and china, animal bones and teeth, and clay tobacco pipes.

When I started mudlarking again in 2013, my best find was a lock plate which I believe came from a wooden chest. My most recent favorite find is a large bronze medal, commemorating three German Kaisers who died in 1888. It is a beautiful medal with three heads in profile. It took me a year to find my first coin, but I have now amassed a nice collection. My favorites are a Saxon coin and a hammered coin from Edward III. I also love mocha ware with different patterns and Bartmann roundels. I found one with the name of Pieter van den Anker, a Dutch Merchant in London who imported German stoneware.

I am drawn to anything decorative or brightly colored, and I particularly love glass. I have always been creative. Painting, producing stained glass, and photography are my obsessions. I started making glass panels for my own amusement, but I discovered that people wanted me to make them with their own glass finds. I have made four small ones for other people, and they seem happy! As well as the panels, I have used brightly colored glass found at Tilbury to make a small lampshade. With the ceramic sherds, I have decorated a plate, a small tabletop, and a large garden planter.

My scariest experience happened when I had only been mudlarking for a few months. The tide was starting to come in, and I couldn't find the steps to exit the foreshore. I carried on walking and looking for them. I came to a spot where the shore was already blocked by the rising water, and it was impossible to go further. I realized I must have walked past the steps. I turned and started running back with my heart pounding in a total panic. Luckily, I got back to the steps in time, but it scared the life out of me.

Over the years, I have made really good friends among the mudlarks. They have enriched my life, and we have had some good laughs together. I like the community because so many people have similar interests, and their knowledge is amazing. My ability to identify finds varies, but I have learned a lot from other people. The mudlark sites on Facebook are very useful for the identification of finds.

Portraits by Tom Harrison.

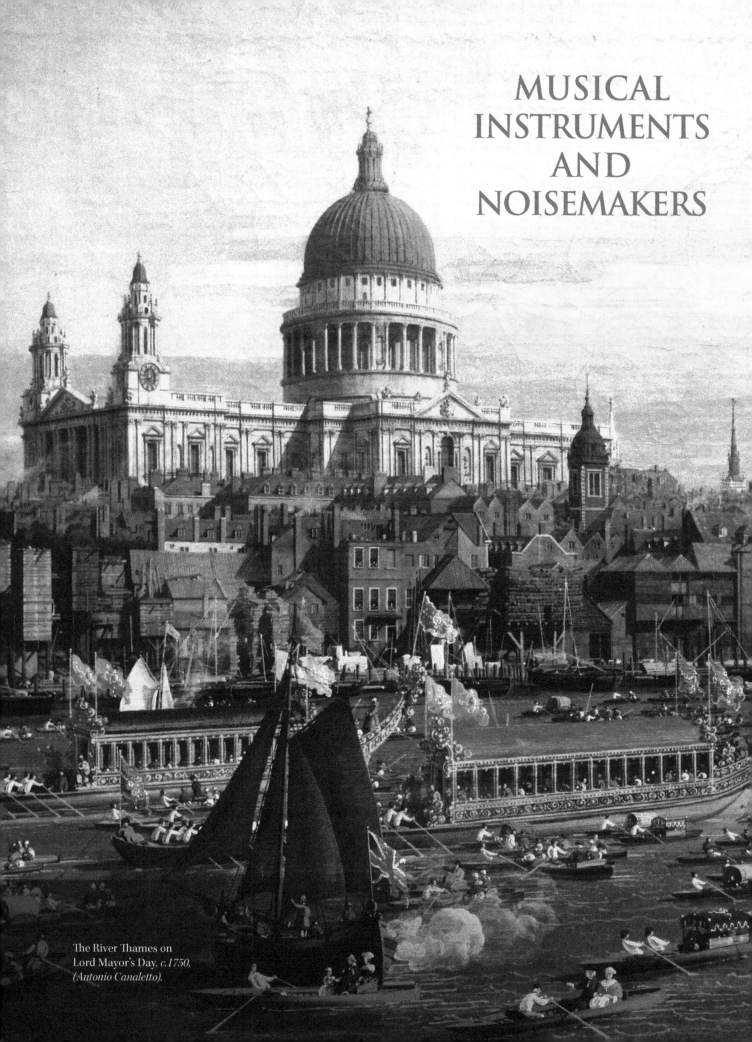

MUSICAL INSTRUMENTS AND NOISEMAKERS

The River Thames on
Lord Mayor's Day, *c.1750,*
(Antonio Canaletto).

For centuries, the River Thames has been a natural stage for music and entertainment. In 1662, King Charles II married the Portuguese princess, Catherine of Braganza. To celebrate the arrival of the new queen in London, an extravagant procession called the "Aqua Triumphalis" took place, and it was described as "the most magnificent Triumph that certainly ever floted on the Thames." Approximately 10,000 boats of all shapes and sizes accompanied the royal barge as it sailed down the Thames to Whitehall Palace in London. They arrived "to the sound of trumpets and other musick." The river pageant was followed by feasting and fireworks.

One balmy, summer evening in 1717, the Thames played host to the world premiere and debut of

Handel's Water Music, performed by a 50-piece orchestra on a barge sailing serenely up and down the river. On a boat behind the open barge sat music-loving George I, who was in the company of his opulent socialite friends while being serenaded. George enjoyed the music so much that he instructed the orchestra to play the entire piece three times as they sailed up and down the Thames.

Shortly before Queen Elizabeth II's Silver Jubilee in 1977, the British punk rock band Sex Pistols performed live on a boat trip down the Thames to herald the release of their famous song, "God Save the Queen." In 1979, The Clash recorded their music video for the song "London Calling" on a boat floating on the River Thames in the pouring rain. In 1986, Pink Floyd guitarist David Gilmour purchased a boat called Astoria and converted it into a recording studio. Parts of the last three

Painting of George Frideric Handel (left) with King George I of Great Britain, traveling by barge on the Thames River while musicians play in the background. The painting is an artist's rendering of the first performance of Handel's Water Music in 1717 (Edouard Jean Conrad Hamman).

Illustration of medieval long horn trumpet in the Museum of London (Coral Pearce).

Pink Floyd albums were recorded in the floating studio on the River Thames, including The Division Bell.

In 2012, during the Queen's Diamond Jubilee, almost 1,000 boats from around the British Commonwealth sailed down the Thames in a maritime parade 7.5 miles long to celebrate the Queen's 60th anniversary on the throne. The boats were organized into groups, each led by a "Herald Music Barge" carrying ensembles playing different genres of music and new works by thirteen modern British composers. On the last barge in the parade, the London Philharmonic Orchestra and the Royal College of Music Chamber Choir performed the James Bond theme song along with many other well-known songs associated with buildings and monuments along the river. I was one of the millions of people who crowded along the Thames to catch a glimpse of the Queen as she sailed past on her royal barge.

Although most live performances and concerts were canceled in 2020 because of the global pandemic, Liam Gallagher, from the band Oasis, performed live on a floating barge in the River Thames in December 2020 (bottom left). The virtual event called "Down By The River Thames" was streamed globally, and Liam played classic Oasis songs such as "Morning Glory" and "Champagne Supernova."

As you can imagine, with all of these performances on the River Thames, many musical instruments and noisemakers have been accidentally dropped in the water over the centuries. One of the most extraordinary instruments ever found in the river is a medieval long horn trumpet made of brass (top). According to Hazel Forsyth, this trumpet is "the oldest surviving example of a medieval musical instrument from Europe, and the only known example of a medieval European straight trumpet." The long trumpet is comprised of four sections and could be dismantled for carrying. A decorative flag or pennant may have been suspended from the hole in the rim of the bell. The trumpet was possibly used at sea for signaling from ship to ship, and it may have been dropped overboard while its ship docked in London in the late 1300s.

Liam Gallagher performs on the Thames for The Tonight Show on December 4, 2020 (Facebook.com/liamgallagher).

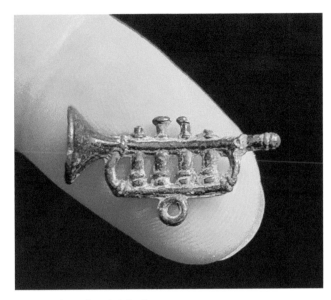

Trumpet charm (Nicola White).

Complete brass bugle found in the Thames (Michael Dower)

A few years ago, Nicola White found a cute little trumpet (top left) made of pewter. It has a suspension loop at the bottom of the trumpet, so it could have been attached to a charm bracelet or worn as a pendant from a necklace.

As Michael Dower was mudlarking, he made a fascinating discovery (top right). "I was walking on the foreshore in Limehouse (London). There were six people in front of me, all in a line searching the beach, so I thought I was not going to find anything here. As I walked to the nearest ladder to leave, I found the bugle, photographed it, and showed it to the people larking near me," describes Michael. The bugle could have been used by the light infantry who were a select group of soldiers sent ahead of the army to disrupt the enemy by taking out officers and strategic targets. Bugle-horn-shaped badges were worn by light infantry soldiers from the late Napoleonic to the early Victorian period. Long before light radios and walkie talkies were invented, trumpets and bugles were used to direct the soldiers and transfer commands around the battlefield with the use of sound.

One of the oldest musical instruments found in the Thames is a bone flute (right) discovered by mudlark Alan Murphy that dates back to the 11th–13th centuries. The flute is carved from the tibia bone of a sheep or goat. It is cylindrical, flaring at one end to a cork fipple forming the blow hole. Fipples are used to regulate the air passing through the instrument to achieve a double octave. On the shin side of the bone, a finger hole was created by a square perforation. Perhaps a sailor lost this pipe when he was in London.

Medieval bone flute (PAS).

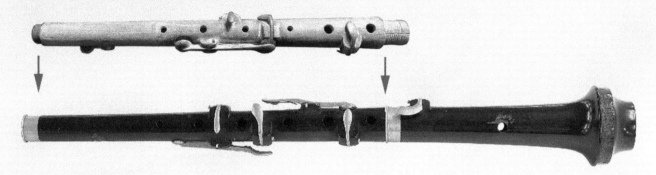

Top 19th-century piccolo oboe piece found along the Thames (Nicola White). Above: Piccolo oboe (Gardiner Houlgate).

Three years ago, Nicola White found a mysterious musical instrument (above), which she was not able to identify. After she posted the instrument on Twitter, Christopher Laspa in Toronto identified it as an early 19th-century piccolo oboe. It is made from a dense hardwood (boxwood or rosewood), and the keys are made of brass. The piccolo oboe is the smallest and highest pitched member of the oboe family. This woodwind instrument could have been played in a military band before it was dropped in the river.

iron tongue attached at the apex of the head. It is played by placing the frame between your teeth and plucking the metal tongue which vibrates and resonates. The constant pitch is modified by changing the shape of the mouth and position of the lips, tongue, and cheeks to create different tones and melodies.

For centuries, jaw harps were a popular instrument among sailors because they are small, compact, and lightweight. I can imagine sailors carried jaw harps in their pockets and played them to pass the endless hours sailing on open seas. They probably entertained the other crew members on board the ship with their music. Jaw harps are still used by musicians even today. For instance, their distinctive sound is prominent in Johnny Cash's recording of "God's Gonna Cut You Down," The Who's song "Join Together," and Red Hot Chili Pepper's song "Give It Away."

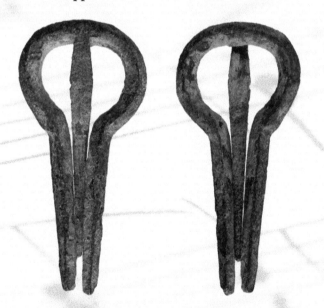

Post-medieval jaw harp (Tony Thira).

Jaw harps (also called Jew's harps) are the most common musical instrument found by mudlarks in the Thames. They are normally broken or encrusted in rust, but mudlark Tony Thira found a complete jaw harp (above) from circa AD 1500–1800. The instrument consists of a circular head with two tapering arms and a flat

Medieval pilgrim's whistle (PAS).

Along the Thames foreshore, mudlarks have also found whistles dating from medieval to modern times (above). They were produced in various shapes and sizes with ornate decoration. One of the most interesting ones is a medieval pilgrim's

Post-medieval whistle with floral decoration (Tom Main).

18th-century hawking whistle (Florrie Evans).

whistle from the 15th century. It has been hollow cast in the shape of a man's head with a short tubular mouthpiece. With an integral loop at the top of the head, the whistle was suspended as a pendant from the pilgrim's neck. Pilgrims believed that the sharp blast from a "holy" whistle would drive away evil.

A few years ago, mudlark Tom Main found an ornately decorated whistle (top left) dating to AD 1600–1800. The pewter whistle has a spherical sound box with a circular hole to release the air. It is connected to a perforated, hollow pipe used to blow air and create the sound. The whistle would have been worn as a pendant using the suspension loop projecting from the top. The outer surface of the whistle has an eye-catching, floral decoration comprised of lines, pellets, and heart shapes.

On the Thames foreshore, Florrie Evans found a small 18th-century pewter hawking whistle (top right) with the profile of a stylized horse at the top. Florrie says it has a "wonderfully piercing and high-pitched sound—perfect for calling a bird like a hawk or falcon! I love the fact that it is an oral connection with the past." Since the 9th century, falconry has been popular among the wealthy upper classes in Britain. Falcons, hawks, and other

birds of prey were used to hunt and catch food for the table. A falconer would use a high-pitched whistle to call the bird while in flight.

In 2008, mudlarks Ian Smith and Tony Pilson discovered a medieval pilgrim's bell (below) from Canterbury dating to the late 14th–early 15th centuries. Around the perimeter, the bell is inscribed with the words, "CAMPAN THOMEA" (Thomas' bell). It was designed to be suspended on a cord or chain from the pilgrim's neck. When Thomas Becket was killed in AD 1170 by knights associated with King Henry II, it is believed that the bells of Canterbury cathedral rang without being touched. Pewter bells were sold as inexpensive souvenirs to medieval pilgrims visiting Canterbury because of their association with Becket's

Medieval pilgrim's bell (PAS).

death. As the pilgrims wore the bells around their necks and walked along the pilgrimage routes, they would ring out and serve as a reminder of the holy saint's martyrdom.

A mudlark found a large crotal bell dating to the 18th–19th centuries. (below) With its leather, 8-shaped strap, this brass bell would have been suspended from the neck of livestock. A shepherd or farmer would have been able to keep track of an animal's location because of the audible sound emitted from the bell as the animal walked or moved its neck. The crotal bell has been decorated with four radiating petals on either side of the sound slit. The engraved initials "RW" could be the maker's mark of Robert Wells Foundry who were established in 1755 and produced crotal bells in Aldbourne. This crotal bell is still fit-for-purpose and rings when shaken.

19th-century badge in the shape of a miniature bell lyre (Jason Sandy).

Brass crotal bell from 18th–19th centuries (PAS).

I n 2020, I found a 19th-century cap or uniform badge in the shape of a miniature bell lyre (above). This portable musical instrument was often used in military or marching bands. A bell lyre is comprised of tuned bars mounted within a metal, lyre-shaped frame and carried on a pole supported by the belt worn by the player. The bars are struck with a mallet, and the instrument sounds like a xylophone.

These musical instruments, whistles, bells, and badges depicting instruments found in the Thames are wonderfully personal items. They were once proudly played or worn by their owners before they disappeared into the muddy waters of the river. I would love to have heard the music once played from these instruments. From Handel to Pink Floyd, composers and musicians have been inspired by and attracted to the Thames as a historic location to play their world renowned songs. Long may the Thames continue to be a stage for music and entertainment to be enjoyed by all!

Tower Bridge (Antoine Buchet).

PAIGE WALKER

I've always really enjoyed hunting for things. We used to go geocaching a lot as a family and would search for animal skulls too. When I was four years old, we went on holiday to Cornwall and looked for pretty shells, patterned pottery, and sea glass on the beach. My sister and I were excited to learn about Mary Anning, and we visited the Jurassic Coast to look for fossils.

When I was five years old, we were planning an outing into London. My mum was looking for something cool and interesting to do, and she discovered a guided mudlarking walk. We had never heard of it before, but thought it would be fun because it sounded like beachcombing and hunting for interesting things! A lady showed us what to do and where to go. I really enjoyed it, so we bought our own mudlarking license and went back. A man on the foreshore told us that he used to find lots of clay pipe bowls, but he said we probably wouldn't find one as they are so hard to find nowadays. That made me really determined to find one! And sure enough, within an hour I had found a perfect pipe bowl in the mud! I was so happy, and from then on, I was addicted. After that, I started researching what I could find on the Thames foreshore and discovered the videos that some of the other mudlarks make about their finds. I love searching and finding something interesting or old, and then researching it afterwards. I like thinking about the person who owned the object before it ended up in the river and wondering how or why it was in the river.

What were they doing or thinking at the time? Who was the last person to hold it, and what was their life like?

My favorite finds are two "pork pie" inkwells. I found one buried in the footpath where we walk our dog. I could see a bit of brown pottery poking out of the ground. I carefully dug it out with my mum's car keys. I was absolutely stunned to pull out a perfect inkwell. It was my dream find and something that I didn't expect to find so close to home and on a route that we walked so often! I had learned all about inkwells from the mudlarking videos, and I knew what it was straight away. I spent so much time wondering how it got there and if a child dropped it from their school bag between a nearby farm and the school down in town. The inkwell also has a finger-print and a thumb print on it, and I wonder who they belonged to. It was the most extraordinary find. My second inkwell which I dug up on the Thames foreshore is also perfect. When I realized it was another inkwell, I literally gasped out loud!

I have also found a piece of medieval pottery with fingerprints in it, an old button, a tiny complete pipe bowl from the 16th century, a modern gold wedding ring, a piece of Bellarmine pottery with a face on it, a doll's glass eye and ear, some bullets, a fossilized shark tooth, a King George III halfpenny, a vulcanite Tizer bottle stopper, and some glass marbles. My dream find would be a 17th-century trader's token.

Portraits by Tom Harrison.

SEAL THE DEAL

18th–19th-century brass seal matrix (Jason Sandy).

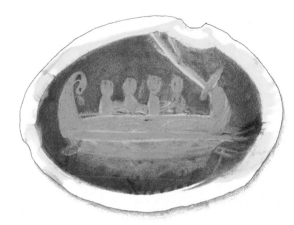

While taking a well-deserved break from his archaeological studies at University College London, Alan Ross made an amazing discovery as he walked along the River Thames at low tide. On a day he will never forget, Alan spotted something which resembled a cough drop laying on the surface of the exposed riverbed. When he picked it up and turned it over, he discovered that a ship with rowers was delicately carved into the convex surface of a brownish-red, semi-precious carnelian gemstone. The extraordinary object (above) is an illustration of a Roman "intaglio" (engraved gem) depicting a rowing galley with a figurehead of a goose or swan.

Carved with various motifs, intaglios were typically made from semi-precious gemstones or glass which were mounted in signet rings or a seal matrix and used to stamp, authenticate, and seal official documents or letters. After placing a blob of thick, melted wax on a document, the signet ring was pressed into the soft wax, leaving the impression of the intaglio which contained the personalized symbol of the owner. The recipient of the document would recognize the unique symbol which proved the authenticity of the document.

The cutting and style of Alan's intaglio indicates that the stone was probably carved in the 3rd century AD, and the nautical illustration could refer to the Classis Britannica, the British fleet of the Roman navy that controlled the English Channel and waters around the Roman province of Britannia. According to Alan, it is possible that the intaglio "could have belonged to a captain in the Classis Britannica or to a commander in a successor fleet." Alternatively, "a signet depicting a warship would have been a suitable device for a merchant who desired a talisman against piracy when on the high seas," explains Alan. The intaglio is now in the Museum of London's permanent collection.

Several years later another mudlark made a similar discovery (right). While searching for colorful glass beads along the Thames foreshore, Johnny Hines crouched down to look closer for the tiny, elusive objects. Out of the corner of his eye, he spotted a modern plastic crystal. As he reached to pick it up, an unusual oval-shaped object caught his attention. As he turned it over, he saw that a dolphin had been delicately cut into a dark brown onyx stone in the Nicolo style over 1,600 years ago!

As I was mudlarking near a medieval dock in Central London, I found a 700-year-old brass seal matrix (below) with an integral suspension loop on the reverse, which indicates that it would have been worn on a chain or leather cord around the neck. In the center of the seal is the head of a stag, which was a common symbol in medieval times attributed to the Saint Hubert, the patron saint of hunters. Around the circumference of the round seal are the Latin words CREDE MICHI [MIHI] which mean "trust me." The words were hand-carved in reverse so that, when pressed into melted wax, the letters are legible.

Top left: Illustration of Roman carnelian intaglio carved with a ship and rowers (Coral Pearce). Top right: Roman intaglio engraved with a dolphin (PAS). Bottom right: Medieval seal matrix (Jason Sandy).

Inspired by historic Roman precedents, the Stuarts and Georgians in England created their own type of seal matrices in the 18th century using glass intaglios featuring natural and classical motifs such as mythological gods and creatures, busts of Roman rulers and English monarchs, etc. Although some 18th-century intaglios are made of precious gemstones, craftsmen often used colored glass as an inexpensive alternative. According to Ward Oles, a researcher of 18th-century material culture, the glass intaglios were made from soda lime glass, both vitreous and opaque. The glass was usually colored with mineral or metallic/oxide additives such as cobalt for blue, manganese for purple, etc.

A Scot named James Tassie created large quantities of glass intaglios in his workshop in London in the 18th century. He mass-produced intaglios by pressing repetitive designs into the molten glass before it hardened. This three-sided, "spinning" glass intaglio (above) was found by David Hodgson in the River Thames. Dating to AD 1707-1714, a bust of Queen Anne, her coat of arms, and a crown surmounted by an orb and scepters are illustrated on the different sides of the glass intaglio.

When mudlarking at night along the old docks in London, Mike Walker found a brass fob seal (below) with an exquisite glass intaglio. Based on the style of the seal, it is most likely from the late Georgian period. Set in a conical brass frame, the intaglio is made of dark green glass and is engraved with a highly detailed bust of a classical figure. Mike explains, "A loop on the top would have attached the seal to a watch chain, probably alongside other items such as a watch winder and pipe tamper."

For wealthy customers, James Tassie would carefully hand-carve custom-made designs into the surface of the glass. The vibrant, colored glass intaglio (left) discovered by Florrie Evans on the River Thames foreshore was hand-carved with interwoven cursive letters surmounted by a crown.

Top right: Sealing wax on envelope (Tiko Aramyan/Shutterstock.com). Top left: Three-sided, spinning glass intaglio (David Hodgson). Bottom left: Red glass intaglio inscribed with cursive letters and crown (Florrie Evans). Bottom right: Georgian glass fob seal with classical bust (Mike Walker).

Another fine example of a Georgian seal matrix (above) was found by Oliver Muranyi-Clark. A crown surmounted by a bull's head is depicted on the flat surface of the Georgian intaglio made of green glass. Holding the carved glass in place, the circular setting is scalloped around the perimeter with a domed, eight-spoke openwork cartwheel shape which allows light to pass through the glass. A handle or attachment loop would have been fixed to the central aperture.

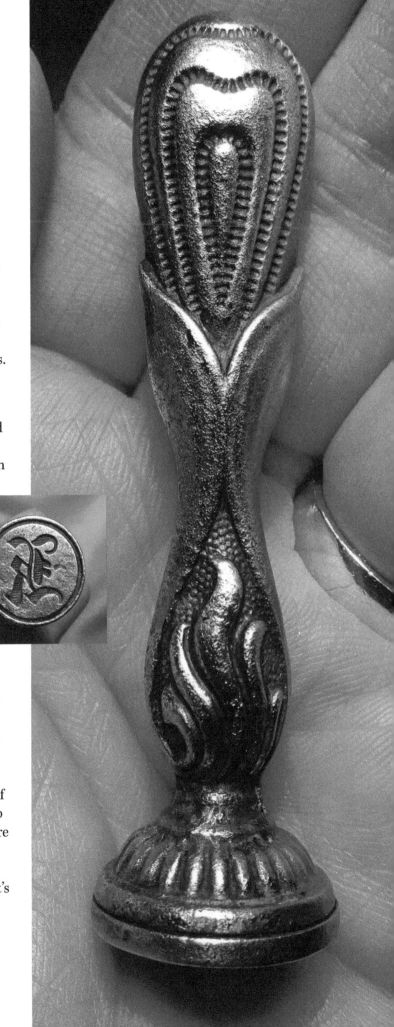

One of my own favorite finds is a highly decorated seal matrix from the 18th–19th centuries (right). The handle is shaped like the stem of a flower with a heart-shaped bud emerging from the top. At the bottom, undulating flames rise from the scalloped base. Underneath the seal matrix, the Gothic letter K has been engraved and articulated with a series of incised lines. Fortunately, it is still "fit for purpose," and I enjoy sealing the envelopes with hot wax when I send my friends handwritten letters.

Lost centuries ago in the River Thames, signet rings and seal matrices are wonderful personal items which reveal rare insights into the lives of Londoners and even Romans who lived in early settlement of Londinium. Although we have not yet been able to link these finds to specific individuals, the intaglios and seals are highly personalized to represent the status and wealth of the owner. Through the unique motifs carved into the various types of seals, we can understand more about the culture and customs of the times long ago. Next time you find a small, circular piece of glass on your local beach, double check to see if it's a glass intaglio!

Top left: Georgian glass seal matrix bull's head and crown (Oliver Muranyi-Clark). Right: 18th-19th century brass seal matrix (Jason Sandy).

TOBIAS NETO

My interest in history and archaeology dates back to when I was a teenager. It was not until I was given a metal detector as a Christmas present back in 2014 that I put into practice my desire to learn more about objects from the past and their history.

I'm fortunate to live by the River Thames in London. Daily dog walks on the Thames foreshore always fascinated me. I often noticed a variety of pottery sherds and other unidentified small objects scattered on the foreshore during low tides. Then a question would pop up: "What's buried in the mud?"

Once I learned about the permits issued by the Port of London Authority allowing people to search the foreshore of the River Thames, I decided to apply for one. That was when my hobby of searching for old things from the past started. Although I use a metal detector to search, I consider myself a mudlark too—the act of searching with the help of "eyes only."

The real thrill of searching is not knowing what is out there and what you may find during the low tides of the Thames, whether using eyes only or a metal detector. As the River Thames hides a huge amount of historic artifacts—either camouflaged among the rocks, buried in the mud, or exposed during low tides—the chances of finding something are always high. Very rarely do I come home with empty pockets. Most of the time, these discovered artifacts are unknown to me. But, with a bit of research, I always learn new things about history and the experiences of past Londoners. Although I am more familiar with certain artifacts which I frequently encounter, the Thames always surprises me with something new to me or rare or otherwise unknown.

Over the course of the last eight years, I have made a number of significant Thames finds, from the Iron Age period, through the Roman Empire, from the Middle Ages to the Tudor Dynasty, from post-medieval through to the 19th century and modern times. Some of my finds were originally from this country, but others arrived here from abroad. Although I seem to be constantly managing my storage space, they are all kept safely with me. My plan is to have them all displayed somewhere someday to fascinate and intrigue future generations of detectorists and mudlarks.

In my large collection of finds, one of my favorites is a silver Drachm coin of King Khosrow II of the ancient Persian Sassanian Dynasty dating to AD 590-628 which might have arrived in London with the Vikings and been lost in the Thames. I donated this find to the Museum of London. Another favorite is a medieval sword pommel circa AD 1250 with an inscription IHESV MERCI (MERCI JESUS) that would have possibly belonged to a knight on his way to the Crusades, again now in the Museum of London.

Finally, the find of which I am most proud is the Thames V.C., a Victoria Cross medal awarded to a recipient for the Battle of Inkerman in 1854. My find has been designated as being of national importance, and it is now held at the National Army Museum.

Portraits by Tom Harrison.

ANCIENT SACRED RIVER

At the end of the last Ice Age, the retreating glacial ice cut deep river valleys in the chalk hills, and groups of hunter-gatherers began to visit England, tracking herds of animals along the River Thames. Both the animals and early humans came to the Thames Valley in search of fresh water and food. The Thames provided plenty of natural resources and was used as a vital transportation link.

Pilgrims leaving Canterbury, The Siege of Thebes, *1455-1462 (John Lydgate).*

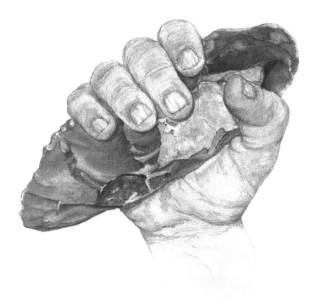

Illustration of Mesolithic tranchet hand axe (Coral Pearce).

Because of its important role, the River Thames was highly revered by early inhabitants who considered its waters to be sacred. During the Stone Age, beautifully crafted flint tools were purposely deposited in the river as votive offerings to the river gods. While mudlarking along the Thames in London, Alan Murphy found a stunning Mesolithic tranchet hand axe made of flint (above). It was knapped between 8,300–3,500 BC and used for hunting, cutting, and scraping. Stone tools, like the tranchet Alan found, attest to the great skill, ingenuity, and workmanship of the Stone Age flint-knappers. According to the Museum of London, over 400 Stone Age flint axes have been found in the Thames, which were possibly deposited in the river purposely as an act of worship and thanksgiving to the life-sustaining waters.

Searching in West London along the exposed riverbed at low tide, a mudlark discovered a Neolithic polished stone macehead from 2900–2100 BC, which illustrates an exceptional level of craftsmanship (right). Originally from Norway, the stone was carved into a macehead and polished so that the transverse stripes of the natural stone created an ornamental effect. This mace would have been a highly valued object. Weapons were symbols of power and authority, so perhaps they were placed in the river to demonstrate humility, self-sacrifice, and acknowledgement of the power of the river gods.

During the Iron Age, Celtic tribes also deposited valuable, highly decorated offerings in the River Thames. While constructing Battersea Bridge in 1857, workmen made one of the most important discoveries in Britain's history as they were dredging the Thames riverbed. They extracted an ancient bronze shield (above right) from the thick mud. Produced around 350–50 BC, the shield is formed from sheets of bronze and decorated within

Battersea Shield (Jason Sandy).

the raised circular and undulating shapes and embellished with red glass. The so-called "Battersea Shield" was probably used during ceremonies to display the wealthy owner's power and to command respect.

Neolithic Macehead (PAS).

Workmen made another extraordinary discovery while dredging the River Thames near Waterloo Bridge in 1868. Decorated with repoussé ornamentation in the La Tène style, a unique Iron Age helmet with horns from around 150–50 BC was pulled from the dense mud of the Thames (right). Although ancient Greek literature describes Celts with horned helmets, this is the only Iron Age helmet with horns ever found in Europe. Iron Age warfare was about posturing and prestige, so this spectacular helmet could have been worn to intimidate enemies or impress onlookers during a ceremony or parade. Considered to be two of the finest examples of Celtic Art in Britain, the Battersea Shield and Waterloo Helmet are on permanent display in the British Museum in London.

Waterloo Helmet (Michal Wal).

The Pilgrim's Story from the Canterbury Tales,
Ellesmere Manuscript, *England, 15th century.*

Throughout the Middle Ages, many people went on pilgrimage to visit holy shrines. On their journeys, they would buy religious badges made of inexpensive pewter to wear on their clothing and hats as souvenirs on their way home. Over the last 40 years, mudlarks have found a large concentration of pilgrims' badges near medieval docks and ferry points where pilgrims arrived back from their travels. Following their safe return to London, it is possible that pilgrims purposely

deposited their badges into the sacred river to express their thanks to God. Some pilgrims traveled very long distances to sacred sites in Santiago de Compostela, Rome, and Jerusalem.

In medieval England, Canterbury was one of the most visited holy sites. Many of the pilgrim badges found in the Thames are from Canterbury. Written between AD 1387 and 1400, Geoffrey Chaucer's famous book, *The Canterbury Tales,* describes a group of pilgrims who exchange stories as they walk from London to Canterbury during a pilgrimage to visit the shrine of

The Martyrdom of St Thomas Becket, Book of Hours,
Use of Sarum, Flanders or Northern France, 14th century.

Saint Thomas Becket. Many pilgrim badges found in the River Thames represent Becket, the former Archbishop of Canterbury (right). After falling out of favor with King Henry II, Becket was murdered in Canterbury Cathedral by four knights in AD 1170. One of the best pilgrim badges of this highly respected saint was found by Tony Thira in 2016. Dating to the 14th–16th centuries, this openwork pilgrim badge (left) depicts the martyrdom of Thomas Becket within an architectural frame surmounted by a cross with trefoil terminals. A knight stands ready with his sword drawn as Becket bows his head with his hands folded together in prayer.

Pilgrim badge depicting murder of Thomas Becket (Tony Thira).

After Becket's assassination, the monks in the cathedral supposedly took his blood and diluted it with water to create a miracle-working cure for illnesses. According to legend, it could even bring the dead back to life. At Becket's shrine, small pewter containers called 'ampullae' containing a small quantity of the healing "water of Saint Thomas" were sold to pilgrims.

John Dunford found a Medieval pilgrim ampulla (right) from Canterbury dating to AD 1220–1420, which was hollow-cast and decorated with bands of triangular patterns. On one end, Becket sits on a throne with his right hand raised in benediction. On the other end, a knight's sword strikes Becket's staff which he uses in self-defense. There

are suspension loops on both sides of the vessel where a leather strap was secured so that the ampulla could be worn as a pendant around a pilgrim's neck.

Saint Thomas Becket Pilgrim Badge (Tommy Donnellan).

Over the years, hundreds of pilgrims' badges, bells, and ampullae have been found in the River Thames, which suggests that they were purposely deposited in the water for religious reasons. Thanks to the generous donations from mudlarks, the Museum of London has the largest collection of medieval badges in the world.

Throughout the history of London, the flowing waters of the River Thames have been considered to be sacred. Valuable, ornate objects such as the Battersea Shield and Waterloo Helmet were deposited as votive offerings to the River Thames by Celtic tribes. Medieval pilgrims could have placed their religious badges into the Thames possibly as a propitiatory gesture to gain favor or blessings.

Pilgrim's ampulla (PAS)

JOHN DUNFORD

Growing up in the 1950s, every schoolboy had a collection of marbles, cigarette cards, and a length of string for conker season in his pocket. We also had an assortment of copper coins spanning five different monarchs—Queen Victoria, Edward VII, George V, George VI, and Elizabeth II. These coins, which I carried around in my pockets, got me interested in history and collecting.

In the early 1960s, I attended Gordon's secondary school in Gravesend, a two-minute walk from Fort Gardens. I spent many hours exploring the fortifications and straying onto the Thames foreshore. I can remember arriving home from school with shoes plastered in Thames mud. My mother was very cross as my only school shoes were ruined. She had very little interest in the half a dozen clay pipes I had rescued from the river.

In 1978, I started metal detecting, and in 1980, I was invited to join the Society of Thames Mudlarks. Working alongside archaeologists from the Museum of London on building sites along the river, club members recovered many coins and artifacts spanning thousands of years.

One of the most amazing finds I have found is a Roman gold clasp with a freshwater pearl attached. I found this on the floor of London's Roman Amphitheatre, and the clasp is currently on display in the Guildhall Art Gallery. Part of the amphitheater has been preserved in the basement of this building.

While searching a heap of building spoil from the City of London, I rescued a rare pilgrim's ampulla depicting Thomas Becket. He is shown holding his staff and wearing his miter. On the back of the ampulla, Becket is kneeling with four knights in each corner, one with a raised sword ready to behead him. This was recently on display in the Museum of London.

It is very rewarding to view your finds on display in the Museum of London. I also donated an Iron Age bone comb with decoration to the museum. This is the only Iron Age comb in the Museum of London's collection which has been recorded with a find spot.

I always wonder who used this coin or artifact last? Was it an accidental loss or a deliberate act of deposition? I especially enjoy finding personal items which can be linked to a specific person. Once I found a printing block with the name of Sir William George Armstrong, who lived from 1810–1900. He was an inventor of modern artillery and became a Lord.

Another find I feel I can possibly link to a person is a knife handle inscribed "R D 1598." One side has a human figure dancing with angels, and the other side depicts a skeleton with a sword and head in his hands. I believe this could have belonged to one of Elizabeth I's favorite court members, the 2nd Earl of Essex, Robert Deveraux. He was executed at the Tower of London in 1601 and was the last person to be beheaded on Tower Green.

I have spent many happy hours, weeks, months, and years walking the Thames foreshore. Watching the river wildlife and chatting to fellow searchers is a great hobby. Over the years of my membership with the Society of Thames Mudlarks, I have been a committee member several times.

Portraits by Tom Harrison.

MODERN
SACRED
RIVER

Today, the Hindu community living in London still considers the River Thames to be sacred and use it as a substitute for the holy Ganges River in India. Deified as the goddess Ganga, the Ganges River is an important place of pilgrimage in India. "As the Ganges is not very accessible to the Anglo-Hindu community in London, it could be that they are utilizing the next best thing—a river that has an impact on their lives and their surrounding landscape," suggests Nikola Burdon from the Museum of London. Hindus in London deposit a wide variety of colorful offerings in the Thames. Over the years, I have discovered many Hindu offerings (facing page and top left) in the river.

A few years ago, Anna Borzello found a cluster of beautiful statuettes of the Hindu god, Ganesh, connected by colorful ribbons (above right). "I found this object lying in thick mud. The statues appear in particular spots along the river, and I like that these finds reflect the demographic living nearby," explains Anna. Hindus deposit

sacred objects in flowing water to energize them and release their powers. Ganesh (shown below) is considered to be the god of new beginnings, success, wisdom, and "remover of obstacles." A Hindu probably placed these statuettes in the flowing water of the Thames as a request for Ganesh to provide success and wisdom and to remove barriers in their circumstances.

Facing page: Hindu Diwali lamps (Jason Sandy). Top left: Hindu offering (Jason Sandy). Top right: Ganesh statuettes (Anna Borzello). Bottom right: Hindu god Ganesh (Illustration by Chinalingalagramam).

When I find Hindu votive offerings in the River Thames, I am reminded of a once-in-a-lifetime journey I experienced along the Ganges River in Varanasi, India. Before dawn, we rented a boat and set out on the peaceful and sacred Ganges (above left). As the sun rose, we sailed past sunken temples half submerged in the river, and we watched hundreds of Hindu pilgrims on the expansive ghats (steps) along the river (above right) as they immersed themselves in the holy waters of the Ganges.

When I am mudlarking along the Thames in London, I especially enjoy finding colorful lamps, which were used during the celebrations of Diwali, known as the "Festival of Lights." On a cold November morning shortly after Diwali, I found over 30 colorful, ornately decorated Hindu lamps (page 132) at a sacred spot along the River Thames. The lamps, which contain images of the Hindu gods

Ganesh and Shiva, were lit and set afloat on the Thames, which created an amazing spectacle of flickering light as the candles slowly floated down the river.

On the exposed riverbed at low tide, I also find a variety of Hindu "yantras." Carved into the surface of a brass plate, the Sri Yantra is a beautiful and complex sacred geometry which has been used for worship, devotion, and meditation for thousands of years (below left). Representing the cosmos at the macrocosmic level and the human body at the microcosmic level, the Sri Yantra is conceived as a place of spiritual pilgrimage, which is comprised of nine interlocking triangles, surrounded by two circles of lotus petals encased within a gated frame called the "earth citadel."

I have also discovered many numerical planetary yantras (below right) made of solid lead. The yantra is decorated with 9 Sanskrit numbers within the so-called "magic square" formed by nine equal squares. If you add up the numbers contained in three of the squares diagonally, horizontally or vertically, the sum of the three numbers is always 36. The number 8 located in

Top: Munshi Ghat and Kedar Ghat in Varansi (Patrick Barry). Bottom: Yantra photos (Jason Sandy).

the upper center square indicates that this is a Rahu Yantra, named after the feared Hindu god, Rahu. It is believed that devoted worship of a Rahu Yantra can protect you from danger caused by hidden enemies, wrong diagnosis of illness, and deceit from those around you. As an act of worship, this yantra is placed into flowing water to appease Rahu.

While mudlarking, I have recovered several beautiful Hindu Rakhi bracelets. Raksha Bandhan is a Hindu festival that celebrates brotherhood and love. The word "Raksha" means "protection," and "Bandhan" is the verb "to tie." Traditionally, during the festival, sisters tie a Rakhi bracelet around their brothers' wrists as a symbol that the brother will always look after and protect his sister. After the procession, the bracelets are purposely placed in a river (e.g., Ganges or Thames) and immersed in the running water in order to energize and release their protective powers. One of the Rakhi bracelets is formed in the shape of a gold-plated eye with a red iris to ward off evil (top right). A floral Rakhi bracelet I found (bottom right) has an abstract eye formed with gemstones and decorated with colorful beads.

Used for a similar purpose, the "evil eye" pendant (below) I discovered in the River Thames is a symbol which has been used to ward off evil for over 5,000 years. In many cultures, it is believed that an evil glare can cause misfortune, bad luck, or injury. As a talisman, the "evil eye" symbol is worn to "stare back at the world" and keep you safe from harm.

Throughout the history of London, the flowing waters of the River Thames have been considered to be sacred. Votive offerings were purposely deposited in the river from the Mesolithic Period until today, and hundreds of these beautiful, ornate objects have been discovered by mudlarks in the River Thames. These unique artifacts reveal the importance of the sacred river. In the Museum of London, there are many glass display cases which exhibit votive offerings recovered from the River Thames. If you would like to read more about the sacred river, I would highly recommend the delightful book, *Thames: Sacred River*, by historian Peter Ackroyd.

Hindu jewelry found in the Thames (Jason Sandy).

ANNA BORZELLO

I started mudlarking in 2015, but it was in my mind long before then. I grew up in London, and I have photos of my 15-year-old self dancing on the Thames foreshore. Even then, I knew there were clay pipe stems among the pebbles, and it seemed crazy that centuries-old objects were scattered like litter in a public place. It was only after returning to the city, after a decade working in Africa, and with my children settled in school, that the time felt right. One day I put on my boots and set off to the river—where I have gone, whenever I can, in all weathers, day or night, tide permitting.

Mudlarking is both meditative and addictive. It is soothing to scan a stretch of riverbed, and I have always loved being near the water to enjoy the dancing light, the wash of waves, and the moments of stillness before the tide turns. There is a "lucky dip" (grab bag) feel as the water pulls back, revealing traces of London's 2,000-year-old past. After three hours of finding nothing, there's always a chance that the next wave might uncover the one elusive object that will make my morning.

I studied history at school, but the past felt shadowy and unreal. Mudlarking has changed that. Finds are like time-portals—the top from a 17th-century moneybox leads to a rowdy Elizabethan theater and a boat hook reveals a Victorian dockyard. I feel the frustration of the Georgian gentleman who lost his cufflink and the grief of the woman who threw her love token into the Thames. Research expands the stories into tales of the slave trade, the fashion for flowing wigs, and the medicinal value of crumbled Egyptian mummies.

I don't have a favorite find, but it would be difficult to part with my collection of 15,000 dress pins, painstakingly picked up from the foreshore one by one. I was puzzled the first time I saw a sliver of metal lying in the mud. Why was it there? I discovered that pins secured the clothes of Londoners for centuries. The story of their fall from grace—from high value items to virtually valueless via a history of trade wars, industrialization, and fashion—feels like seeing the world in a grain of sand, as William Blake put it.

Mudlarking has become a way of life. My car is scattered with old bones, and my clothes are always muddy. I planned my kitchen redesign around display shelves for my finds. Most days, I photograph an artifact, research its history, and post it on Instagram. "Let me consult my diary," I tell the hospital, as I scroll through the tide table to make sure the date doesn't clash with a good low tide.

When I started mudlarking, I enjoyed the transgressive feeling of being on an often-empty foreshore while commuters streamed to work above me. There are more people on the river now, and passers-by shout down, "What have you found?" rather than, "What are you doing?". There is a generous and interesting mudlarking community, and I have made many good friends. They share my notion that a fun night out is climbing down a ladder in the rain to search for musket balls by headlamp in the Thames mud.

Portraits by Tom Harrison.

FANTASTIC
BEASTS
OF THE
THAMES

Can you imagine seeing a hippo swimming in the River Thames or a rhino drinking from its cool waters? Millennia ago, London was home to a wide variety of animals typically associated with Africa, not Europe. During the Paleolithic Age, ancient beasts such as straight-tusked elephants, hippos, rhinos, cave lions, wolves, hyenas, brown bears, giant deer, and large oxen (known as aurochs) freely roamed the fertile Thames Valley and grazed in the grassy floodplain along the river. At that time, the banks of the Thames extended to present day Trafalgar Square, and these exotic animals thrived in the warm, tropical climate. During major excavation work under this popular tourist site in the 19th century, a 125,000-year-old hippopotamus tooth and remains from a prehistoric elephant were discovered.

Along the River Thames, mudlarks have also found traces of these ancient beasts. Several years ago, Stefano Ambrogi discovered part of a skull (above left) from a woolly rhinoceros in the river. Bones from woolly rhinos have also been found in the Thames Estuary and along the river under Battersea Power Station. Although they died out about 8,000 years ago, woolly rhinos (above right) were once a common sight in the London area. With their thick fur and dense layer of fat to keep warm in the extreme cold, these prehistoric rhinos survived the last Ice Age.

At low tide along the Thames foreshore, Alan Murphy discovered two fossilized teeth (top right) from woolly mammoths who have been extinct for around 10,000 years. Woolly mammoths (bottom right) lived during the Pleistocene epoch and were approximately the same size as modern African elephants, weighing about 6 tons. With their thick coat of fur, they were well adapted to London's cold climate back then. Their long, curved tusks and large trunk were used to move objects, forage, bathe, and fight. Their four molar teeth were replaced six times during their lifetime, and this

is potentially the reason why several mammoth teeth have been found in the Thames. In 1864, a complete 200,000-year-old steppe mammoth skull with tusks was found in Ilford, London. It's hard to imagine these giant beasts walking through the London area hundreds of thousands of years ago when it was covered by a massive polar ice sheet.

Facing page: Collection of Thames fossils (Sam Caethoven). This page, top to bottom, left to right: Woolly rhinoceros skull (Stefano Ambrogi). Illustration of woolly rhino (Mauricio Antón, Public Library of Science). Woolly mammoth teeth (Alan Murphy). Illustration of woolly mammoths (Mauricio Antón, Public Library of Science).

Millions of years before these large herbivores and carnivores roamed the Thames Valley, other prehistoric creatures inhabited the London area. As Nick Stevens was searching the surface of an abandoned barge bed on the Thames foreshore, he spotted a large, fossilized shark's tooth belonging to a prehistoric Megalodon. It is the largest species of shark ever recorded and has been extinct for millions of years. Dating from the Early Miocene to Pliocene epochs, the Megalodon thrived and feasted on the abundant aquatic life native to the warm seas around the sub-tropical British Isles. It fed on whales, dolphins, squid, and even turtles. Growing up to 18 meters (59 ft) in length and weighing approximately 65 tons, this prehistoric shark had approximately 10 tons of biting power. Although they lived approximately 3.6–23 million years ago, some people believe that Megalodon still roam the earth's deepest oceans, which is the premise for the 2018 Hollywood film, *The Meg*.

Fossil collector and mudlark, Sam Caethoven, has collected numerous smaller, fossilized sharks' teeth (below) in the Thames Estuary. Dating to the Eocene period, they were eroded out of the London Clay and are approximately 49–56 million years old. The most common sharks' teeth which Sam finds are from Striatolamia, a sand tiger shark. Dating to the Early Paleocene to Late Miocene periods, this extinct species of shark is around 10.3–61.7 million years old. Sam has also discovered larger teeth from Otodus sharks, which lived from the Paleocene to Pliocene epoch. Growing up to 12.2 meters (40 ft) long, they were one of the top predators of their time. Otodus sharks preceded Megalodon sharks.

Every year mudlarks discover numerous fossils in the River Thames (page 138) providing evidence of the diverse wildlife native to England millions of years ago. Sam explains why so many fossils are found in the river: "The Thames cuts through Eocene and Paleocene clays underlain by Cretaceous chalk and overlain by Pleistocene gravels, all of which yield fossils. The ancestral Thames has changed course over the millennia and was historically wider and further north until the effects of major glaciation caused the river to be diverted, laying down terraces of sediments and gravels during the Pleistocene that is extremely rich in fossils. In the Thames Estuary, there are also Red Crag and Corallian Crag deposits, yielding fossils from the Pliocene (1.8–3.6 million years ago) and earlier fossils including Megalodon and earlier sharks as well as rays, crabs, lobsters, corals, and bryozoa.

"The Eocene age London clay yields fossil remains from sharks, rays, bony fish, crabs, lobsters, fish, sea snakes, and invertebrates such as nautilus. These are more commonly found in the estuary but can also be found further upriver. Some of the fossils in the Thames are local and others are imported. Chalk is also found naturally at the estuary, but there is also a lot of imported chalk which was brought in to form the soft tops of barge beds for use in London's thriving river trade. Chalk contains fossils and flint fossil casts, the most common of which are

Fossilized sharks' teeth (Sam Caethoven).

sponges of many varieties. The most easily recognizable fossils from the chalk are echinoids (sea urchins). Bivalves, gastropods, and brachiopods can also be found, as can belemnites and ammonites."

Some of my favorite fossils from the Thames are micraster fossils (above left). They are heart-shaped, fossilized sea urchins which come in a variety of colors. Living between 35–100 million years ago, micrasters are an extinct genus of echinoids dating to the late Cretaceous to the early Eocene periods. They are simply beautiful creatures, which I love to collect from the gravel beds along the river (above right).

Over the years, Sam has found many echinoids in the Thames (right). For centuries, it was believed that these echinoids possessed magical powers and were harbingers of good luck. In Britain, echinoids have been called "Sugar Loaves," "Shepherd's Crowns," "Thunderstones," "Snake's eggs," and "Poundstones." Some people refer to them as "Fairy Loaves" because they look like small round loaves of bread. These echinoids were sometimes used as charms believed to help the baking of bread,

a precious commodity centuries ago. They were also kept in dairies because they were thought to prevent milk from curdling. Fairy Loaves also supposedly protected families against witchcraft. Therefore, they were placed on the windowsills of their homes as a good luck charm and talisman to protect against evil. Although I'm not superstitious, I do keep some of these fossils on my windowsill because they are lovely little objects to look at and enjoy.

Top left: Micraster fossil (Jason Sandy). Top right: Micraster fossil (Sam Caethoven). Right: Collection of Thames echinoids (Sam Caethoven).

I also enjoy finding beautiful, spiral-shaped ammonites (above) in the Thames. They are approximately 65–240 million years old and lived at the same time as the dinosaurs before they went extinct at the end of the Cretaceous Period. Ammonites were cephalopods with a ribbed, spiral shell similar to a nautilus and would have had eight arms, which they used to propel themselves backwards through the water. After millions of years in the Thames, the incredible, spiral shapes of ammonites are still perfectly preserved—nature's beauty frozen in time.

One of the most interesting fossils that Sam has found is a Basinotopus crab (below), which eroded out of the London Clay in the Thames Estuary. Dating to the Eocene period, it is approximately 49–56 million years old. If you look closely, the fossilized crab's shell looks like a Chinese dragon's face with a wide mouth, round cheeks, nose with nostrils, and squinting eyes. It's bizarre, but stunningly beautiful.

Top: Ammonite fossil (Jason Sandy). Left: Basinotopus crab fossil (Sam Caethoven).

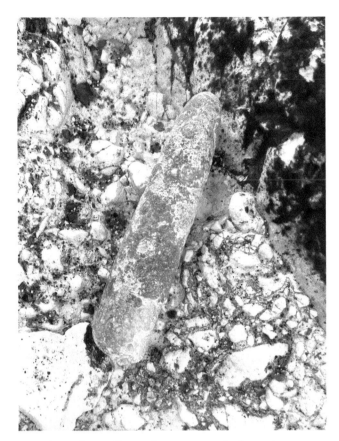

1252, King Henry III was given a magnificent white polar bear by the King of Norway as a royal gift. It was kept in the menagerie at the Tower of London castle along the Thames which housed other exotic animals including lions, leopards, tigers, elephants, baboons, eagles, pumas, and even a jackal.

The polar bear was a huge, hungry beast, and it soon became too costly to feed. So, the caretakers let the bear swim in the castle moat and Thames to catch fish to eat. A collar and a "stout cord" were attached to the bear to keep it from escaping. Each day, excited Londoners would gather along the riverbank to watch the bear plunge into the Thames and emerge with a sturgeon or salmon between his jaws (below). What a fascinating sight that would have been!

Sam has also collected numerous belemnite fossils (above) from the Thames. They originate from an extinct squid-like cephalopod that lived around 100 million years ago. Dating to the Late Triassic to Late Cretaceous periods, belemnites had a cone-shaped skeleton, a pair of fins, and ten hooked arms which were used to swim and capture prey. Made of calcite, the pointed guard is typically all that survives as a fossil. There is much folklore which surrounds these bullet-shaped fossils. They were used to supposedly cure rheumatism and even crushed and ground into a powder to cure sore eyes, which actually had the opposite effect and irritated the eyes.

I n the Middle Ages, unusual animals were also spotted in the Thames. In 1457, two whales, a narwhal, and a walrus fascinated Londoners as they swam upstream from the English Channel. Even a polar bear was seen swimming in the Thames catching fish in the 13th century. What was this hypercarnivorous bear doing in the river? In

Top left: Belemnite fossil (Sam Caethoven). Bottom right: Polar bear catching fish (Miia "Myrtti" Ranta).

Frost Fair in 1814 (Tableau by Julia Fullerton-Batten).

During the early 17th and early 19th centuries, Britain experienced a series of extremely cold winters known as the Little Ice Age. Because of the restricted flow of the river caused by the narrow arches of the old medieval London Bridge, the Thames would freeze upstream from the bridge. According to historic records, the river froze over 24 times from 1400 to 1832, when the medieval London Bridge was demolished and rebuilt with wider arches. During the Great Frost of 1683–1684, the Thames was completely frozen for over two months with ice over 11 inches (28 cm) thick. Londoners took advantage of these rare opportunities to be on the ice, and vendors set up booths and tents on the frozen river to sell their goods. During these "Frost Fairs," all sorts of entertainment were on offer, including ice skating, horse and coach racing, gambling, dancing, football/soccer, and nine-pin bowling. In the last Frost Fair, which lasted four days in 1814, a colossal elephant was led across the thick ice on the Thames near Blackfriars Bridge (above). Londoners must have been shocked to see a heavy elephant walking on the ice-covered river. Professional photographer Julia Fullerton-Batten recreated this historic spectacle in a short film called "1814 Frost Fair," which is available to watch on Vimeo.

For centuries, raw sewage and trash have been carelessly dumped into the River Thames. During "The Great Stink" in 1858, the overwhelming smell of the fecal matter and industrial effluent in the river became untenable. The Victorian sewer system alleviated some of the problems, but the discharge of raw sewage into the Thames during heavy rainfall continued.

The Thames was declared "biologically dead" in 1957 by the Natural History Museum in London. Fortunately, the cleanliness of the water has dramatically improved in recent years, and wildlife has returned in abundance. The Thames is now considered to be the cleanest metropolitan river in the world. Over 125 species of fish, 400 types of invertebrates, and even seahorses (right) now thrive in the river. Cormorants, Egyptian geese, Canadian geese, swans, grey herons, and many types of ducks, seagulls, and other birds live along the Thames. According to researchers from the Zoological Society of London, over 2,800 grey seals (bottom) and almost 800 harbor seals live in the Thames and are sometimes seen as far upstream as Richmond and Twickenham in West London. Whales are also sometimes seen swimming in the Thames, which is once again teeming with bountiful wildlife as it returns to its natural state. Will hippos be seen once again in the Thames in the future?

Top: Seahorse found in the Thames (Nicola White). Bottom: "Freddie the Seal" by Hammersmith Bridge (Broni Lloyd-Edwards).

SAM CAETHOVEN

I've been a fossil hunter for many years now and have enjoyed collecting natural and man-made curios, antiques, and lost objects since childhood. Since I work in Central London, it is almost impossible to get out to the beach on a workday to take advantage of the long, summer days and low tides to satisfy my inner magpie. This felt like a lost opportunity which I thought mudlarking might fill, so five years ago I signed up to an organized foreshore walk to try it out before investing in a permit. I bought my first foreshore permit by the end of that day.

As a fossil hunter, I'm used to thinking of my finds in the context of deep time, being millions of years old rather than mere centuries. You witness the evolution of our planet and the species that inhabit it, seeing adaptations and extinctions as environments change. Human history can feel quite trivial against this backdrop, but in fact, mudlarking takes your mind on a similar journey. People come and go, leaving behind objects and traces of their impact on the landscape. Although reading different traces and artifacts, the mindset is much the same and brings the same wonder. The most common find, potsherds, tell a story of evolution and migration as people import and trade in wares, fashions evolve with taste, cultural and political climates change, and new technologies emerge. For an inquiring mind, even a basic object can be thought-provoking and revealing when you set about learning to understand it.

Mudlarking has connected me deeply and personally with London. The river has revealed to me all the layers of human history that have passed through this city-port, seeking to conquer, trade, pay pilgrimage, find refuge, or make a living. What I find provides a tangible connection to people who likely never thought they'd ever be pondered by another person centuries into the future. I take delight from placing my fingers in the fingerprints of a medieval potter when holding a fragment of the vessel they made, and marveling at the craftsmanship of the artisan who made a glass bead.

The truth is that mudlarking is about luck and legwork. Many days you'll find nothing notable, but the thrill is in the possibilities—you never know what you might find. Most days I don't find anything special, but occasionally and often unexpectedly, I'll find something exceptional. Some of my favorite finds include a rare Roman bone hairpin with a cuboid head, elaborate Tudor buttons, and a medieval, secular pewter badge in the shape of a purse filled with money intended to attract wealth by means of sympathetic magic!

The foreshore is an escape in time and space; set apart from, yet in the midst of, a thronging capital. Alongside lapping water, wildlife, and the muffled sounds of life going on somewhere beyond, even the air tastes different. It's a space I really enjoy being in. Whatever else, I know I will always find a sense of well-being, calm, and precious headspace on the foreshore.

Portraits by Tom Harrison.

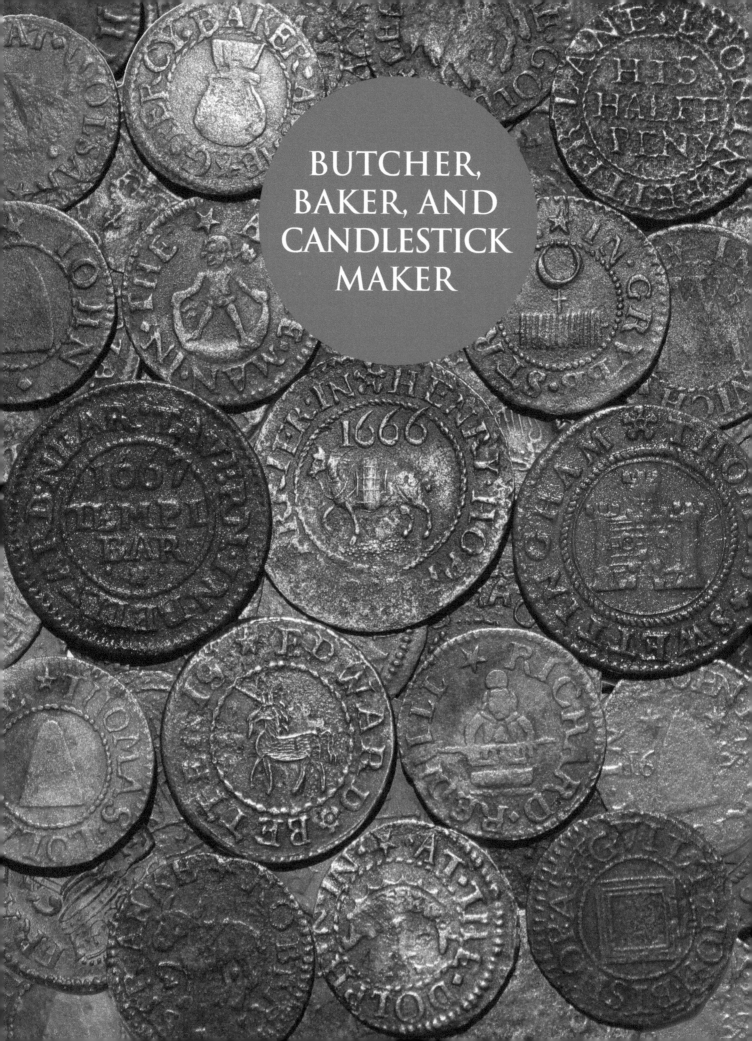

BUTCHER,
BAKER, AND
CANDLESTICK
MAKER

Startled by my loud alarm clock, I awoke to a dark, cold, and rainy morning in London. I seriously contemplated staying in my warm, cozy bed instead of going mudlarking. But, the "thrill of the hunt" got me up and out onto the damp foreshore.

I searched for several hours and disappointingly found nothing of interest, so I decided to find a warm café for breakfast and hot coffee. As I was leaving, I noticed a dark patch of the riverbed, which had recently been eroded away by the waves of passing boats. There, lying on the top of the black mud, was a round disc (right). As I picked it up, I couldn't believe my eyes! Stamped on the front of the copper token was a horse and the infamous date: 1666—the year when London was destroyed by the Great Fire of London. My heart was pounding with excitement!

The inscription on the 17th-century trade token says, "HENRY HOPPING CARRIER IN CVLLVMPTON, HIS HALFPENY 1666." Since the token depicts a packhorse and says "CARRIER," we can assume that Henry Hopping owned a business in Cullompton, Devon, which specialized in transporting goods with his packhorses. I wonder if Henry was in London delivering goods with his packhorses when the token was lost? Hopefully, he was not caught up in the Great Fire of London. Or, was Henry in London after the Great Fire to deliver construction materials with his packhorses to rebuild the capital which lay in ruins?

A few years ago, Micah Moore found a rare 17th-century trade token (right) from a vintner (wine merchant) named Brian Appleby. Dated 1657, the token is from Pudding Lane, the street where the Great Fire of London began. Appleby's shop was located close to Thomas Farriner's bakery where the fire started.

On September 2, 1666, the hot coals left in Thomas's oven sparked a small fire in his bakery which quickly spread and engulfed the City of London. The all-consuming fire raged for three days and destroyed most of the city. To escape the intense heat and destructive fire, people grabbed as many of their belongings as they could carry, boarded boats, and crossed the River Thames. During the perilous river crossing, personal possessions were probably accidentally dropped into the River Thames, which could explain how this token could have been lost in the river. It's hard to imagine what the last person to touch this token experienced during the Great Fire.

Facing page: 17th-century trade tokens (Jason Sandy).
Top: Trade token from 1666 (Jason Sandy).
Bottom: Trade token from Pudding Lane (Micah Moore).

Over the past ten years, I have been very lucky and have found over 30 different trade tokens in the River Thames. I simply love these copper tokens because they are so personal. Each token represents a different shop owner or trader who lived in London in the 17th century and reveals insightful information about their lives. Some of the most interesting people and occupations stamped on the tokens I discovered are:

- Robert Stranke, a butcher on Radcliffe Highway, London
- George Percy, a baker from Wapping New Stairs, London
- Richard Redhill, a candlestick maker from Long Acre, Covent Garden, London (A)
- John Bishop, a milliner (hatmaker) at the Guildhall in Oxford

- John Corne, a cobbler (shoe maker) in Martines LeGrand, London
- George Hide, a grocer from Grubb Street, London (B)
- Sary Heit, owner of the Woolsack tavern in Houndsditch, London
- Robert Redway, owner of the Lion tavern in Fetter Lane, London

- Stephen Porter, owner of the Stag tavern in Bell Yard, London (C)
- Thomas Swettingham, owner of the Castle tavern in St. Paul's Chaine, London (D)
- Thomas Lole, owner of the Sugarloaf tavern in Wheelers Street, London

Top: Castle tavern trade token (Jason Sandy). Above, left to right: Trade token from a candlestick maker, grocer's token from Grubb Street, Stag tavern trade token, Castle tavern token (Jason Sandy).

Because of the lack of small denomination coinage issued by the government in the mid-17th century, custom-made pennies, halfpennies, and farthings were produced between 1648 and 1674 for all different types of businesses and traders such as butchers, bakers, and candlestick makers, along with cobblers, milliners, grocers, mercers, fishmongers, fruiterers, tobacconists, chandlers,

coffee-house owners, among other traders. These trade tokens could be used in shops locally and in other towns. On the front of the tokens, images or symbols illustrated the type of business. Tokens were often stamped with the issuer's name, location of the business, year of issue, and denomination. Unlike standardized coins issued by the govern-ment, trade tokens are very special and unique. Mudlark Tom Main found a beautiful, heart-shaped trade token (above) from William Baldwin in Milton, dated 1667. A few years ago, John Higgin-botham discovered an extraordinary token (below) with the depiction of a hunting dog carrying a duck in its mouth. Dated 1651, the token was issued by the "Dogg and Ducke (tavern) in Southwarke."

While I was mudlarking along the River Thames in 2018, I found an interesting trade token (top right) dated 1650 and inscribed with the words "THE BLEW BELL AT THE OLD BALEY." The Blue

Bell was a pub located near the Old Bailey (the Central Criminal Court of England and Wales) and the notorious Newgate Prison which was in use for over 700 years, from 1188 to 1902. The pub was named after the infamous bell that tolled 12 times at midnight as a "death knell" to give condemned prisoners a last chance to repent before having their "necks stretched" at the gallows the following morning. Beginning in 1605, the clerk of the nearby St. Sepulchre-without-Newgate church rang a handbell outside the condemned man's cell

Top left: Heart-shaped trade token (Tom Main). Bottom left: Trade token from the Dogg and Ducke tavern (John Higginbotham). Top right: Trade token from the Blue Bell pub (Jason Sandy).

Execution Bell on display in the St. Sepulchre-without-Newgate church (Jason Sandy).

in Newgate Prison the night before his execution, and he would proclaim:

All you that in the condemned hole do lie,
Prepare you, for tomorrow you shall die.
Watch all, and pray, the hour is drawing near,
That you before Almighty God will appear.
Examine well yourselves, in time repent,
That you not to eternal flames be sent,
And when St. Sepulchre's bell tomorrow tolls,
The Lord above have mercy on your souls.
Past twelve o'clock!

The blue-colored "Execution Bell" still exists and is now on permanent display in the church of St. Sepulchre-without-Newgate across from the Old Bailey. I was so intrigued after finding the token, I had to go see it for myself. With the Blue Bell token in my pocket, I visited the beautiful, historic church and viewed the Execution Bell in a glass display case (above left). It was an eerie experience! I could just imagine how many poor prisoners heard that bell ringing before their execution in the notorious Newgate Prison centuries ago.

*S*hortly before the pandemic lockdown in 2020, I found an unusual trade token (below) depicting a mythical unicorn. The token was issued by Edward Betteris, a grocer and fish-monger in Old Fish Street near St. Paul's Cathedral in Central London. Edward died in July 1666, two months before the Great Fire of London.

When I posted the token on Facebook, a friend did some research and discovered Edward's will and last testament in the National Archives (UK). I purchased a digital copy online, but I was unfortunately unable to read the Old English calligraphy handwriting in the will. So, I asked my followers on Instagram if they were able to translate it into modern English for me. Janet Foster and Joel Lefever successfully deciphered the cryptic text and sent me a good translation (facing page).

Dated June 13, 1666, the will gives us a unique insight into Edward's wishes after his death. He started by saying that he is "sick and weake in body, but of sound and perfect mind and memory." Upon his death, Edward explained that he would like to live eternally in heaven. He wrote, "first and principally to commend my Soul unto the hands of Almighty God my Creator & of Jesus Christ mye only Saviour and Redeemer...to have free pardon and forgiveness of all my sinns and to inheritt

Unicorn trade token from Edward Betteris (Jason Sandy).

life eternall in the Kingdom of Heaven." After his debts and funeral expenses were paid for, Edward bequeathed 20 shillings to his son, Robert, and his daughter, Sarah. His possessions listed as "Goods, Cattle, Chattles, Money, Plate, Debts and Estate" were to be sold and the money used "towards the education and bringing upp of my said Children until they shall bee fit to putt forth Apprentised to some conveniente Trade."

When his children turned 21-years-old, they received further money from his will. Edward also designated money for his sister Mary, brother-in-law Thomas, cousin Francis, and friend Joseph. He doesn't mention his wife in the will, so it is possible that she died before 1666. I am so pleased that I found Edward's will and have learned more about his life and death in the 17th century. This unicorn trade token is a real portal to the past.

Trade tokens are simply magical. Each one is a tiny time capsule that reveals fascinating information about the people, their shops, and livelihoods in the 17th century. Many of the tokens were produced before the Great Fire of London in 1666. Because the raging fire destroyed most of the buildings and official documents within the City of London, trade tokens are now an important record of the original names of 17th-century taverns, inns, pubs, shops, businesses, street names, and people who would have been lost forever.

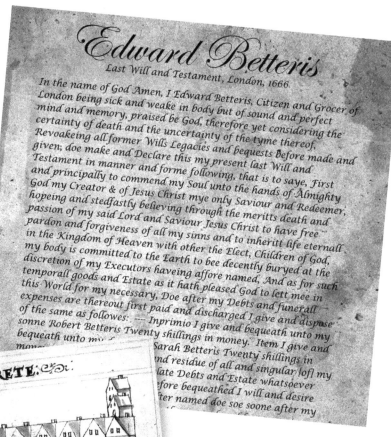

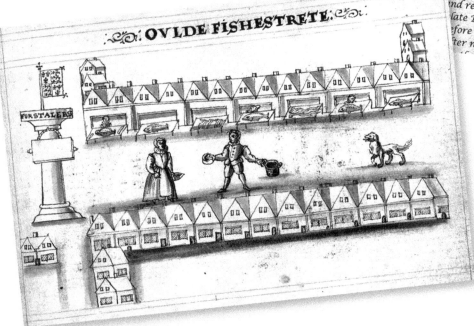

Above left: Historic illustration of the shops in Old Fish Street in the 17th century. Above right: Illustration of Edward Betteris's will (Jason Sandy).

JAYDEN SANDY

I was born in London and became interested in history for many reasons. My parents took me to all of the main museums in London, and I enjoyed visiting historic buildings, bridges, and monuments, especially the Tower of London. When I was younger, my favorite TV show was *Horrible Histories.* I liked the show because it tells the secrets of history that we don't learn in school, and it is presented in a funny and silly way. I started watching it a while ago, and it is another reason why I fell in love with history.

My favorite part of British history has to be the Tudor period because of Henry VIII. He has been my favorite British monarch since I was very young. In fact, I even found a silver coin from his son, Edward VI, when I was mudlarking. I took the coin with me when we visited Henry VIII's famous warship, the *Mary Rose*, in Portsmouth. In school, we have been studying the reign of Mary I and Elizabeth I which inter-

ested me a lot because of various events like the defeat of the Spanish Armada, the Counter-Reformation, and the Elizabethan Golden Age.

The first I ever heard of mudlarking was from my dad as it is his major hobby. Sometimes he would take me down to the foreshore to go "treasure hunting," as I used to call it. I was about six years old when I properly started mudlarking and going down to the foreshore most weekends with my dad. It became a big part of my life as we would go on many mudlarking expeditions together. Sometimes I would take my close friends down to the foreshore with me because they were also interested in history.

For me, the thrill of mudlarking is finding out about the history behind the objects I bring home. I have learned so much about the history of Britain from all the coins, pottery, jewelry, pipes, buttons, and more. Also, just knowing how much you can find out from an old hair comb on the foreshore shocks you. It makes me want to keep coming back to look for more things.

One of my favorite mudlarking finds is a post-medieval bone dice which I found outside the Tower of London during the annual open day. I was so intrigued when I found it because the dice could have been used by the prisoners for entertainment when they were locked up in the Tower of London. Because of *Horrible Histories* and history lessons at school, I know quite a few people such as Anne Boleyn, Catherine Howard, and Lady Jane Grey. It was really interesting to find out what they would have been doing while imprisoned in the Tower of London awaiting their fate.

In 2019, when I was ten years old, my dad and I were invited to speak about mudlarking at a conference in Wildwood, New Jersey. In front of an audience of over 200 people, I presented my ten best mudlarking finds and explained the history behind the artifacts. Although I was nervous on stage in front of a big crowd, it was so enjoyable to answer all of the people's questions about British history and show them all the artifacts that I found. The audience was intrigued to hear about the history of the objects.

Portraits by Tom Harrison.

LOST,
FOUND,
AND
RETURNED

chrisdorney

As Steve Brooker, aka "Mud God," was mudlarking along the river wall in East London, he heard a faint female voice calling him from above. As he looked up, Steve was surprised to see the face of Hollywood actress Helen Mirren staring down at him from her garden along the top of the river wall. Moments earlier, her daughter was throwing some freshly cut grass clippings into the River Thames, and her expensive gold ring slipped off her finger and flew into the river. Helen called down to Steve to ask if he could look for the lost ring. With decades of experience, Steve was able to spot the gold ring lying among the grass clippings on the exposed riverbed at low tide. He kindly returned the cherished ring to Helen, had a friendly chat, and continued mudlarking. She and her daughter were very grateful that the lost ring was returned so quickly.

There are many heartwarming stories about objects dropped in the Thames that have been discovered by mudlarks and returned to their original owners or living descendants. One of my favorite stories is about an unusual French coin, which Simon Bourne found in the Thames.

When Simon initially spotted a coin (below) while mudlarking, he thought it was a

common 10-pence piece. To Simon's surprise, it was a French coin that had been converted into a dog tag for a soldier during World War I. It was worn smooth on one side and engraved with a winged emblem and inscription "RFC–N. Posener–19385–Jew."

The letters "RFC" are the initials for the Royal Flying Corps which became the RAF (Royal Air Force), established at the beginning of World War I. On the database of the National Archives (UK), Simon was able to find out more about Posener's life in the military. The records confirmed the name matched his ID number. According to the archives, Posener served at the end of World War I and several years after the war (1918–1928).

By searching on the website ancestry.co.uk, Simon was able to find more information including the

Facing page: Steps from the shore of the River Thames that lead up to the Thames Path in London (chrisdorney/Shutterstock.com). Above: Hand-engraved dog tag from WWI (Simon Bourne). Top right: Photograph of Nathan Posener in uniform (courtesy of Posener's family).

full name, Nathan Posener, and previous address on Commercial Road in East London, which is only a short distance from where Simon found Nathan's dog tag on the foreshore. Simon was determined to track down Posener's descendants and return the dog tag to the family.

He contacted the local newspaper, hoping that they could help him locate friends or family members who might still be living in the area. Once Simon submitted the story, it was printed and also published online, and he didn't have to wait very long for a response. Two weeks later, the reporter who ran the story contacted Simon and said that

a reader had recognized the surname Posener and contacted his friend, John Silverman, who is the grandson of Nathan Posener. John's mother (Nathan's daughter) was still alive and had recently turned 90 years old. Simon spoke to John on the phone, and he was delighted to hear the story about the discovery of the lost dog tag, because his family knew nothing about it. After John told his mother that her father's dog tag had been found in the Thames, she said it "made her year."

Soon afterwards, Simon met John in person and returned the dog tag to him (top left). John explained that Nathan wasn't actually a pilot in the Royal Flying Corps. In the First World War, the lightweight wings and tail of the fighter planes were constructed of a wooden framework, which was covered in cloth, stretched tight, and painted to stiffen the cloth. Nathan was a master tailor who served in the RFC by sewing the cloth onto the wings of the airplanes. He was stationed in France, which explains why he used a French

franc to make himself a dog tag. Nathan probably engraved it himself, as he was a skilled tailor, equipped with the necessary tools.

Nathan survived the war and went on to live a long life. In March 1987, he died aged 94 in Hampstead, London where his daughter now lives. After returning the medal to Nathan's descendants, Simon was thrilled and stated that "returning long-lost items to their rightful home is a positive thing that few of us 'treasure hunters' ever get the chance to do."

While mudlarking along the River Medway, which is a tributary of the Thames, Nicola White discovered a large brass plaque (below) on the exposed riverbed. After gently cleaning the plaque, she could read the engraved writing with a soldier's name, service number, and date he joined the military (bottom). It reads, "R.M.L.I., C. 13524. A. WILKES., 2.9.12." R.M.L.I. stands for "Royal Marines Light Infantry." Originally, it would have been fixed to the bottom of his military kit bag, which was made of fabric. After over 100 years in the river, the fabric has disintegrated, leaving only the brass plate.

Born in 1884 in Westminster (London), Alfred joined the Royal Marines in 1912 and served in World War I. Nicola did a lot of research and was able to track down the descendants of Alfred who now live in Canada, and she kindly returned the kit bag bottom to them.

Top left: Simon returning the dog tag to John (Simon Bourne). Middle right: Mysterious brass plate on the Thames foreshore (Nicola White). Bottom right: Plate engraved with the soldier's name: A. Wilkes (Nicola White).

As Britain commemorated the centennial of the First World War in 2014, the discovery of this Victory Medal on the Thames foreshore in 2015 was a significant find and poignant reminder of the courage and bravery displayed by the British troops in the Great War. Between 1914–1918, approximately 8.7 million soldiers served in the British Army, and almost 890,000 soldiers died in the conflict.

In 2015, a London bus driver discovered a soldier's medal from World War I (top) while mudlarking along the Thames. On a windy and rainy day, Matthew Virgo spotted what he thought was a large coin on the surface of the foreshore. After cleaning the coin at home, he realized it was a medal engraved with the soldier's name and number: F A French, 19028. Matthew posted a photo of the medal on a Facebook forum, and members of the group were able to research and find out that Francis Arthur French (bottom) was born in Harpenden, England, in 1899. He fought in both the First and Second World Wars before dying in 1958.

Made of copper and lacquered in bronze, the medal has a winged figure of Victory depicted with her left arm extended and holding a palm branch in her right hand. Surrounded by a laurel wreath, the words, "THE GREAT WAR FOR CIVILISATION, 1914-1919," appear on the back of the medal.

Matthew contacted Francis Arthur French's relatives and offered to return the medal. He explains: "It's just really exciting, it's one of those things you don't expect to happen, and when you do, you can't describe it. It was just such a brilliant feeling finding this part of history. It's amazing to find the relatives."

A few years ago, mudlark Jason Davey unearthed a military dog tag (above) from the mud of the Thames riverbed. The tag belonged to Casper James LaMotta, an American soldier who served overseas in the Army Air Corps during World War II. Although the dog tag was rusted, a name and address for his next of kin was still clearly visible: "FRANK LAMOTTA, 57 HOUSTON ST, NEWARK, NJ." According to his certification of enlisted service, Casper James LaMotta was a corporal in the 823rd Air Engineering Squadron of the Army Air Corps, and he died in 1980.

Jason was determined to track down the descendants of Casper, so he posted a photo of the dog tag on Facebook. Joseph Bilby, assistant curator of the National Guard Militia Museum of New Jersey in Sea Girt, reposted the picture on the museum's Facebook page, and the grandson of LaMotta's relatives saw the post. Bilby says, "It's an example of how social media can work in a positive way and help people out and bring people together." Within 12 hours, the dog tag found in London was connected with family members in America. Jason generously returned the lost dog tag to the descendants of LaMotta. At some time in the future, the

Top left: Victory medal from WWI (Matthew Virgo). Bottom left: Photo of Francis Arthur French in uniform (courtesy of French's family). Top right: WWII military dog tag stamped with the name: Caspar J LaMotta (Frank LaMotta).

family hopes to host Jason at their family-owned Krug's Tavern in New Jersey to share a burger and a beer in honor of Casper LaMotta (right).

A mudlark stumbled across the scene of a crime a few years ago. A thief had dumped a hoard of stolen medals into the Thames, hoping to get rid of the incriminating evidence. The five medals had been awarded to American tennis player, Peter Fleming, for his performance in the Wimbledon Tennis Championships.

Dating to 1978, 1982, 1985, 1986, and 2002, the four runners-up medals are made of sterling silver,

and the semi-finalist medal is made of bronze. On the front of all of the medals, a classical female figure is depicted in front of a tennis net holding a trophy depicting Victory in her left hand and supporting a globe with a laureate band between her right hand and right knee (bottom left).

On the back of one of the medals (bottom right) is inscribed, "THE LAWN TENNIS CHAMPIONSHIPS, MEN'S DOUBLES, RUNNERS-UP, P. FLEMING, J. P. McENROE, 1978." During the late 1970s and

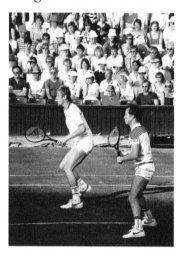

1980s, Peter Fleming teamed up with fellow American John McEnroe (right) and dominated the men's doubles game, winning 50 doubles titles, including four at Wimbledon in 1979, 1981, 1983 and 1984. After the stolen Wimbledon medals were recorded on the British Museum's Portable Antiquities Scheme, they were returned to Peter Fleming in the United States.

Top left: Caspar LaMotta's certification of enlisted service and photo of Caspar LaMotta (courtesy of LaMotta's family).
Top right: Peter Fleming and John McEnroe (Brittle Heaven). Bottom: Wimbledon tennis medal awarded to Peter Fleming (PAS).

On a warm, summer day in August 2020, I was mudlarking along the Thames in West London. On the south side of the river, there is a towpath through a dense forest with a beautiful, scenic trail along the river, which is a popular location for dog walking, jogging, and cycling. As I was searching the exposed riverbed at low tide, I unearthed what I thought was just another Victorian coin (top left)—a common find in this area.

Upon closer examination, I discovered that the unusual 19th-century halfpenny was worn smooth and engraved by hand with some letters (top right). Surprisingly, the coin was inscribed with a name and address: S. SMITH, 13 DELORME ST, FULHAM PALACE RD. I quickly searched online to see if this address still exists. Sure enough, there is a Victorian house still located at this address.

After I posted the photos on a Facebook forum, Karis Lacy kindly offered to research Samuel's history. On the website of the National Archives,

Top left: Victorian halfpenny freshly unearthed from the riverbed (Jason Sandy). Top right: Dog tag hand-engraved with Samuel's name and address (Jason Sandy). Bottom right: Photograph of Samuel Smith and young Peter Shayers with the dog (Joan Shayers).

Karis found Samuel Smith was listed in the Census of England and Wales, 1911. According to the census, Samuel's daughter was listed as Norah Smith, born in 1903. On the website findmypast.co.uk, Karis discovered that Norah had married Stanley Shayers in 1928, and they had a son named Peter Shayers. The website listed Peter's postal address based on the Electoral rolls up to 2014. In September 2020, I wrote Peter a letter and offered to return the dog tag. I wasn't sure if he still lived at this address, so I didn't know if I would ever get a response.

A month later, a handwritten letter arrived in the mail. I had goosebumps, and my hands were shaking with

Handwritten letter from Joan Shayers (Jason Sandy).

excitement as I carefully opened the letter. Unfortunately, Peter (aged 89) passed away in May 2019, but his widow (Joan Shayers) kindly responded to my letter. Although Samuel served in the military during the First World War, the pendant I found was not his service "dog tag." It is literally his dog's tag which his favorite dog had lost, possibly while on a walk along the riverside.

Along with the letter, Joan included old photos of Samuel Smith (above)

Message in a bottle (Nicola White).

who was born in 1867. The dog appears in a photo with Samuel and his grandson, Peter, whom I sent my letter. I really enjoyed seeing photos of Samuel and his dog who lost its collar tag over 100 years ago. Joan and I have become friends and have regular contact via phone and letters.

Over the years, Nicola White has retrieved over 100 bottles from the river with personal messages rolled up inside (left). One of them contained a scribbled, handwritten

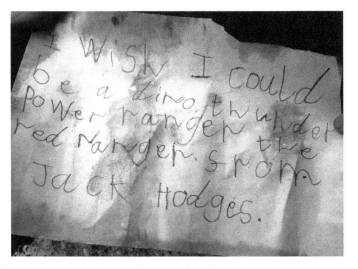

Top to bottom: Handwritten note by Jack Hodges (Nicola White).
Photo of Jack reading the note and Jack in his Power Ranger suit
(courtesy of Jack's family).

message (top left) from a young boy: "I wish I could be a dino thunder power ranger the red ranger, from Jack Hodges." Touched by the boy's innocent wish, Nicola was determined to track him down and fulfill his request. Unfortunately, the bottle and note contained no contact details.

Within three hours of posting the message on social media, Nicola's Twitter followers had found the boy. To Jack's surprise, Nicola kindly sent him a red Power Ranger suit. As you can imagine, he couldn't believe his wish had come true! In return, Jack sent Nicola a letter of thanks including photos of himself dressed as the Power Ranger (bottom left). In 2020, I posted this heart-warming story on my Instagram account, and the Hollywood actor, Jason Faunt, who plays the red Power Ranger, saw my post. He commented: "Amazing message. I know a couple of red rangers happy to make an introduction!" Jason offered to speak directly to Jack. I was excited that this Hollywood celebrity was willing to contact the young boy who had thrown the message in a bottle in the Thames. Dreams do come true!

The absolute thrill of mudlarking is finding a long-lost artifact and returning it to the owner or their descendants. I especially enjoy when the descendants have old photographs of the person who lost the artifact. Seeing the person brings the history to life and makes the experience so personal. To know that you are the first person to touch this object since it was dropped by the person in the photograph is a wonderful feeling. It's a tangible connection to them as if you were reaching back through time, personally meeting them and shaking their hand. You wonder what they were thinking when they accidentally lost or purposely discarded the artifact. As Simon explained, the ultimate experience is to meet the descendants in person and return the long-lost personal item. It brings the extraordinary story to a beautiful conclusion.

STEPHANIE MILLS

It was my lovely, late husband John "GM" Mills who got me interested in mudlarking, quite soon after he started. From a young age, I often found coins on the pavement, so I was interested in trying out mudlarking. John took me to an event on the Tower Foreshore in 2008 organized by the City of London Archaeological Society (COLAS). I didn't find anything, but I was keen to go again. We ventured to Wapping, and I was hooked after finding a button. Mudlarking soon became a hobby we both enjoyed together. We went as much as possible, in all weathers. Some days we were mudlarking until 2 AM and "up with the lark" at 4 AM.

We both grew up in Dagenham, East London, and John liked to mudlark in Wapping as his grandma had lived there. My great granddad came from Deptford, and in the 18th–19th centuries, my ancestors worked as shipwrights along the Thames. The thought of potentially picking up our ancestors' dropped coins is exciting.

John had always been interested in history, and he enjoyed working at a coin collector's shop in his teens. In 2007, Steve Brooker introduced him to Thames mudlarking. At the start, I didn't really have any interest in history, but I slowly gained some knowledge about the artifacts and coins we found. John was extremely knowledgeable and enjoyed researching our finds, so he did most of the research which enabled me to catch up with home life, as having four children, working part-time, and mudlarking kept me very busy.

In late 2013, during a meet-up with other mudlarks, John felt strangely unwell. We didn't even make it down to the river and went back home. He suffered further episodes and was sadly diagnosed with a Glioblastoma brain tumor. His prognosis was very poor, with only 6–12 months to live. Fortunately, he survived another two years and three months. John was well-liked and respected, and he was overwhelmed by the love and support of the mudlarking and metal detecting communities. During John's illness, we made it to the foreshore a few times with the help of other mudlarks. John sadly passed away in February 2016, aged 54.

After I lost John, I had offers to meet other mudlarks, but I found it very difficult to return to mudlarking, although I knew in time I would. About two years later, I arranged to meet Rae Love (a lovely friend to John and me) on the foreshore. During my first few visits back, I struggled without John by my side and hardly picked anything up. That gradually changed and after a few more visits with Rae, my confidence grew, and my luck started to change. I soon started to love it again.

I've met lots of friendly mudlarks along the river, and members of the Society of Thames Mudlarks have been very supportive and helpful to me, especially Rae. I don't know if I'd have started mudlarking again without her help. My son and my son-in-law are both Thames mudlarks too, so it's nice to spend time with them on the river. I love searching the foreshore. It's very relaxing to be by the river, and the excitement of what I might find keeps me returning. It's a very special place I will always share with John.

Facing page: Tom Harrison. This page: Coral Pearce.

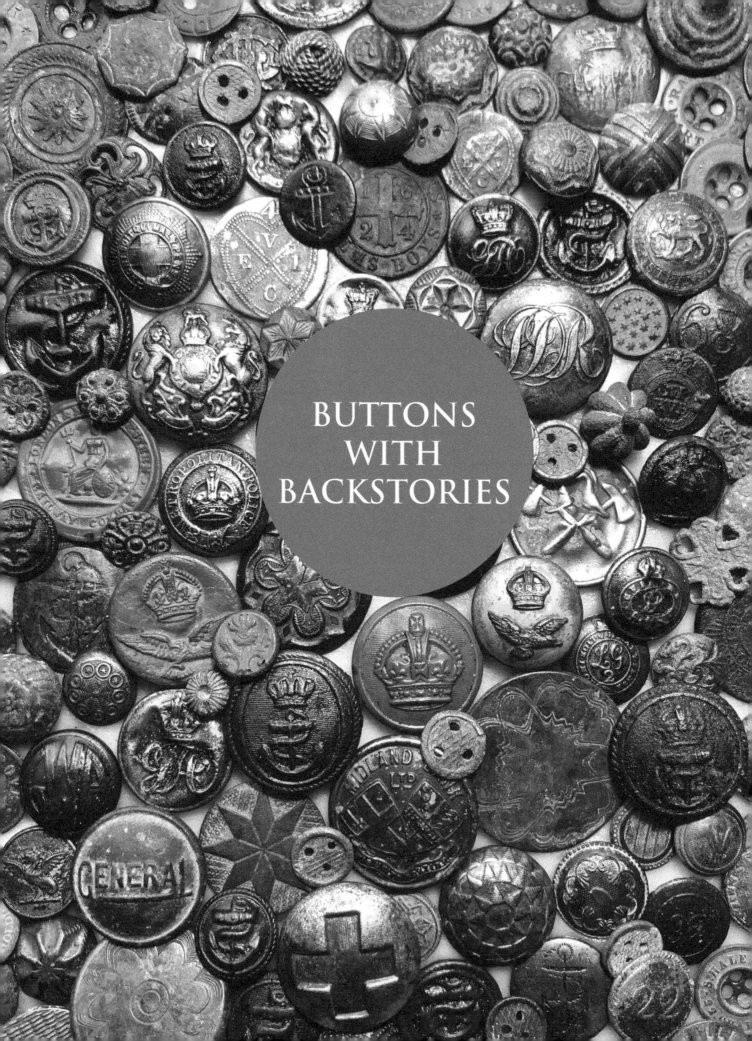

BUTTONS
WITH
BACKSTORIES

How many times have you lost a button off a favorite coat or shirt? It's so frustrating, isn't it? As you can imagine, people inevitably snared and lost buttons as they worked or got in and out of boats along the River Thames. Over the past 40 years, mudlarks have found thousands of buttons on the exposed riverbed, which range from medieval to modern times.

Buttons serve a practical purpose, and it's hard to imagine life without them. Not only are buttons functional, they were often highly decorated, beautiful works of art and craftsmanship. Researching buttons can tell us a lot about styles and fashions throughout the ages. Buttons are also wonderful personal items because they tell us a lot about the people who wore them. They represent all members of society—from policemen, firemen, postmen, train conductors, customs officers, and bankers, to uniformed servicemen and women such as sailors, pilots, soldiers, and household guards who protected the kings and queens of England. Although these people are long gone, their brass buttons have been perfectly preserved by the Thames mud and remind us of the great men and women who bravely served their country and their city.

In 2020, mudlark Florrie Evans discovered an exquisite pewter button (above left) depicting King Edward VI, son of King Henry VIII and Jane Seymour. Upon Henry's death in 1547, Edward became king when he was only nine years old. Unfortunately, he died six years later in 1553. When Florrie found the button, she recognized Edward because there had been a similar 16th-century portrait of him (above right) hanging in the fine art gallery where she worked. The portrait was painted by Flemish artist and court painter, William Scrots. According to the Museum of London, the button was probably produced in the 18th or early 19th century and worn on a school uniform of Christ's Hospital, which was founded by Edward VI in 1552, the year before he died. Even today, school children at Christ's Hospital wear Tudor-styled uniforms adorned with buttons depicting Edward VI.

Following the wedding of King Charles II and the Portuguese princess, Catherine of Braganza, in 1662, crowds gathered along the River Thames to welcome them as they entered the city by boat in a sensational, floating pageant called the "Aqua Triumphalis." To commemorate this joyous celebration of love, buttons and cufflinks decorated with a symbol of two hearts surmounted by a crown (right) were worn by Londoners. Although Charles had numerous mistresses and many illegitimate children, the crown and hearts motif endured as a popular symbol of love and marriage.

Buttons were also worn as status symbols and to demonstrate one's wealth. Some were made of gold or silver and set with semi-precious gemstones. Others were produced with elaborate and extravagant motifs. One of my favorite buttons I found in the Thames (above) is ornately decorated with heart-shaped cyclamen leaves and flowers from the 19th century.

Facing page: Historic buttons in Jason's collection (Jason Sandy). This page: Victorian button (Jason Sandy). Pewter button (Florrie Evans). Portrait of Edward VI (William Scrots). 17th-century button (Jason Sandy).

As I was crawling on my hands and knees along the exposed riverbed on a sunny Sunday morning, I was pleasantly surprised when I spotted an 18th-century button decorated with a face in the shape of the sun (above). It was produced for the Sun Insurance Company, which was established by Charles Povey in 1706. Povey was a businessman who survived the Great Fire of London in 1666. He witnessed firsthand the devastation and destruction caused by the fire. Before the Great Fire, people and businesses did not have insurance. As a result, they lost everything! Povey started the first insurance company to protect people's livelihoods and to help them get back on their feet again after a disaster. It's amazing that the company was started as a direct result of the Great Fire of London and is the oldest insurance company in the world. The company is now called RSA Insurance Group. Many historic houses and buildings in the UK still have the sun logo on

them because they were previously insured by the Sun Insurance Company.

The 18th century was the golden age of button making in Britain because of the high demand. Georgian men and women were dressed to impress from head to toe. The most ostentatious Georgians were the Macaronis, Dandies, Fops, and Popinjays who were excessively vain and completely obsessed with their appearance, clothes, and hairstyles. I absolutely adore the Georgians because of their extravagant and eccentric fashion and decadent, flamboyant lifestyles. They worn decorative buttons on their coats, waistcoats, and breeches. The buttons they lost in the Thames are evidence of the popular fashions of that time period.

Over the years, I have found numerous buttons from the 18th century which are decorated with elaborate geometric and floral motifs (left). "Dandy" buttons were

Top: Sun Insurance Company button (Jason Sandy).
Bottom: 18th-century button (Jason Sandy).

intentionally oversized to create an unmissable fashion statement. Some of the large Georgian buttons were purposely designed to dazzle in the sunlight to attract attention (right).

While I was mudlarking along the historic docks in East London, I discovered a pewter button decorated with a large heart formed by a double band of pellets and subdivided into four sections containing the letters V E I C (below). After a bit of research, I discovered that it is a uniform button from the infamous East India Company. I found it at a location where they had docked their ships centuries ago to unload the precious cargo from the Far East.

Although a heart is depicted on the button, the company has a dark history. In 1600, Queen Elizabeth I granted the East India Company a royal charter. By establishing a trade monopoly with China and the Indian subcontinent, the company grew into a massive organization. At its height, the company handled half of the world's trade, importing cotton, silk, indigo dye, salt, saltpeter, tea, pepper, cloves, nutmeg, cinnamon, ginger, and opium. To increase their profits, the company ruthlessly exploited and plundered the natural resources of the Indian subcontinent under the threat of its private army of nearly 260,000 soldiers, which was twice the size of the British Army at that time.

Following the Indian Rebellion of 1857, the East India Company was dissolved, and power was transferred to the British government, which established the British Raj. In 1876, Queen Victoria was proclaimed the Empress of India. Finally in 1947, India, Pakistan, and Bangladesh gained their independence from centuries of British rule, which began with land grabs and military force from the powerful East India Company. This 18th-century uniform button revealed this sad chapter in British history.

A few years ago, I found a 19th-century gilded livery button depicting a wyvern, which is a mythical creature that is half dragon and half serpent (below). Typically decorated with a twisted rope under a symbol, livery buttons were worn by household servants who provided a domestic service to wealthy English nobles and aristocrats. Gilded buttons were often worn by boatmen, coachmen, and upper servants to indicate their connection to a specific household. Based on the wyvern symbol, I believe this button was probably worn by a servant to the Leighton or Rich family in the 19th century. There were several Leightons who served in the Houses of Parliament, which are located beside the Thames. I wonder if the button was lost by a boatman who was rowing his master up the river?

Top: Illustration of dazzling buttons from 1777 (William Humphrey). Above left: East India Company button (Jason Sandy). Bottom right: 19th-century livery button (Jason Sandy).

I always enjoy discovering sailors' buttons (top left) on the Thames foreshore. Each button represents a different sailor and their incredible stories of conquest, adventure, warfare, heroic victories, and devastating defeat. For centuries, sailors, mariners, and naval officers lived along the river in London. From the 16th–19th centuries, the riverside parishes such as Wapping, Whitechapel, Mile End, Stepney, Shadwell, Ratcliff, and Rotherhithe were home to the largest maritime community in Britain. Even famous admirals and explorers lived in houses near the Thames. For instance, Sir Walter Raleigh and Admiral Horatio Nelson had houses in Blackwall. Captain James Cook lived in Wapping, and Captain Christopher Jones resided across the river in Rotherhithe. If only these buttons could speak and reveal the personal stories and experiences of the sailors!

When I picked up this Royal Air Force fighter (RAF) pilot's button from World War II (bottom left), I could almost hear the air raid sirens blaring, sharp blasts from the anti-aircraft guns, the low hum of approaching German bombers, and the deep thuds of exploding bombs in the distance, coming precariously closer. During the Battle of Britain (1940–41), the Royal Air Force defended Britain against large-scale attacks by the German Luftwaffe. The British RAF was grossly outnumbered, but their bravery and sheer determination defeated the Luftwaffe and prevented them from establishing a foothold in Britain. Over 540 RAF pilots and aircrew were killed, and over 43,000 civilians died during the bombing raids.

Some of these brass RAF buttons have a compass concealed inside them. In case the fighter pilot crashed behind enemy lines, they could use the secret compass to help them escape. This RAF button is a poignant reminder of the brave and courageous pilots who sacrificed their lives to protect our freedom and independence.

In 2018, Monika Buttling-Smith discovered a uniform button (facing page) with the initials ARP which stand for "Air Raid Precautions." This button was worn by a member of this organization responsible

Top left: Sailor and navy buttons (Jason Sandy). Bottom left: Royal Air Force button (Jason Sandy).

for the protection of Londoners from the danger of air raids in World War II. The ARP consisted of wardens, messengers, ambulance drivers, and rescue parties who liaised with local police and fire brigades. Starting in 1939, they also enforced the "black out" of all windows in homes and businesses. During the London Blitz, the ARP managed the air raid sirens, directed civilians toward bomb shelters, and reported bombing incidents. Renamed the Civil Defence Service in 1941, approximately 1.5 million men and women served in the organization during the war. Unfortunately, almost 7,000 workers were killed during the Nazi bombing raids in Britain.

The most common buttons mudlarks find in the River Thames are "fly" or "suspender" buttons from the 19th and early 20th centuries. They are easy to recognize because they are circular and have four holes in the center. Conveniently, the name and address of the clothes maker or business appear around the perimeter of the button. A few years ago, Malcolm Russell discovered a Victorian fly button with the inscription: BLACKETT, WEST SMITHFIELD ST (below). According to Malcolm's research, the Blackett family originated in North East England and moved to London during the Industrial Revolution. In a directory from 1793, T. Blackett was listed as a tailor and salesman based at 21 West Smithfield. In the 19th century, the business was located at 31 West Smithfield and was managed by James Blackett, who produced the characteristic blue and white striped aprons for the butchers working in the neighboring Smithfield Market. From the Middle Ages, Smithfield Market was the main meat market located in Central London. It is still the largest wholesale meat market in the United Kingdom and one of the largest of its kind in Europe.

Veteran mudlark Tony Pilson amassed an astonishing collection of over 2,500 buttons after mudlarking for more than 30 years. Some of his earliest buttons are from the 14th century. In 2009, Tony generously donated his entire button collection to the Museum of London, where they are currently being researched. The collection includes buttons of all shapes and sizes made of silver, pewter, and semi-precious gemstones. Each button represents a different person who lived or traveled through London over the centuries. Buttons are wonderful little time capsules of the lives of the people who wore them and the fashions of bygone ages.

MALCOLM RUSSELL

I've been engaged in a lifelong love affair with exploring the past: as a teenage excavator of Victorian rubbish tips in the industrial Midlands, as a history and archaeology student, and now as a mudlark. I first discovered mudlarking after moving back to London following a decade living in the United States. Seeking a way to reconnect with the city and its history, as well as a distraction following the death of a close friend, I happened to chance upon a review of Ted Sandling's book of Thames finds, *London in Fragments*. I soon made my first foray onto the foreshore and returned excitedly clutching a bag of broken clay pipe stems, smashed pottery, and indeterminate bits of iron. I was captivated by the fact that flotsam and jetsam from two millennia of urban life were lying around, right in the middle of London. It took me several frustrating months to learn how to search among the rocks, rubble, mud, and shingle for often tiny lost or discarded objects. Since then, I've recovered thousands of artifacts from the mud-archive of the Thames, from Roman gaming counters to Tudor rings, and from 18th-century wig curlers to contemporary spells.

Aside from the raw dopamine hit released by making a find, what draws me back to the foreshore is that mudlarking offers a disruptive, and at times perhaps even a radical way of engaging with the past. It democratizes the "doing" of history, cutting out middlemen such as archaeologists, professional historians, and museum curators, and putting the raw materials right into the public's hands. Because its finds are the stuff of ordinary men and women, it helps to bring the forgotten lives of London's marginalized people out of the shadows and into the light and provides a rich resource for the writing of a people's history.

Mudlarking also introduces a welcome serendipity to engaging with the past, challenging the historian's default mode of linear chronology. This is because, unlike a conventional archaeological site, there is no stratification on the Thames foreshore. Layers of the past lie undone, chaotically strewn together. When I mudlark, I never know what corner of history I'm going to end up visiting. Mudlarking constantly challenges my ideas about where my interests lie and reveals unforeseen connections across time.

Finally, the foreshore draws attention to London's history as a global city. Remnants of London as England's busiest port, center of overseas trade, place of immigrants, and capital of empire, are among the most evocative and provocative finds I've made. I've recovered coins from across the Roman world, seals once attached to cloth made by continental religious refugees, glass beads that facilitated the brutalities of the transatlantic slave trade, hundreds of pipes used to consume plantation-grown tobacco, and ammunition used to gruesomely suppress resistance during the "Scramble for Africa." I even found a turn-of-the-century Chinese-made opium pipe, hailing from when popular fascination with supposed East End Chinese opium "dens" blended with the racist fear of the "Yellow Peril" to populate pulp novels and press reports.

It's been said that English history is not well understood because so much of it took place overseas. In its own modest way, mudlarking can help redress this, and it is one theme running through my book *Mudlark'd: Hidden Histories from the River Thames*, published in 2022.

Portraits by Tom Harrison.

WEAPONS AND WARFARE

F or millennia, battles have been fought along the River Thames. At low tide on the exposed riverbed, mudlarks have discovered evidence of warfare. These weapons recovered from the river reveal the stories of these battles throughout the ages, and the plight of Londoners who lived through these turbulent times.

In 54 BC, Julius Caesar invaded Britain, and his army attacked the Celtic tribes living in the Thames Valley. Celtic Queen Boudica raided the early Roman settlement of Londinium in AD 61 and burned it to the ground. In the 9th century, Vikings sailed up the Thames several times and plundered the Anglo-Saxon settlement in London. During the English Civil War in the 17th century, the Parliamentarians fought against the Royalists along the river for control of London. In World War II, the Docklands were the strategic target of

Nazi bombers which inflicted extensive death and destruction along the river during the London Blitz (above). More recently, the bridges across the Thames have suffered several terrorist attacks. Between 1939 and 2000, the IRA (Irish Republican Army) tried unsuccessfully to blow up Hammersmith Bridge three times. In 2017, Westminster Bridge and London Bridge were the scenes of grotesque acts of terrorism when innocent pedestrians were brutally attacked and killed.

Long before the Romans established a settlement along the River Thames in 43 AD, transient hunters and gatherers were attracted to the Thames valley because of its rich resources and wildlife, which grazed in the grassy floodplain along the river that was teeming with fish and bird life. The early inhabitants of the Thames valley made weapons out of flint stone to hunt and protect themselves against attackers. Several years ago, mudlark David Hodgson discovered one of the earliest Stone Age axeheads (above) in the River Thames. Dating to the Paleolithic Age, the axehead is circa 3.3 million years old.

Along the river in Chelsea, a club made of alder wood (below) was recovered in several pieces. It was possibly used as a war club or flax beater. Radiocarbon dated to 3530–3340 BC, the pieces were carefully reassembled. Miraculously, the anaerobic (no oxygen) mud of the Thames preserved this wooden club for thousands of years. The artifact conjures up images of a stereotypical caveman carrying around a big wooden club.

In West London, many spectacular Bronze Age and Iron Age weapons including swords, rapiers, palstaves, spearheads, and axeheads (above) were recovered from the river. They were passionately collected by Thomas Layton, a 19th-century businessman and antiquarian. In the "London before London" gallery in the Museum of London, there is a large "River Wall" which showcases many of these prehistoric weapons from Layton's collection.

One of the most interesting artifacts in Layton's collection is a Bronze Age dagger and sheath (right), which was found in the river in West London. The iron dagger has a broad blade bound with bronze strips and was probably imported from southern Germany or Austria around the 6th century BC.

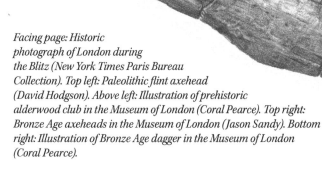

Facing page: Historic photograph of London during the Blitz (New York Times Paris Bureau Collection). Top left: Paleolithic flint axehead (David Hodgson). Above left: Illustration of prehistoric alderwood club in the Museum of London (Coral Pearce). Top right: Bronze Age axeheads in the Museum of London (Jason Sandy). Bottom right: Illustration of Bronze Age dagger in the Museum of London (Coral Pearce).

In February 2021, mudlark Lukasz Orlinski discovered a complete Bronze Age spearhead (above) on the Thames foreshore. Dated to 1200–1050 BC, the blade is triangular with a pair of small loops at the junction between the lower blade edge and the socket. A wooden shaft would have been fixed into the socket to create the spear. During the Bronze Age, tribes of people living along the river would have used these types of spears in battle or for hunting purposes.

A Bronze Age sword (below) was also found by a mudlark in the River Thames and dates from 1140–1020 BC. The beveled blade of this Wilburton type flange-hilted sword is leaf-shaped. There are visible nicks along the blade edge which could indicate that the sword was used in battle.

On the foreshore in Fulham (West London), a Roman sword (below) was found within an elaborately decorated sheath made of bronze. It is the standard type of sword used by the Roman legionary in the 1st century AD. Comprised of bronze plates decorated using a delicate repoussé technique, the scabbard is a beautiful work of art. On the upper plate, two hounds are shown attacking a stag above the symbol of Rome, a she-wolf suckling the twins, Romulus and Remus.

In the 9th century, the Anglo-Saxon settlement in London endured a series of vicious and brutal attacks from Vikings who sailed up the Thames from the North Sea. Some historians believe that London Bridge was destroyed in AD 1014 during a ferocious Viking attack led by Olaf Haraldsson, King of Norway. Many Viking axes, spear heads, and swords were found during renovations to London Bridge in the 1920s. These weapons are evidence of the bloody battles fought between the Saxons and Vikings.

Medieval London was a fortified city, completely enclosed by a thick, continuous stone wall punctuated by large, imposing gates that provide secure access in and out of the walled city. The defensive walls were originally built by the Romans in the 3rd century AD, and they were strengthened and increased in height in the Middle Ages. To protect the city from foreign invaders who might sail up the Thames, the mighty and magnificent Tower of London (above) was constructed in the 1070s by the Normans at the eastern end of the fortified city.

Although mudlarking on the foreshore in front of the Tower of London is now prohibited, veteran mudlarks discovered some extraordinary artifacts (below) outside the castle river wall several years ago. Medieval swords, daggers, arrowheads, a halberd spearhead, and a shield boss were recovered from the riverbed at low tide. Some of these mudlarking finds are now on permanent display in the Tower of London. Medieval swords and daggers were both practical fighting weapons and status symbols. The exquisite decoration on them reflects the wealth and status of their owner.

One of the most unusual artifacts discovered by Tony Pilson is a 15th-century wrought-iron hand cannon (above). It is the smallest of only three early guns of this type found in England. The barrel was made by forming a central tube of iron straps held together by bands and hoops, which were heated and then cooled to fit tightly around the barrel.

In the Middle Ages, London was home to many knights. The Knights Templar established a base in London along the River Thames around AD 1148. This order of crusading monks protected Christian pilgrims on their journey to the Holy Land, and they became some of the wealthiest and most powerful knights in Christendom. Within the Temple Church in Central London, stone effigies of the most famous Templar knights line the floor. They are dressed for battle, wearing chainmail armor, helmets, and clutching their shields and swords which pierce the heads of snarling beasts below the knights' feet.

Top: Tower of London castle (Bob Collowan). Left: Swords and daggers on display in the Tower of London (Jason Sandy). Above: 15th-century hand cannon (Jason Sandy).

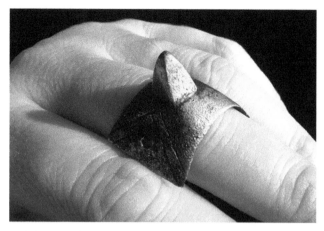

While mudlarking early one morning, I spotted something very rare at low tide—a brass knuckle guard from a medieval knight's gauntlet (above) from AD 1350–1400. In Canterbury Cathedral, the bronze effigy of the Black Prince has similar knuckle guards which have a large, central spike. It is an incredible feeling to hold this artifact, knowing that the last person to wear this knuckle guard was a wealthy 14th-century knight!

In 2020, Mark Vasco Iglesias discovered a piece of iron chainmail (below) from a medieval knight. It was worn as protective armor during battle. Chainmail is comprised of small, interlocking rings which are riveted together by hand in a pattern to create a strong mesh. It was a tedious and painstaking job to make chainmail. Mark estimates that 60 to 70 individual rings are contained in the piece of chainmail he found. The tiny rivets are still visible on the rings.

In January 2021, Monika Buttling-Smith found a beautiful medieval arrowhead from AD 1200–1300. It would have been attached to the tip of a wooden shaft and shot from a longbow. The tip of this iron arrowhead is missing, which could indicate that the arrow was fired and hit a target. Will Sherman, an arrowsmith and fletcher, kindly made a replica of this medieval arrowhead (below) for Monika. The dangerously sharp arrowhead has been beautifully crafted.

In the 1970s, mudlark Brian Pitkin discovered a 17th-century Walloon sword (right) on the Thames foreshore. This type of sword had a wide, double-edged blade which was used in battle for piercing and slashing the enemy. The soldier's hand was protected by the ornate, S-shaped guard and a unique thumb ring. Walloon swords were used by the military and civilian gentry.

Top left: Medieval knight's knuckle guard (Jason Sandy). Left: Medieval chainmail (Mark Vasco Iglesias). Above right: Medieval arrowhead (Monika Buttling-Smith). Right: 17th-century Walloon sword (Graham duHeaume).

Several years ago, a mudlark recovered a complete 18th-century flintlock pistol (top left) from the riverbed. The waterlogged conditions and anaerobic mud perfectly protected the timber and metal from corrosion. The name of the pistol is derived from the flint stone which is tightly held by the cock (hammer) of the pistol. When the trigger is pulled, the flint strikes the frizzen, which produces sparks that ignite the gunpowder and fires the lead shot from the gun. Flintlock pistols were made in a variety of sizes and were used in warfare and for self-defense.

Cannonballs, grapeshot, and musket balls (below) are a relatively common find on the Thames foreshore. Many of them were manufactured along the river in the Tower of London and Royal Arsenal

in Woolwich. Over the years, I have found a few cannonballs and hundreds of musket balls.

A few years ago, Monika discovered a heavily encrusted 18th-century bayonet (top right) on the foreshore. After carefully restoring the artifact with the help of Graham duHeaume, she was able to identify it as a 1770 Heavy Dragoon carbine bayonet. Monika explains that it was "designed for mounted dragoons to carry at speed into battle, then dismount and fight. When the action got too close, they could stab the enemy with the bayonet. It is a cruel weapon, and holding it, you can almost smell the gun-smoke, mud, and blood of battle."

Under a bridge in West London, Graham's son discovered a .442 caliber Webley British Bulldog revolver (above). In Victorian times, these pistols were popular because they were lightweight, portable, and could be easily concealed. Since the gun was found under a bridge, it is highly likely that this pistol was purposely discarded in the river, possibly after a crime or murder.

Top left: 18th-century flintlock pistol. Top right: 18th-century bayonet (Monika Buttling-Smith). Left: Iron cannonballs, grapeshot, and musket balls (Jason Sandy). Above: Webley British Bulldog revolver (Graham duHeaume).

During the London Blitz in World War II, the Nazi Luftwaffe dropped more than 12,000 metric tons of bombs on London and killed over 43,000 Londoners. Unfortunately, several of these bombs fell into the river and did not explode. A few mudlarks have stumbled upon unexploded ordnances (UXOs) as they were walking along the exposed riverbed at low tide.

While mudlarking in West London, Tobias Neto spotted what he thought was "a large bottle covered in mud" on the foreshore (above). When Tobias picked it up, he noticed some German writing on the heavy, encrusted object. He suddenly realized it was a German bomb from World War II and called the police. "By the time the bomb squad arrived, I had moved the object and placed it securely behind a ladder fixed to the wall as tide was coming in quite fast," explains Tobias. "It was a risk I took, but it had to be done. The water had submerged the area, and the police rescheduled it for the next low tide on the following day. I returned to the spot the next day and waited for the police. The bomb was still there, exactly how I had placed it. The whole Putney

Top: World War II bomb (Tobias Neto).
Right: World War II bomb (Mike Walker).

Bridge area was sealed off again by the police. The bomb squad arrived, disarmed the bomb, and took it away."

In June 2017, Oliver Muranyi-Clark found a rusty bomb (below) on the foreshore in front of the London Eye, a world-famous tourist attraction in Central London. After his friend, Mike Walker, took some photos of the bomb, "we decided it probably was what we thought it might be and so best to get out of the vicinity and phone the police bomb squad," explains Oliver. "The whole London Eye and surrounding area had to be evacuated and cordoned off, it was quite an experience. Mike and I were, of course, loving the excitement being in the middle of everything! Fortunately, nobody got injured, so that was very lucky really as it could have turned out differently for sure." With a police helicopter circling overhead, the bomb from World War II was safely removed by the bomb squad.

When mudlarking in Greenwich in 2015, mudlark Nicola White spotted an unexploded grenade (below) lying on the foreshore. When Scotland Yard's ordnance experts arrived, they decided

it was not safe to remove the 70-year-old grenade, so it was detonated on the foreshore around 9:30 PM. The controlled explosion could be heard three miles away, and nearby residents complained about being woken up by a loud detonation.

One of the largest and most explosive "artifacts" in the River Thames is an American ship called the SS *Richard Montgomery* (below), which was built during World War II. After the ship was loaded with over 6,000 tons of munitions, she sailed from Philadelphia to the Thames Estuary where she anchored en route to France to deliver the supplies to the Allied troops. On August 20, 1944, the SS *Richard Montgomery* ran aground on a sandbank. According to a survey conducted in 2004, the bombs are so severely deteriorated that they could explode spontaneously at any time. If a single bomb exploded causing a chain reaction, it could blast water and debris nearly 10,000 feet into the air and create a 16-foot-high wave, according to a BBC News report in 1970. The deadly cargo has not yet been removed because of

the high risk and expensive cost. Even at high tide, her three masts are still visible above the water line. It's a ticking time bomb sitting on the bottom of the Thames!

Shortly before Remembrance Day (UK) in November 2020, I discovered a complete World War II helmet (above) called a "Home Front Zuckerman" helmet in the river. It could have been worn by members of the Fire Guard who played an important role in extinguishing fires and saving many homes and buildings in London. The helmet is a poignant reminder of the heroism and sacrifice of those who protected London during World War II.

Unfortunately, murder weapons such as guns and knives are still disposed of in the Thames. A few years ago, I arrived at Blackfriars Bridge in Central London to go mudlarking, and there was a large team of police officers on the foreshore. They were equipped with metal detectors and were searching for a murder weapon that had been thrown in the river by the suspect. Throughout history, the Thames has been the scene of many crimes and battles. I wonder how many more weapons lie concealed in the mud, waiting to be discovered so they can tell their interesting stories.

Top left: Hand grenade (Nicola White). Left: Masts of SS Richard Montgomery *in the Thames Estuary (Clem Rutter). Above: World War II Zuckerman helmet (Jason Sandy).*

MONIKA BUTTLING-SMITH

Growing up, I traveled all over Europe with my family in our trusty VW camp-ervan. I remember feral cats at the Roman Forum and gelato at Pompeii. In Sper-longa, where Emperor Tiberius had built his coastal palace, you could sail a little boat right into the grotto, dive off, and swim around the marble sculptures. It was magical! My dad was keen on military and naval history, so he would march us over battlefields and naval ports. He adored sailing in any form. On our river outings, my dad was always Long John Silver, and I was Jim Lad. He loved storytelling and would slip facts seamlessly into his tales.

I don't recall a first official mudlark. I have visited the foreshore on and off since childhood. When my mum was having chemo from 2012 onwards, I started going to the river more often. It's a peaceful place to just walk and contemplate life. Every now and then, I'd pick something up. One day I extracted a Jacobean latchet shoe with perfectly incised stars and moons on the leather heel piece. That was the start of obsessive mudlarking for me. I began finding better things and researched each one.

I love the randomness of my gifts from Father Thames—it's hard to get bored! Recent finds include a medieval battle-axe, a Tudor farthin-gale pin, a 17th-century half-heart padlock, and wooden spindle from a 16th-century spinning wheel. Occasionally, wildlife will catch your breath: a heron snatching an eel, or a crow dropping a sherd of pottery at your feet. Drama too! I watched white witches perform healing ceremonies at the start of the Covid pandemic. I spotted the Queen on the golden royal barge in the Jubilee flotilla, and I cheered on the super-fit Doggett racers. I've spied teenagers stealing their first kiss, and I've rescued dog-walkers cut off by the tide. I have handed in modern weapons to the police and collected plastic on every lark. The river gives so much to us, but it also needs our care.

My favorite find is usually the last cool item I have plucked from the mud. Old favorites include my Roman oil lamp, last held by a slave girl in ancient Londinium, and my bronze Medieval Pax which was kissed by every member of the Catholic High Mass congre-gation for over two hundred years until the very face of St. Peter was worn smooth. I also treasure my Georgian Rococo penknife, perhaps used by William Blake to trim the very quill that wrote *Jerusalem*. These finds set my imagination on fire!

I am a born-and-bred Londoner, and I am incredibly proud of my city. I like to share my finds so that everyone can touch London's history. I get such a thrill from letting a child swish my tall-ship machete that has traveled the trade routes, last used by a Jack Tar sailor to slash though tropical jungles in search of fresh water. I enjoyed chatting to a musician who was learning to play the Jaw harp and letting him hold one last played by Thames-side dockers back in the 12th century. Visitors bring their own curiosity and life experiences to the objects I display, and seeing their enthusiasm is pure joy for me.

Portraits by Tom Harrison.

DEATH
ON THE
RIVER

For millennia, the River Thames has been a life-giver as well as a life-taker. Early man was first attracted to the Thames Valley because of its life-giving waters. The river was a natural resource which provided fresh water and an abundant supply of food. London grew up along the river and thrived because of the Thames.

Conversely, the river has the power to kill. In January 1928, fourteen people died when the Thames burst its banks and flooded Central London with the highest water levels ever recorded. One of the worst Thames disasters took place on September 3, 1878, when the paddle steamer *Princess Alice* collided with the steam-collier *Bywell Castle*. Approximately 700 people died when the paddle steamer sank within four minutes of the collision near Thamesmead. It is still the largest peacetime disaster on the river. In 1989, the pleasure boat *Marchioness* sank between Southwark Bridge and Cannon Street Bridge in Central London. Fifty-one people drowned after the pleasure boat hit a 1,457-ton dredger.

For millennia, people have been attracted to the Thames by its dark, sinister powers. The Thames is a river of lost souls. It calls out to those who wish for death—the forlorn, the neglected, and those who are suffering. It is a gateway for them to reach their final destination. Flowing directly into the sea, the river provides a macabre way of disappearing without a trace. The deep, enigmatic waters provide an eternal escape from tortured minds and evils of the city. After Waterloo Bridge was opened in 1817, it became known as "Lover's Leap", "Arch of Suicide," "Bridge of Sighs," and the "Bridge of Sorrow" because of the tragic number of jumpers from the bridge.

Suicide victims do not normally wish to be seen or to be found. They remain anonymous and unlamented as their lifeless bodies float calmly to the sea and disappear forever, swallowed up by the flood of human tears. The Thames is a river of the dead, a harbor of lost souls. The mother of a suicide victim in 2004 claimed that "The river is haunted—it draws people in." Like the ferryman Charon who transports the souls of the newly dead across the river Styx to Hades in Greek mythology, the dark waters of the Thames also carry the dead to the Underworld.

Not all suicide victims are washed out to sea. Disturbingly, I have seen three dead bodies in different locations along the river which washed up on the shore. Alan Murphy was also traumatized by a gruesome discovery. "In 1987, I was

under a pier, and I felt something touch the back of my neck. When I looked up, there was a dead body on top of a beam where a guy had come in the night before. As the water went out, he'd got stuck. I never went back to that location again, not at that time of the morning anyway. That was a bit of a wake-up call," explains Alan. Sadly, on average about 50 people die each year in the River Thames. Most of them are suicide victims.

For centuries, the Thames has been littered with refuse and corpses. An illustration (above) called "The Silent Highwayman" by John Tenniel depicts the appalling state of the Thames in 1858. In Charles Dicken's book, *Our Mutual Friend* (1865), the thriving trade of retrieving human corpses from the Thames is described. Gaffer Hexam goes out at night in his small boat to find the floating bodies and steal any valuables he could find on them.

Facing page: Skull on Deadman's Island (Simon Bourne). This page: The Silent Highwayman on the Thames *(Punch Magazine, Volume 35 Page 137; 10 July 1858).*

There is a morbid fascination with water and death in our culture. In a twisted way, death is sometimes portrayed in a poetic and tranquil way. One of the most iconic paintings depicting death was produced by John Everett Millais in 1852 along the Hogsmill River, which is a tributary of the River Thames. Ophelia, from Shakespeare's play Hamlet, is floating peacefully on the surface of the water. She was a noble woman who was madly in love with Hamlet. After Hamlet kills her father, Ophelia falls into a stream from a willow tree. Air trapped in her flowing dress keeps her temporarily afloat until it is saturated, and she slowly disappears under the water. More than 150 years later, professional photographer Julia Fullerton-Batten returned to the exact same spot along the river where Millais produced his famous painting. With her production crew, Julia re-created this scene (above) of Ophelia floating in the river.

When you step onto the Thames foreshore, one of the first things you will notice is the amount of bones lying around. In some areas of the foreshore, the riverbed looks like a graveyard (below) and is literally covered several inches deep

Top: Shakespeare's Ophelia floating peacefully on the river (Tableau by Julia Fullerton-Batten).
Bottom: Bones on the foreshore in Greenwich (Jason Sandy).

in bones. From the slaughterhouses, butchers, skinners, tanneries, pubs, and inns located along the river, the bones of the processed animals were simply discarded in the river. Because they do not biodegrade over time, they have accumulated on the riverbed. Bones from horses, cows, sheep, goats, foxes, dogs, and many other animals have been retrieved from the riverbed. Steve Brooker even found a monkey skull. The largest skeleton ever discovered in the River Thames is from a North Atlantic right whale that had been killed in the 18th century and towed back to London to be processed.

Nearly 300 human skulls have been recovered in the river, dating back to the Neolithic and Iron Age. A number of Roman and early British skulls have been dredged from the riverbed near Chelsea Bridge. The stretch of river near Battersea Bridge was once known as a "Celtic Golgotha," a place of skulls.

At Strand-on-the-Green in West London, over 100 human skulls were discovered in the late 1920s. There have been similar finds in Kew and in Hammersmith. No one knows whether these skulls were ritualistically placed into the river or if they are evidence of ancient battles on the river. Oddly, the skeletons have not been found—only the skulls.

Some of the oldest human remains found by mudlarks in the Thames date back to the Neolithic period. While searching the exposed riverbed at low tide in 2018, Martin Bushell discovered part of the oldest human skull (below) ever found in the Thames. Radiocarbon-dated to 3,600 BC, the

5,000-year-old skull is from a young adult who was possibly a farmer in the local area. The skull fragment is now on permanent display in the Museum of London.

As Simon Hunt went rowing on the Thames one morning in 2021, he discovered a 5,000-year-old femur bone lying among the pebbles on the exposed riverbed. He picked it up, placed it in his boat, and continued rowing up and down the river. Simon took the bone home in a plastic bag and called the police. After tests were carried out in police labs, experts confirmed that the leg bone belonged to a person who lived between 3,516–3,365 BC.

In 2018, Chelsea McKibbin spotted a human mandible (below) as the tide was coming in. She took it to a local police station, and the bone was radiocarbon dated to 740–685 BC. "Never have I felt more of a humbler connection to past humans. I'm sad to think of the possible circumstances surrounding how this young individual came to rest in the Thames," explains Chelsea.

Located at the mouth of the River Medway which flows into the Thames Estuary, there is an uninhabited island that is called Deadman's

Bottom left: Neolithic skull fragment (Martin Bushell).
Bottom right: Neolithic mandible with teeth (Chelsea McKibbin).

Island. On the desolate, windswept island, the corpses of convicts were buried who died on board prison ships called "hulks," which were moored near the island in the 18th century. During a survey in 2016, the remains of more than 200 humans were found on the deserted island. With tidal ebb and flow over the past two centuries, the wooden coffins have eroded out of the mud, and the bodies are slowly being swallowed up by the sea. The foreshore around the island is littered with human remains (left), and it is one of the most haunting and eerie islands of the world.

Before access was prohibited, mudlarks Simon Bourne, Stephen Johnson, and Steve Trim visited the island and documented what they saw. They found arms, legs, ribs, vertebrae, jaw bones with teeth, and other human bones covered in barnacles (bottom left). Near the island, they also spotted a human skull (page 184) lying on the surface of the mud. "The skull was obviously several hundred years old and looked like it had been in the water for many years. Looking into the empty eye sockets felt like a direct link to the past—it was probably from one of the prisoners or cholera victims. We left it where it was found, reported it to the police to investigate, and returned to shore in a sombre mood," explains Steve. Describing his experience, Simon said: "I came away thinking about the suffering these people endured before they died. The unfortunate ones were subjected to appalling conditions on board the prison hulks. When a disease struck, it would wipe out large numbers of prisoners." It is now forbidden to set foot on the island.

Over the years, mudlarks have also discovered several artifacts that are associated with death and mortality. Memento mori rings engraved with skulls (facing page, top) have been found. The inner band of of this ring is inscribed with the haunting words, "Remember to dye."

In Latin, memento mori means "remember thy death" or "remember that you have to die." Skull bead rosaries and necklaces were worn as a reminder of one's mortality and the temporary, transient nature of life on earth. One of the most

Top left: Bones lying on Deadman's Island (Simon Bourne).
Bottom left: Jawbone with teeth and barnacles (Simon Bourne).

interesting memento mori artifacts was found by Caroline Nunneley (bottom). Hand-carved from animal bone, the delicate face of a woman (possibly Virgin Mary) is depicted on one side. She is wearing a wimple or cloth headdress, which was fashionable in the late medieval period. On the other side, the sinister face of a skull has been carved. Dating to AD 1450–1550, this artifact could have been used as a bead on a rosary as a reminder about human mortality or to encourage the wearer to enjoy life.

Fortunately, there are heart-warming stories which give us hope in humanity. From a young age, Londoner Jonny Benjamin struggled with mental health problems. In his early 20s, he was diagnosed with a schizoaffective disorder, a combination of schizophrenia and a bipolar disorder. Jonny was hospitalized in January 2008, but he escaped and went to Waterloo Bridge in Central London to commit suicide by jumping into the river. A compassionate stranger spotted Jonny on the bridge and gently talked him down before he could leap to his death. He said, "It will get better, mate. You will get better." They continued talking for 25 minutes, which was long enough for the emergency services to arrive and take Jonny back to safety in the hospital. After reaching a healthier state of mind, Jonny launched a social media campaign called "#FindMike" that went viral in January 2014. He didn't know the name of the Good Samaritan who saved him, so

he nicknamed him "Mike." Two weeks later, Jonny was reunited with Neil Laybourn who came forward after his girlfriend saw the campaign on Facebook.

In 2016, Jonny started an initiative called "Think-Well" to establish mental health education in schools and break down the stigma surrounding mental illness and suicide. "I wanted to let people know that it's OK to have suicidal thoughts and feelings. I also hoped to show people that through talking about it, and by having someone else listen, it is possible to overcome the darkness that overwhelms a person when they feel helpless. This is something that I learned from my exchange with Neil on the bridge, and a message that I've been trying to pass on to others," explains Jonny. Since 2017, Neil has worked full-time for Jonny's mental health campaigns, and they ran the London Marathon together that year. In May 2018, Jonny was awarded an MBE (a highly coveted "Member of the British Empire" award) and published a book about his experiences called *The Stranger on the Bridge*.

Although the River Thames has claimed many lives over the centuries, Jonny's story gives us hope that this darkness can be overcome through the kindness of others and talking openly about mental health issues.

Top: Gold memento mori ring inscribed with the words "Remember to dye" (PAS).
Bottom: Memento mori bead depicting a woman and skull (PAS).

CAROLINE NUNNELEY

Being a Thames mudlark is the greatest joy and privilege. As a teenager, I spent months on a Saxon archaeological dig. In that time, I handled only fragments of animal bones, whereas in three years as a mudlark, I've been lucky enough to find Roman, possibly Saxon, and many medieval and Tudor artifacts.

As part of my degree, I studied Old English, Old Norse, and Middle English. I loved Chaucer, and read about the medieval pilgrims setting off from the Tabard Inn in Southwark on their journey to Canterbury. Many years later, I had an idea what mudlarking was, but it wasn't until 2018 that a friend bought me Ted Sandling's book, *London in Fragments*, which made me realize people still did this and were finding remarkable evidence of London's history. The object in the book I most desired was a tiny 17th-century pipe bowl. So, I bought my license, went down onto the foreshore, and soon found

one. Since then (excluding Covid lockdowns), I've traveled to the river every week and still feel the same level of excitement and anticipation as I did on that first visit.

It began as a solitary pastime for me, spending hours on my own, figuring out how the tides work, and where I might find objects. Soon, I started to make friends, and became part of a community of like-minded, history-obsessed people who celebrate each other's finds and generously share their respective knowledge.

I've learned so much from my finds. I'm especially fascinated by the social history. I've also learned about our shameful colonial past and

the terrible truth about the British Empire, the legacy of which continues today and is only now being taught in schools.

Because of my fascination with medieval life, my most precious finds are two pieces of pilgrim badges associated with Thomas Becket. One badge is in the shape of his bust, which is a bit battered but recognizable with his cope, miter, and forlorn expression. The other badge shows Becket's leg upon his horse as he returned from exile in France. This significant 14th-century artifact was most likely bought in Canterbury and worn proudly on the journey home to London. It has been graffitied with stars on the horse's leg and with the owner's initials on the reverse.

The foreshore is a magical place. It stretches for miles as it meanders through the city, both part of and separate from the metropolis. The river has been a rubbish dump throughout its 2,000 year history. Because it's tidal, the river drops objects onto its foreshore twice a day, perfectly preserved if they've been buried in its anaerobic mud. I count it as a wonderful visit if I come away with an everyday object. These personal finds connect me most intimately to their historic owners -- their fingerprints on a sherd of pottery, the base of an ointment pot, a bodkin that was used daily to thread clothing together, or a farthing token that gives the name and address of a 17th-century trader. Whatever I pick up links me directly to past Londoners and teaches me something about the city's long and colorful history. It doesn't need to be made of gold for me to consider it treasure.

Portraits by Tom Harrison.

A THREAD THROUGH TIME

Along the exposed riverbed at low tide, it is difficult to spot the smallest artifacts because they are camouflaged among the stones, broken glass, and rusty ironwork. I wear sturdy knee pads and gloves so I can crawl on my hands and knees, searching for these little, evasive treasures such as brass pins. When you first start mudlarking, it takes a while to "get your eye in" and spot these tiny pins. After you find the first one, you start to notice them everywhere (right).

Over the years, pins have been washed out of drains and were dropped as people got in and out of boats. Several mudlarks are obsessed with collecting brass pins, and they can spend hours bent over picking them up. Since she began mudlarking in 2015, Anna Borzello has patiently and painstakingly collected over 15,000 pins (top) from the Thames. "I remember the wonder of finding my first pin on the foreshore—it felt brilliantly incongruous that something so domestic and so tiny was lying in such abundance in the mud in Central London. I like the dreamy, meditative feel of picking up the pins," describes Anna.

Other mudlarks such as Florrie Evans and Charlie Dixon also have large collections of handmade pins of all shapes and sizes, which they have beautifully displayed in pin cushions (left) at home. Florrie's Victorian pin cushion is in the shape of an elegant woman's shoe. The post-me-

Top: Anna's pin collection (Anna Borzello).
Middle right: Pins lying on the foreshore (Jason Sandy).
Bottom: Spheric pin cushion with Thames pins (Charlie Dixon).

dieval pins within the 19th-century pin cushion (right) are a beautiful combination.

Long before the invention of zippers and Velcro, pins were used to hold all types of garments and headwear together. "Pins tell the history of modern England—from the method of production to the history of dress. They were once such high-end, luxury items, bequeathed in wills, and owned only by the rich. Now pins are mass produced and barely merit a second thought. I calculated that in the 15th century you could buy 30 sheep for 100 pins," explains Anna. The elaborate dresses of Queen Elizabeth I were held together with thousands of pins.

In the 14th century, the English parliament passed an act restricting the pin maker to only sell his pins on the first two days of January of each year in order to limit the sale of these "luxuries." Well-to-do ladies flocked to buy them with so-called "pin money" given to them by their husbands or families. When pins became more plentiful and cheaper, ladies bought other luxuries with their pin money—a term which still exists in the English language to this day.

The pin-making industry was a very important and lucrative business for many centuries in England. Hundreds of thousands of pins were exported all over the world. To regulate the trade and quality of the pins, the Worshipful Company of Pinmakers was founded in the 14th century in London.

Pins were made by hand, and there were approximately 18 different

steps in producing a single pin. They were created by drawing brass wire through a die to the required length. It was cut and sharpened at one end, and the head was formed by coiling finer wire around the other end. In the last step of the process, the brass pins were polished to create a golden appearance. They were often sold in bunches, and several mudlarks have found intact bunches of pins (middle) on the foreshore which are still bound together with brass wire.

To create a sharp tip at the end of the pin, animal bones were cut and notched with parallel grooves. The brass wire was placed in the groove of the notched bone and sharpened to a point using a file. Malcolm Russell and several other mudlarks have found so-called pinners' bones (bottom) in the river.

Pins were not only used for utilitarian purposes. They were transformed into decorative objects which were worn as fashion accesso-

Top: Post-medieval pins in a Victorian pin cushion shoe (Florrie Evans).
Middle: A bundle of 61 brass pins (PAS). Bottom: A pinner's bone (Malcolm Russell).

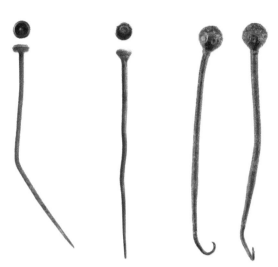

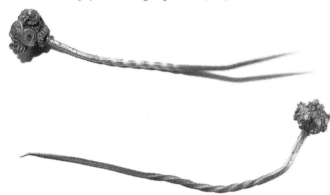

Top, left to right: Iron Age bronze pin (PAS). Roman bronze pin (PAS). Anglo-Saxon brass pin (PAS). Tudor gold pin (Stuart Wyatt). 16th-century gold pin (PAS). Bottom: Highly decorated gold pin head (PAS).

ries and to display one's wealth. One of the earliest ornate pins found by a mudlark in the Thames dates back to the Iron Age. The bronze pin (above left) from 500–200 BC is 154mm (6 inches) long and tapers to a point. The disc-shaped head has a ridge around the perimeter with a decorative rib above and below. Although missing now, either enamel or coral would have been placed in the hollow top of the pin head.

Many decorative pins have been discovered from the Roman period. A beautiful example (above center) is 119mm (4.7 inches) long and is made of bronze. It has a globular head which is inlaid with enamel. In the center, there is a circular bronze ring containing white enamel surrounded by a ring of red enamel. Around the perimeter of the red enamel, there are seven evenly spaced grooves cut into the smooth, bronze disc.

Dating to AD 720–850, an Anglo-Saxon pin (above right) was found in the Thames. It is 62mm (2.4 inches) long. The head is subtly faceted and decorated with ring and dot motifs. A circular collar is located at the junction between the pin head and the circular shaft.

The Tudors especially liked their decorative pins, and some of them are beautiful works of art. A few years ago, Stuart Wyatt found an exquisite gold pin (top right) from the 16th century. The pin head is decorated with four circular features formed by semi-circular rings around a central globe. The

ornamentation resembles miniature Tudor ruffs, which were fashionable in the 16th century.

Malcolm Duff also discovered a beautiful gold pin (above) dating to the 16th–17th centuries. Measuring 32mm (1.3 inches) in length, the pin has a globular head and a shank with a square cross-section which has been twisted to create an elegant effect. Surrounded within twisted wire rings, filigree circular pellets adorn the pin head.

Several years ago, John Mills discovered one of the most remarkable pieces of Tudor gold in the Thames. It is an extremely ornate pin head (right). Although it is only 11mm (0.4 inches) in diameter, it is highly decorated with applied fili-gree circlets and knops.

Set with small turquoise gemstones, the flower heads are surrounded by petals of gold, openwork decoration made of fine twisted wire. Only a wealthy aristocrat or member of the royal family could have afforded this expensive gold pin which has been acquired by the Museum of London. The extraordinarily fine details of these delicate pins display the skilled workmanship of the Tudor craftsmen.

For centuries, pins continued to be worn as fashion accessories. Marie-Louise Plum discovered a beautiful brass pin (top left) from the early 20th century. The pewter top of the pin is formed in the shape of a fox's head with eyes wide open, a long, tapering nose, and pointed, upright ears.

Clothwork and needlework were thriving industries in England for many centuries, and needles were important tools of the workers. Originally, bone needles would have been used with thick thread to sew coarse, woolen fabrics together, and were also utilized for leatherwork. Over the years, mudlarks have recovered a wide variety of bone needles (top center) from the Thames. Brass needles have also been found, which are much thinner and sharper for precise and delicate needlework.

Top, left to right: Fox head pin (Marie-Louise Plum). Carved bone needles (Giovanni Forlino, PAS). Georgian ivory needle case (Florrie Evans). Bottom: Carved bone bodkin with ear scoop (Monika Buttling-Smith).

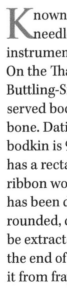

A few years ago, Florrie Evans discovered a rare, ivory needle case (top right) carved from an elephant tusk. Dating to the 18th century, it has a hollow, tapered body with a removable, domed lid. The finial at the top is carved in the shape of a miniature beehive.

Known as a lacing or threading needle, a bodkin is a sharp slender instrument used to make holes in cloth. On the Thames foreshore, Monika Buttling-Smith discovered a well-preserved bodkin (left) carved from animal bone. Dating to the 17th century, the bodkin is 90mm (3.5 inches) long and has a rectangular slot through which ribbon would be drawn. The terminal has been delicately carved into a rounded, concave ear scoop. Wax would be extracted from the ear and applied to the end of a thread or ribbon to prevent it from fraying.

In the 16th and 17th centuries, it was fashionable for women to wear bodkins in their hair. It was also a convenient way of carrying this multi-purpose tool. Florrie Evans found an ornate bodkin (far left) made of brass. The body of the bodkin has a thin, rectangular cross section, and the tip tapers to a point. The head is shaped like a small scallop shell, which would have been visible when the bodkin was used to secure a woman's hair in place.

A stunning silver bodkin (near left) was discovered by Giovanni Forlino in January 2022. Dating to 1625–1650, the bodkin has a decorative finial in the shape of an ear scoop. Along the length of the pin, the body has been engraved with various shapes created with delicate, incised lines. A long, stemmed flower with petals and diamond-shaped head is depicted above the rectangular ribbon slot. The letters "E N" are formed with small dots, which are presumably the maker's or owner's initials.

E arly one morning as I was mudlarking in Central London, I discovered a large, brass thimble (below) dating to the 15th century. Each individual dimple on the surface has been meticulously stamped by hand. Some of the irregular holes were accidentally punched through the thin sheet of domed brass.

Above: Post-medieval silver and brass bodkins (Florrie Evans, Giovanni Forlino, PAS). Right: Medieval brass handmade thimble (Jason Sandy).

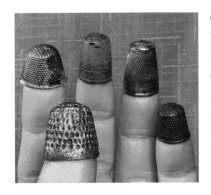

Over the years, I have found many thimbles (left). They are in great condition and are still fit for purpose. It is a very satisfying experience to pluck an old thimble from the mud and put it on your finger, knowing that the previous owner lived hundreds of years ago.

Worn to protect the fingertip from being pricked by a needle while sewing, the design of thimbles has changed very little over the years. Mudlarks have discovered a wide variety of brass and silver thimbles (next page) which are beautifully decorated with various patterns and motifs. Some of the most exquisite thimbles were made in Nuremberg, Germany, which was a well-known center of thimble production in the 16th–17th centuries. Thimbles were not only a utilitarian object, they were also produced to commemorate events and even given as love tokens.

Since at least the Iron Age, people have been weaving along the Thames. Dating to 400–100 BC, John Dunford recovered an extraordinary weaving comb (right) from the river which has been carved from bone. It would have been used to comb the threads into position on a loom.

In the Middle Ages, the wool trade was the backbone and driving force of the English economy. Wool became the principal export to mainland Europe, which relied on the quality of fine English wool. European weavers were willing to pay top prices for it. By the end of the 15th century, England dominated the global wool market. In the 16th century, cloth represented 90% of England's exports and remained the main export until the Industrial Revolution.

At the height of the wool and cloth trade, London controlled almost 80% of these exports. In London, many companies flourished and became very wealthy through the wool and cloth trade. The Worshipful Company of Clothworkers and the Worshipful Company of Drapers (wool and cloth merchants) amassed great wealth and power by the end of the 16th century. The Drapers were granted a monopoly of the retail sale of woolen cloth in London and set the standards for the trade.

Mudlarks have found evidence of the weaving and cloth making trades in London. Loom weights and spindle whorls have been recovered from the exposed riverbed. Spindle whorls are circular discs fixed to a wooden stick, and were used for winding yarn using a spinning motion. Dating between 1450–1550, several spindle whorls made of glazed stoneware (bottom) have been discovered. They have convex sides and flat upper and lower surfaces and are decorated with bands of horizontal, incised lines. They range in diameter between 23–27mm (0.9–1.1 inches) and were probably imported to London from Langewehe, Belgium.

Wool exports began to be taxed in 13th century, followed by cloth exports in the 14th century. As proof that the correct tax had been paid, lead seals were attached to cloth as a means of identification, regulation, and quality control of cloth between the 13th and 18th centuries. Appointed by the government, "alnagers" were officials who assessed the quality and measurements of every cloth and ensured that the appropriate tax had been

Top left: Medieval and post-medieval thimbles (Jason Sandy). Middle: Iron Age weaving comb (PAS). Bottom: Post-medieval spindle whorls (PAS).

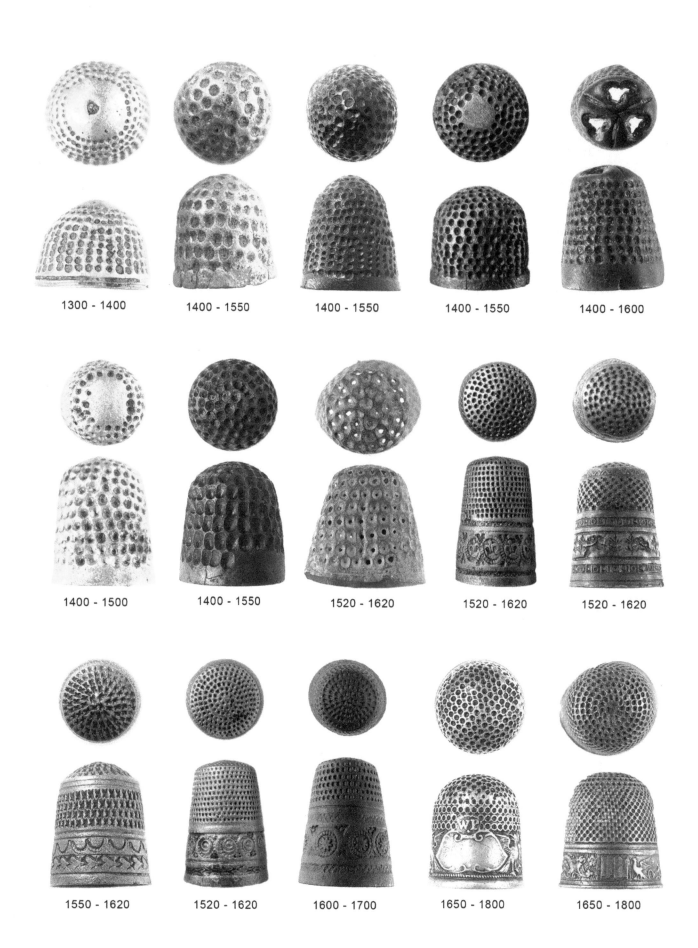

1300 - 1400   1400 - 1550   1400 - 1550   1400 - 1550   1400 - 1600

1400 - 1500   1400 - 1550   1520 - 1620   1520 - 1620   1520 - 1620

1550 - 1620   1520 - 1620   1600 - 1700   1650 - 1800   1650 - 1800

Thimble designs throughout the ages from the PAS (Collage by Jason Sandy).

paid. To uphold the outstanding reputation of English cloth, they had the authority to search and confiscate cloth which did not comply with the high-quality standards. Until 1724, it was illegal to sell cloth in England without an alnage seal fixed to it.

There were mainly two different types of cloth seals—two-disc (top) and four-disc seals which were joined by a connecting strip. One disc had a rivet, and one had a hole. They were folded together at the edge of the cloth and hammered together with a die, which stamped information into the surface of the lead disc. The seals were often stamped with the mark or sign of the county, city, or borough where the cloth was made. Other stamps on seals depicted the initials and busts of English monarchs, coat of arms, shields, crowns, roses, and fleur-de-lis. Animals, floral patterns, and other symbols were also stamped on the seals. The maker's name, initials, personal symbols, and value of the cloth appear on some cloth seals. Over the years, I have found a wide variety of lead seals (middle) in the Thames.

One of the most interesting cloth seals (bottom) was found by Dave Hiddleston. It is a large four-disc cloth seal from Colchester and stamped with the date 1618 and inscription, ENGLISH COLCHESTER SAYE. A cross and three coronets appear within an ornate shield in the center. Although it is missing now, a large disc on the back of the cloth seal depicted Colchester castle with a

soldier standing in its doorway. Arriving as religious refugees in Colchester between 1565–1570, Dutch immigrants were among the most successful manufacturers of cloth in England in the late 16th–17th centuries. According to Stuart Elton, author of the book, *Cloth Seals: An Illustrated Reference Guide to the Identification of Lead Seals Attached to Cloth*, this lead seal "was actually made by the native English Colchester weavers, who did not have the skills of the immigrants but envied the prices and markets they commanded, and so set about producing impressive seals that they knew would be confused with the Dutch Colchester's own saye seals and would lead to more money!"

Some of the smallest objects found on the Thames foreshore tell the biggest success stories of Britain's global trade. Pins and needles, along with bodkins, thimbles, spindle whorls, and cloth seals reveal the importance of the wool and cloth exports to the British economy for many centuries. In England, entire towns aptly named "wool towns" were built around the wool trade. Beautiful "wool churches" were built solely from the proceeds of the lucrative wool trade. London also prospered and amassed a great wealth by shipping wool and cloth abroad from the River Thames.

Top: Two-part cloth seal (Tony Thira). Middle: Collection of lead seals (Jason Sandy). Bottom: Cloth seal from Colchester (Dave Hiddleston).

CHARLIE DIXON

I first dabbled with mudlarking for a university illustration project before permits were compulsory, and I became a licensed Thames mudlark in September 2019. Since then, I have been fully immersed and enchanted by this amazing hobby. Mudlarking is never far from my mind, and I am always dreaming of what historical treasures could be waiting for me on the banks of this ancient river.

Growing up obsessed with palaeontology, I was fossil hunting since I could walk. I built up quite a collection and even displayed them in a mini museum in my bedroom. I amassed my own personal library of books and visited every museum that I could. This naturally evolved into a fascination with history and archaeology. I have always loved London and its history, but I somehow never realized that thousands of years' worth of its artifacts could be washed up daily by the Thames. When I first learned of mudlarking after being intrigued by the countless animal bones that litter the foreshore, everything suddenly snapped into place. My childhood obsessions with archaeology, palaeontology, and collecting had all come together in the form of one thrilling hobby.

Mudlarking to me is pure anticipation, excitement, and escapism. It's exhilarating that you never know what you're going to find, and the rush of an interesting discovery is almost unmatched. Some of my best finds have come when I was least expecting them. With mudlarking I am never bored, as the searching is only part of the thrill. I relish getting lost in the research, the cataloging and curating of my collection, and the reconstructive drawings of my most special finds. I like giving tours of my collection that is housed in a large, vintage cabinet with over 50 drawers, and similarly I enjoy photographing and writing about my finds for my Instagram account.

I love learning about long-gone Londoners, their lives, and experiences that were so vastly different to our own. I think that's why the older finds fascinate me the most—such as those from the Roman and medieval periods— as I like to imagine how alien and different everything must've been back then.

Two of my most prized finds come from these earlier periods in London's history. Back in October 2020, I got goosebumps as I turned over an unassuming pottery sherd to reveal the perfect image of a hare with its ears folded back as it runs. The depiction is still as crisp and clear as the day it was lost or discarded at least 1,600 years ago. It once belonged to a Roman "hunt cup," and the hare would've been chased by hounds around the complete vessel.

On a quite high tide in July 2021, I noticed a little, green-glazed face nestled among the shingle, staring up at me. He turned out to be a rare and unknown bearded king from a 13th–14th-century miniature, anthropomorphic jug. The realistic portrayal of the face is unusual, as most facial depictions on English pottery at this time were quite crude. Incredibly, the potter's fingerprints can still clearly be seen, almost 800 years after they were left.

As a mudlark, it's easy to take what we do for granted, but I think it's so important to look up from the ground once in a while and appreciate how lucky and privileged we are to have access to this wonderfully ancient river and the incredible objects that it gives us.

Portraits by Tom Harrison.

KEEP IT TOGETHER!

Various cufflinks found in the River Thames by Stuart Wyatt, Mark Jennings, Mike Walker, Mark Paros and other mudlarks (collage by Jason Sandy).

Over the centuries, people have used toggles, clasps, dress fasteners, hooked tags, and cufflinks to hold their clothing in place. Not only were they practical and utilitarian items, they were also highly decorated, ornate fashion accessories that were worn to show off and attract attention. They also displayed one's wealth and social status. These beautiful works of art tell the story of fashion and culture throughout the ages in Britain.

Since the Iron Age, toggles and fasteners have been used to literally keep things together. Mudlark Jason Davey found a decorative Celtic button and loop fastener (above), which has been dated to the 1st century BC. Although the fastener is small, it is a mini-masterpiece of Celtic art. Both discs are cast with abstract motifs, comprised of recessed circular and abstract shapes interspersed with lunate symbols, which are typical of Celtic design. The swirling motif is similar to the decoration on Celtic mirrors from the Iron Age. This button and loop fastener was probably used to secure a cloak or some other garment in place.

In the 16th century, it was very fashionable to wear decorated dress fasteners (top right), hooked tags, and chatelaines. The Tudors wore them in prominent positions on their clothes so the ornate designs were visible. Although they are intricate and beautiful fashion accessories, the fasteners were used for a variety of utilitarian purposes,

mainly to fix clothing and stockings in place. Tudor women often used pairs of hooked fasteners to keep their long dresses from touching the mud as they walked through the filthy streets of London (below). The fasteners were also used to secure their long neck scarves to their clothes to keep them in place.

Demonstrating the creativity of the Tudor craftsmen, dress fasteners were formed in a wide variety of styles and shapes. Produced by casting molten brass into a carved mold, they were beauti-

Left: Celtic button and loop fastener (PAS). Top right: Tudor dress fastener found in the River Thames (Jason Sandy). Bottom right: Historic painting of Tudor woman wearing dress fasteners, Holbein the Younger (Ashmolean Museum, University of Oxford).

fully decorated with openwork patterns, floral designs, abstract geometrical motifs, religious symbols, hearts, animals, and faces. The openwork designs consisted of interwoven lines and circles within a central pattern. Mudlarks have found many of these beautiful works of Tudor art (above).

One of the nicest dress hooks found in the River Thames (above, second row, left) has an ornate, openwork design. The brass clasp has a rectangular bar at the top with a horizontal slot where the fabric would have been attached to the fastener. Within the openwork design, there are three pierced trefoils in a row above a horizontal ridge with a foliate pattern below.

Graham duHeaume and I have also found beautiful Tudor hooked tags with ornate openwork patterns (above, second row, center) dating to the 16th century. They are formed with three distinct features—a rectangular loop at the top, central body with openwork pattern, and projecting hook from the base. The body is decorated with a pinecone above a V-shaped molded design in the center. Playful, perforated circles form the edges of the fastener and create a striking appearance.

A few years ago, Monika Buttling-Smith discovered a rare, hooked tag with the letters "ihs" (above, second row, right) dating to AD 1500–1600. The

dress hook has a circular disc in the center with an integral, trapezoidal lug at the top for securing the fabric. The circular plate has molded decoration within a thick, ribbed border from which the tapering hook projects downwards. The Christogram "ihs" is a monogram symbolizing Jesus Christ. Religion played an important role in the lives of Londoners in the 16th century. The Church of England was formally founded in 1534, when King Henry VIII broke away from the Roman Catholic Church after its leaders refused to annul his marriage to Catherine of Aragon so he could marry Anne Boleyn.

There were many different styles of Tudor dress fasteners. One of the most beautiful types is formed from three ornate, hemispherical domes at the top with a hook projecting from the base. Several mudlarks have found this type of fastener (below). One of them is a dress hook with a scalloped-edged, trefoil-shaped backplate and three domed bosses decorated with a filigree, twisted rope design

Top row: Tudor dress hooks found by Mark Paros and others (PAS/Collage by Jason Sandy). Second row, left to right: Ornate Tudor dress hook (PAS). Tudor hooked tags (Graham duHeaume and Jason Sandy). Hooked tag with Christian monogram (Monika Buttling-Smith). Bottom: Ornate, domed dress fasteners from the PAS and Graham duHeaume.

(right). Each boss has a large annulet encircling a trefoil of smaller annulets. Where the hook is attached to the main body, there is a maker's mark "G. Reed." This silver gilt fastener would have been worn by a very wealthy Tudor woman in the 16th century.

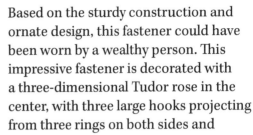

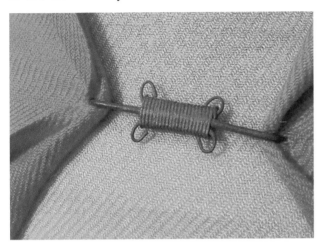

Based on the sturdy construction and ornate design, this fastener could have been worn by a wealthy person. This impressive fastener is decorated with a three-dimensional Tudor rose in the center, with three large hooks projecting from three rings on both sides and bottom. It would have been used to secure three pieces of fabric together.

Chatelaines are another kind of fastener formed with a hooked tag and spiraled brass coils bound together with thin, wound wire (right). Not only are chatelaines beautiful works of art, they served a very functional purpose. They were decorative hooks, which Tudor women slipped over the waistband of their dresses. From the various coiled scrolls, small chains were attached from which useful, everyday items such as keys, thimble cases, pin cases, and tweezers were suspended.

Another type of Tudor fastener was used to secure two pieces of fabric together with a horizontal bar and two hooks on either side (above). I have found several of these brass fasteners, which were made inexpensively by tightly winding a thin gauge wire around thick, sharp hooks (right). The body, formed by thinner wire, was hammered flat to secure the large hooks in place. Four thin, wire loops at each corner create a simple decoration for this utilitarian fastener. The foreboding hooks are very sharp and must have been uncomfortable to wear, especially if they punctured through the fabric or leather and pierced the skin. Perhaps circular, metal mounts were fixed to the fabric through which the hooks were secured to prevent them from ripping through the fabric.

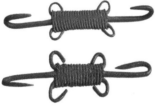

In the image at right, Florrie Evans has attached a chain connected to a Tudor ear scoop (for removing ear wax) to illustrate how a chatelaine was used in the 16th century.

Several years ago, Graham duHeaume found a beautiful example of this type of fastener (left).

Top, center: Domed fastener with filigree design (PAS). Left column, top to bottom: Tudor hooked fastener (Jason Sandy). Ominous hooked fasteners (Jason Sandy). Elaborate fastener decorated with flower (Graham duHeaume). Right column, top to bottom: Tudor chatelaines found by Florrie Evans and Peter Olivant (Florrie Evans and PAS). Chatelaine with chain and ear scoop (Florrie Evans).

Some of the most ornate and coveted artifacts found on the Thames foreshore are 18th-century brass cufflinks, which were decorated with a vast array of designs such as crowns, anchors, balloons, floral patterns, and famous personalities such as kings, queens, and military heroes (page 202). Many of the cufflinks are missing the other half, which most likely indicates how the cufflink was accidentally lost.

Although the first cufflinks appeared in the 1600s, they did not become common until the 18th century. Their development is closely related to the changing fashion in men's shirt designs. Before the 17th century, shirt sleeves were simply tied at the cuff with a ribbon. With the introduction of the French cuff in the mid-1600s, cufflinks served a practical purpose of holding the cuffs together. Cufflinks quickly became a popular fashion accessory and object of personal adornment for sophisticated Georgian gentlemen.

The ornate designs of the cufflinks which are found on the Thames foreshore are an insight into men's fashion during the age of elegance in Georgian and Victorian times. Each set of cufflinks tells a unique story about the person who wore them centuries ago. Many of the cufflinks found in the Thames are simple, and indicate that they served a very utilitarian purpose or were owned by a middle-class man who was not able to afford the more extravagant cufflinks. But, some cufflinks were highly decorated, one-off pieces which could have been made by a jeweler for a specific client or commemorative event.

While mudlarking in London, Mark Jennings found an unusual pair of oval-shaped, brass cufflinks (facing page, top left) dating to 1783–1800. A hot air balloon carrying a gondola boat with four ropes is depicted on the cufflinks. Two figures wearing tricorne hats are shown facing each other inside the boat, which is decorated with guidon flags on either side. A lattice work net surrounds the inflated balloon and is connected to a circular ring below the balloon with a series of thick ropes.

The French brothers Joseph-Michel and Jacques-Étienne Montgolfier developed a hot air balloon in Annonay, France, and undertook the first unmanned flight in September 1783, which lasted only 10 minutes. The first balloon flight with human passengers was conducted in Paris in November 1783. Two years later in 1785, Jean-Pierre Blanchard crossed the English Channel in a hot air balloon and landed in England for the first time. Perhaps these cufflinks were made to commemorate this event and celebrate this feat of 18th-century engineering.

A few years ago, Marie-Louise Plum found an unusual pair of cufflinks decorated with a comical portrait (facing page, top right). "When mudlarking, every now and again, you'll have a happy moment of something literally washing up at your feet," says Marie. "This cufflink was found that way, a proper serendipitous find. It is one of my favorite River Thames finds." According to the Museum of London, the brass cufflink dates to 1750–1800 and portrays a caricature bust in the style of Mr. Punch. Often associated with British culture, "Punch and Judy" is a traditional puppet show featuring Mr. Punch and his wife Judy. Performed typically in a red and white stripped, portable booth, the comical show consists of a sequence of short scenes featuring Mr. Punch clowning around with another character who falls victim to his slapstick comedy. Based on a 16th-century Italian precedent, the figure of Mr. Punch made his first recorded appearance in Britain in 1662. Even today, Punch and Judy puppet shows are still popular among British children.

Although they are relatively rare, several mudlarks have found cufflinks depicting the bust of Queen Anne (facing page, bottom). She is easily recognizable because of her plump face and hair styled in a bun. Despite 17 pregnancies, she never produced an heir and was the last monarch in the House of Stuart. Nevertheless, she was a well-respected queen in the early 18th century, and these cufflinks attest to her popularity at that time.

Another interesting circular pair of brass cufflinks (above) depicts a couple locked in a romantic embrace and kissing. The words "LOVE FOR L(OVE)" appear on either side of the two figures. The perimeter is decorated with a twisted rope design. Based on the imagery and words on the cufflinks, they could have been a gift of love which was worn to show one's affection and relationship status.

Dating to AD 1780–1796, a pair of cufflinks (above) was engraved with a bust representing Admiral Samuel Hood or his brother Admiral Alexander Hood. The profile of Admiral Hood faces right with the words "AD HOOD" below. Both Hood brothers became vice admirals in the British navy. Samuel Hood became a full admiral in 1794, and

served during the Seven Years' War and the American Revolutionary War. During the outbreak of the French Revolutionary War, Hood was the commander in chief of the British Navy in the Mediterranean. Georgian gentlemen probably wore cufflinks depicting Hood because he was an accomplished admiral and hero whom they admired.

Mike Walker (aptly nicknamed "Cuffs") has found many beautiful cufflinks in the Thames. One of the best pairs (above) is made of shiny brass which would have originally glistened like gold in the sunlight. The cufflinks are decorated with two cherubs holding a large, articulated crown above a vessel containing two heart shaped flowers. Although the symbolism of the decoration remains a mystery, we can assume a man of distinction wore these cufflinks judging by the delicate design and workmanship.

One of the most valuable pairs of cufflinks from the Thames was unearthed by mudlark Nick Stevens. They are made of real gold and hand-engraved with a flower motif in the center. The cufflinks are also decorated with a foliate design around the perimeter and vertical, inscribed lines surrounding the flower. Connected by an S-shaped loop on the back, these gold cufflinks were surely worn by a wealthy aristocrat or nobleman in the 18th century.

For well-to-do customers, cufflinks were also produced with precious gemstones in gold and silver settings. To imitate the upper-class fashion trends, the middle class wore inexpensive alternatives. Clear glass (below) was cut to sparkle like real diamonds. Cufflink makers also used colored glass (facing page, top) to imitate real gemstones such as emeralds. Sometimes a silver foil was placed behind glass paste stones to accentuate the appearance of the cufflinks. As new techniques were developed, portraits of military heroes or slogans of outspoken politicians were sometimes pressed into the surface of the glass and set into the cufflinks.

Top: Cufflinks with cherubs and crown (PAS). Bottom: Glass cufflinks (Mike Walker). Facing page, top: Green glass cufflinks in the Thames mud (Jason Sandy). Facing page, center: John Wilkes cufflink (Jason Sandy).

While mudlarking along the River Thames in August 2017, I found a small, unassuming cufflink (below) from the 18th century which contained a glass stone set in a decorated pewter setting. Although the glass stone was worn down by tide and time, I thought I could see some letters through the glass. Using a magnifying glass, I could read the words, "Wilkes and Liberty No. 45," which were barely legible through the cloudy surface of the stone. While researching the cufflink, I discovered that John Wilkes (1727-1797) had been a Member of Parliament and was famous both in Britain and America for his fight against government oppression and for his rebellion against the King of England. In 1763, he wrote an essay (No. 45) in The North Britain newspaper which aggressively criticized the king.

King George III was so outraged by the essay that he ordered John Wilkes to be arrested. Fearing for his life, Wilkes fled the country but was imprisoned upon his return. Cries of "Wilkes and Liberty!" were heard across London, as people desperately sought political change. John Wilkes became an icon and symbol of the powerless against the privileged. Georgian men wore cufflinks with the words, "Wilkes and Liberty No. 45," to show their support for his cause.

After Wilkes' death, many children in England and America were named "John Wilkes" in his honor. A century later, the most infamous was the American, John Wilkes Booth, who was a distant relative of the original John Wilkes. Like his British ancestor, John Wilkes Booth was also politically active and voiced his strong opinions. He was a Confederate sympathizer and strongly opposed the abolition of slavery during the American Civil War. Four days after the Confederate army surrendered to the Union army in Virginia, John Wilkes Booth decided to take matters into his own hands. He successfully achieved his ultimate political goal: he assassinated the United States President, Abraham Lincoln, as he watched a performance at Ford's Theater in Washington, D.C. on April 14, 1865. It was a dark day in U.S. history.

MARIE-LOUISE PLUM

I started mudlarking "seriously" in the summer of 2016. Prior to that, I'd been down to the foreshore many times, but despite my existing love of history and exploration, I had never realized that I could become a full-time, 21st-century scavenger of London's sunken corridor. Legendary mudlark, Steve Brooker, took me under his wing and invited me to join his mudlarking and metal detecting club called "Thames and Field." I learned most of what I know now from members of the club, who kindly shared their knowledge and expertise of reading the river, identifying, and preserving finds, which is utterly invaluable.

From a very young age, two things piqued my interest: investigating and collecting. I discovered that the pleasure in "collecting" objects directly relates to the lived experiences of people and places during significant times in history. As the curator and caretaker of found objects, my purpose is the search for answers to their existence. I want to know what links these finds to human history. All around us are discarded, lost, and forgotten items, reminders of the past, ghost-signs, and whispers of what used to be. There are things we look at every day, yet never really see them. I gather their loose ends, learn as much as I can about what they are and why they exist, and share my findings in the form of written work, visual art, and educational videos.

For me, the thrill of mudlarking is twofold. Firstly, the immediate moment of saving a piece of history, sometimes thousands of years old, is

exhilarating. Although stories gleaned from researching social history are my particular interest, I would never be so foolish as to deny the thrill of finding a delicate, silver hammered coin or devotional pilgrim badge. But once that immediate thrill has calmed, the research can begin. For instance, a clue on a button back mark can transport you to raucous adventures of licentiousness and larceny in the annals of the Old Bailey.

My favorite finds are many, but my stand-out find is a large, sandstone block carved with a skull, crossbones, and three sets of initials which I found at the foot of an 18th-century salt mill. The romantic in me hoped the block was a crude grave marker, perhaps for a soul lost at sea or a salt mill worker who met an untimely death. The sandstone block was examined and recorded by the Museum of London Archaeology CitiZan scheme. Although they too would have liked it to be a grave marker, renowned archaeologist Gustav Milne ruled it out due to a lack of evidence.

I know that mudlarking is my lifelong passion. The return is inevitable. On each tide, for one time only, there is a chance to save pieces of history that will otherwise likely never be seen again. Mudlarking is the riverine, one-armed-bandit of London's rich history—sometimes delivering nothing, other times throwing out priceless treasure. I absolutely choose to accept my addiction.

Portraits by Tom Harrison.

For millennia, personal appearance and hygiene have been very important to people around the world, and many went to great lengths to look after themselves. For instance, Roman women wore make-up, perfume, and fashion accessories, and they styled their hair to enhance their appearance. Roman cosmetic sets, make-up stirrers, perfume bottles, brooches, decorated pins, hairpins, and many more fascinating artifacts (above) have been found in London and are on display in the Museum of London. Similar objects recovered from the River Thames demonstrate that Londoners were very conscious about their outward appearance and wanted to make a good impression.

Since at least the Iron Age, mirrors have been used to see one's reflection. Celts living in the Thames Valley owned elaborate, decorative mirrors, and a few of them have been found in the river in West London. One of the most extraordinary Celtic mirrors discov- ered in the Thames (left) is called the "Mayer Mirror" which is named after the Victorian collector, Joseph Mayer, who donated his collection to the World Museum in Liverpool in 1867. The 2,000-year-old mirror is a spectacular work of Celtic art and is decorated in

Top: Roman artifacts in Museum of London (Jason Sandy).
Bottom: Illustration of Celtic mirror decorated in the La Tène style in the National Museums Liverpool (Jason Sandy).

the "La Tène" style. Dating from the 1st century BC–mid 1st century AD, the elliptical shape of the bronze mirror is engraved with a series of delicate circles, lobes, and interlocking, crescent shapes within three larger circular forms. The undulating, curvilinear decoration is accentuated by an incised, cross-hatch pattern comprised of fine, parallel lines. At the base of the mirror, the handle is formed in a teardrop-shaped open loop with raised, circular bands. On the other side of the mirror, the bronze surface was highly polished to create a reflective surface to see one's face. You can just imagine an elegant Celtic woman styling her long, flowing hair using this mirror.

Small, portable mirrors were also popular throughout the centuries. A few years ago, a mudlark discovered an unusual Roman mirror (top left). Dating to the 3rd–4th century AD, this discoidal mirror was cast in pewter and has a central, circular recess in which the reflective mirror would have been fixed. On the front of the mirror, a series of concentric circles radiate from the center. Each band has a different type of decoration including undulating waves, spiral shapes, and pellets. On the back of the 57mm (2 ¼ inch) diameter mirror, a sexfoil flower and pellet motif appears within the central boss. The thin, integral handle of mirror has two spiral, foliate shapes on either side.

Several years ago, Mark Paros discovered a delicate medieval mirror case (top center) which is decorated with an openwork pattern cast in

pewter. It is the lid of a two-disc mirror case, which would have been hinged together with a pewter lug at the base. Within the circular frame of the mirror case which has beveled edges and a pelleted border, the scene of crucifixion is depicted. In the center, Christ appears with arms raised and hands nailed to the cross. On either side of Christ, the haloed figures of Mary and Saint John appear. The sun and crescent moon are illustrated above the cross. The case would have been fitted with a circular piece of glass and tinfoil backing to create the reflective surface. It is possible that this mirror is a pilgrim's souvenir which was purchased at a shrine during a pilgrimage in the Middle Ages.

Miniature mirrors have also been found in the River Thames which are evidence that children owned mirrors as toys. A beautiful example has been cast in an openwork pattern (top right) and dates to the 17th–18th centuries. The mirror has an integral hanging loop with decorative scrollwork at the top. Between the outer and inner rectangular frames, the openwork pattern is comprised of criss-cross decoration and a diamond fret work pattern which resembles twisted rope. A beaded decoration appears along the edge of the inner frame. On the back, there are three fixing points where a reflective backing sheet would have been secured. You can just imagine a child playing with this miniature mirror and imitating their parent.

Top left: Roman pewter mirror (PAS). Top center: Medieval mirror case depicting the crucifixion (Mark Paros). Top right: A child's toy mirror (PAS).

*Roman hairpin on
the Thames foreshore
(Jason Sandy).*

In Londinium, Roman women wore their hair in braided buns and used decorative bone pins with ornate designs to secure their hair in place. Over the years, numerous hairpins (above) have been found on the foreshore by mudlarks. Carved by hand from animal bones, the finials of the pins have various geometric shapes and styles.

One of my best-ever finds from the Thames is an extraordinary hand-carved bone hairpin (facing page) depicting the bust of a Roman woman with an extremely large coiffure. The nearly 2,000-year-old hairpin provides a unique glimpse into Roman hairstyles of the Flavian period (AD 69–96) when it was fashionable for women to wear their hair in high false curls. Based on the hairstyle illustrated on the pin, the Museum of London has dated the hairpin to AD 43–100. I donated it to the Museum of London where it is now on permanent display in the Roman gallery.

Several years ago, Jason Davey found an exquisite Roman hairpin (left) carved from African ivory in the shape of an elephant. Two abstract birds are depicted under-

neath a thick plinth on which the elephant is walking. These exquisite, decorative hairpins would have been worn to display a woman's wealth and social status.

For millennia, people have been styling their hair with combs. Along the Thames foreshore, mudlarks have found a wide variety of combs from the medieval and post-medieval periods made from ivory, bone, and boxwood. One of the oldest and most complete examples is a medieval comb (right) dating to AD 1200—1500 found by Peter Olivant.

Carved by hand from a single piece of ivory, this comb has a lentoid cross-section with fine teeth on one side and larger teeth on the other side. After centuries lying on the bottom of the Thames, it's amazing that the comb has survived unbroken in the turbulent river currents.

A few years ago, I discovered a delicate, fine-toothed Tudor comb (below) which was hand-carved from animal bone. In the 16th century, almost everyone was plagued with lice and nits (lice eggs) in their hair. The fine teeth of this comb were used to carefully remove the small pests.

Top left: Various Roman bone hairpins (PAS). Middle left: Roman hairpin depicting an elephant (PAS).
Top right: Medieval ivory comb (PAS). Bottom right: Tudor bone comb (Jason Sandy).

In 1545, King Henry VIII's ship called the *Mary Rose* sank during a battle off the coast of Portsmouth, and it was recovered in 1982. On board, 82 Tudor nit combs were found which the sailors had owned. Under a microscope, dead lice are still visible between the comb's teeth. Based on the nit comb's original purpose, the phrases "go over with a fine-toothed comb" and "nit-picking" became common expressions in the English language that are still used today.

From around 1650 until 1800, men and women would cut their hair short and wear a periwig (left) to avoid pesky head lice. It was fashionable to style the wigs with curls and cover the hair in a white powder consisting of a mixture of wheat, cornflour, highly refined starch, and even plaster of Paris. Similar to modern day hair curlers, the hair was wrapped around pre-heated wig curlers, left overnight, removed in the morning, and styled to create an impressive appearance. Wig curlers were made from the same fine, white clay used to produce clay pipes. I have found many Georgian wig curlers (below left) on the Thames foreshore, although most of them are broken. Dating to the 18th century, several complete wig curlers (below right) have been found by Malcolm Russell.

Since the beginning of time, men have suffered from hair loss and baldness. In the 19th century, different remedies and creative cures for baldness were developed. While mudlarking, David Hodgson discovered two lids from Victorian porcelain pots (top right) which had contained bear's grease. The artwork on one of the lids depicts the capture of a Russian bear, and the words, "GENUINE BEARS GREASE," appear on the other lid. This ointment was produced from the fat of furry Russian brown bears, which was believed to strengthen and stimulate human hair growth. Out of desperation, Victorian men would rub the greasy substance on their hairless scalps, hoping to magically cure their baldness.

Sarah Newton found a Victorian glass bottle (right) in the Thames with the molded lettering, "HARLENE FOR THE HAIR." A 19th-century advertisement (below) for the product claims it is a miraculous remedy for all hair ailments and promotes the growth of beards and mustaches, restores grey hair to its natural color, removes dandruff, and cures weak and thin eyelashes.

Top left: Painting of King George II, 1727 (Christian Friedrich Zincke). Bottom far left: Georgian wig curler in the Thames (Jason Sandy). Bottom left: Collection of clay wig curlers (Malcolm Russell). Top right: Victorian bear's grease lids (David Hodgson). Middle right: Victorian glass bottle from Harlene (Sarah Newton). Bottom right: 19th-century advertisement for Harlene.

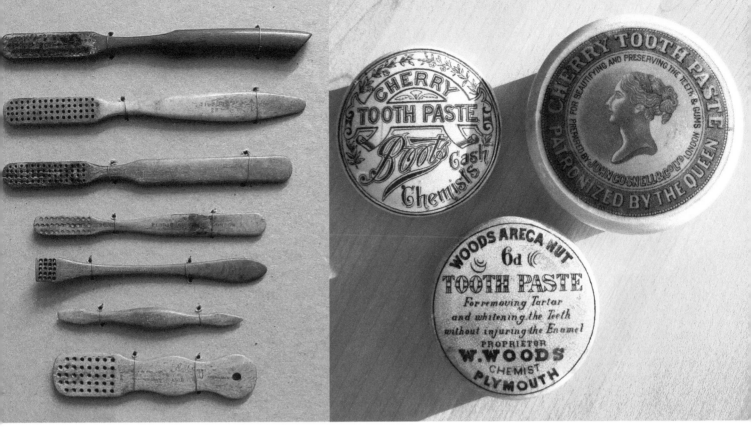

Based on the number of Victorian toothbrushes recovered from the Thames foreshore, we know that Londoners cared about the appearance of their teeth in the 19th century. Mudlarks Candace Kuss and David Hodgson have collected many different styles of 19th-century toothbrushes (top left and right) carved from animal bone. The bristles would have been made of horse or boar hair.

Numerous types of lids from 19th-century pots of toothpaste (top right) have been discovered in the river by Sarah Newton. Cherry was a popular flavor of toothpaste, and was even endorsed by Queen Victoria. According to the label, cherry toothpaste could be used for "BEAUTIFYING AND PRESERVING THE TEETH & GUMS." The inscription on another porcelain lid says: "WOODS ARECA NUT TOOTH PASTE, For removing Tartar and whitening the Teeth without removing the Enamel." These 19th-century toothbrushes and toothpaste lids prove that people cared about dental hygiene and were actively brushing their teeth.

If Victorians did lose an adult tooth, they went to the dentist to have a replacement fitted to maintain their perfect smile. David Hodgson has found many false teeth (below right) in the river dating to the 19th–early 20th centuries. He also retrieved two real teeth fixed to a gold plate (bottom right), which must have been owned by a wealthy Londoner. The dentures were engineered to fit comfortably in the mouth, and the authentic appearance of the false teeth proves that Victorians went to great lengths to conceal their tooth loss. I can imagine that the people who accidentally dropped these false teeth in the river were extremely embarrassed as they walked home with a toothless smile.

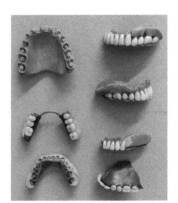

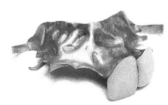

Top left: Bone toothbrushes in various shapes and sizes (David Hodgson). Center: Victorian bone toothbrushes (Candace Kuss). Top right: Victorian toothpaste lids (Sarah Newton). Middle right: Victorian false teeth (David Hodgson). Bottom right: Real human teeth fixed to gold plate (David Hodgson).

Since I was a kid, I have owned a Swiss army knife. I love it because it's a portable, versatile tool containing all different types of practical gadgets such as a toothpick, nail file, nail cleaner, tweezers, scissors, etc. Portable cosmetic and manicure sets have been popular since the Iron Age, and exquisite Roman cosmetic sets are on display in the Museum of London.

A few years ago, John Higginbotham discovered a beautiful, silver manicure set (top left) in the Thames. Dating to the 17th century, the small tools are in the shape of a naked female body. The four implements are suspended from a silver ring at the top and are fixed together with a bracket and single lug so the tools can pivot and be used individually. The cosmetic set consists of an ear scoop, toothpick, and nail cleaner.

Dating to the late post-medieval period, a manicure set made of bone (top right) was found by a mudlark on the south side of the river. Three pivoting implements are attached to an outer frame with an iron pin. They consist of a nail file, nail cleaner, and broken ear scoop.

Long before cotton buds and Q-tips existed, people used small scoops to remove the wax from their ears. I have found several medieval ear scoops (middle left) that have a very simple design. They are formed from twisted, brass wire with a loop at the end for removing ear wax. The projecting wire at the base could be used as a toothpick. These types of simple ear scoops were easily and cheaply produced in quantity, similar to inexpensive cotton buds today.

In the 16th century, the Tudors produced highly ornate ear scoops decorated with zoomorphic patterns. One of the finest examples in the Museum of London is carved from bone into the shape of an elaborate seahorse. A few zoomorphic ear scoops have been recovered from the river. Caroline Nunneley discovered the top of a stunning 16th-century ear scoop resembling a beautiful unicorn (bottom left). Although the horn and ear scoop are now missing, the head of the unicorn

Top left: 17th-century silver manicure set (PAS). Top right: Bone manicure set (PAS). Middle left: Medieval, brass twisted wire ear scoops (Jason Sandy). Bottom left: Tudor ear scoop in the shape of a unicorn (PAS).

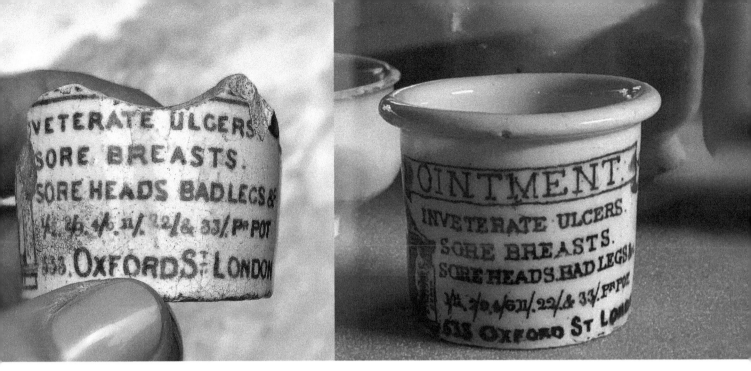

is beautifully carved from an animal bone. The circular eyes are formed with rings and dots, and a long beard extends from the unicorn's chin below the mouth and nostrils. Four diagonally incised lines on either side of the neck represent a mane.

In the 19th century, personal health and well-being were very important to Londoners. The empty jars and lids found in the River Thames are evidence of the wide variety of medicinal products which were in use in Victorian times. At home, Londoners had ointments for everything. Candace Kuss found a tantalizing fragment of a Victorian ointment pot (top left), and I have seen a complete one of these pots in the Museum of London archive (top right). According to the inscription on the pot, the ointment was for "inveterate ulcers, sore breasts, sore heads, and bad legs." It sounds like a cure-all cream!

In February 2022, Michal Knap discovered a beautiful, early 20th-century ointment pot lid (right). The ointment was produced by Thomas Holloway to treat gout, rheumatism, ulcers, and bruises. On the lid, an image depicts a classical scene of Hygieia (goddess of health, cleanliness, and hygiene) and her brother, Telesphorus, carrying a banner listing the business address and price of the ointment.

Since London was founded by the Romans nearly 2,000 years ago, it has attracted people from all over the globe. The small trading post

developed into one of the largest, most influential cities in the world. As people lived in close proximity to each other in the city, they were conscious about their outward appearance and personal hygiene. They wanted to look good and make the right impression in public. Mirrors, hairpins, combs, wig curlers, remedies for baldness, toothbrushes, toothpaste lids, cosmetic sets, ear scoops, ointment pots, and many other historical artifacts recovered by mudlarks from the River Thames reveal the importance of personal appearance, hygiene, health, and well-being to Londoners throughout the ages.

Top:: Victorian ointment pots (Candace Kuss and Jason Sandy).
Bottom right: Holloway's ointment pot lid (Michal Knap).

DAVID HODGSON

When I was very young, my grandfather took me to museums, and I became very interested in our past. I assembled a large collection of items about the history of Lancaster, my hometown. Many people gave me old photos and leaflets to add to it. In 2013, I started mudlarking after I saw people on the Thames foreshore. I asked what they were doing and started talking to them.

For me, the thrill of mudlarking is finding items that have been lost for many centuries or years and discovering and unlocking the history about the items. Every single day is a different day, and you never know what you may find.

I am just over 4 foot 5 inches tall, and my height does give me a bit of an advantage in comparison to other mudlarks. I don't have to bend down too much like other people who are normal height. Some of them end up having back problems from bending over too much, so my height is an advantage.

My best mudlarking experience was finding a large Palaeolithic hand axe, lying halfway up the foreshore among a pile of house bricks and other debris. It's definitely my favorite find. The Museum of London wanted to acquire the rare hand axe, but I was allowed to keep it. However, I have donated other artifacts to the museum. My most curious find is a Victorian solid gold dental palate with real human teeth.

My scariest experience was at Limehouse. The tide was coming in, and I suddenly heard a rumble behind me. Without warning, a sluice opened and blocked my exit from the foreshore. My only way out was to jump over the fast-moving water. I took a big leap and just managed to clear the water which was cascading out. I smacked my right hand against the wall, but I was very relieved I'd made it!

I like to share my knowledge because it helps other people who are beginners to identify their finds. I was very proud to be asked to display my collection at the mudlarking exhibition in Chiswick in 2021 and London's Roman Amphitheatre in Guildhall Art Gallery in 2022. Using my art skills, I made a great effort to display my artifacts, and people were very interested to learn about them.

I also design and make costumes which are used at Comic-Con, along with a group that helps to raise money for UNICEF and other charities. The most popular costume I have designed and made with help of a friend is an Ewok costume, which took six and a half months to produce. I used to work as an extra on different film sets with an agency called 2020. Over the years, I have met many celebrities. The last film I worked on was *Notting Hill* with Julia Roberts and Hugh Grant.

Over the years while mudlarking, I have made many good friends such as Christine, Monika, Jason, and many more. The mudlarking community all has the same interests as I do. They love history and finding items from the past. That's the glue which bonds us together!

Portraits by Tom Harrison.

AT THE DINNER TABLE

Roman oil lamp with lion found by Alan Suttie (Stuart Wyatt).

The Thames is flowing with stories about the people who lived and worked along its banks. Throughout the ages, they have accidentally lost or purposely discarded thousands of domestic items in the river. Spoons, knives, forks, plates, bowls, jugs, tankards, lamps, candlesticks, and many other household objects have been recovered from the Thames by mudlarks. Some people may consider these objects to be mundane and worthless, but the sheer volume of these artifacts shows us how people lived and what they used on a daily basis in their homes centuries ago.

Until electricity became readily available in the 20th century, most homes were lit with lamps or candlelight. In Roman London, people used small oil lamps to illuminate their houses. Several mudlarks, including a ten-year-old boy, have found complete Roman oil lamps on the Thames foreshore.

One of the most extraordinary lamps was discovered by Alan Suttie. After a business meeting in the City of London, he wandered down to the foreshore dressed in a suit and tie—definitely not his usual mudlarking attire. Alan was not expecting to find anything until he spotted a mysterious red object (facing page) lying on the exposed riverbed. To his surprise, it was a highly decorated Roman oil lamp which had been dropped in the river between AD 300–410. Just imagine, the last person to touch this lamp lived in Roman Londinium around 1,700 years ago and probably used this lamp to illuminate their home. It is a rare example of a North African red slip ceramic oil lamp depicting a running lion which symbolizes Christianity. Although these lamps are relatively common in other parts of the Roman empire, this is an unusual lamp to be found in Britain because of its late date and Christian iconography.

In the Middle Ages, candles became a more common way to illuminate houses. A beautiful medieval candlestick (left) was found by John Higginbotham in the Thames. Dating to the 1250–1300, it is a pewter candle holder which was possibly sold as a souvenir to a medieval pilgrim. The circular base is supported by three feet which resemble lion's paws. In the center of the base, there is a cylindrical socket where the candle would have been inserted. The base is decorated with an outer and inner border, formed by alternating pellet and trefoil motifs. Written in medieval French, there is an inscription which states, "May God protect all those who are here and those who made me." You can just imagine a group of pilgrims gathered around the warm glow of the candle as they told stories about their adventures en route to the shrine of a patron saint.

Several years ago, Mark Paros also discovered a rare medieval candle holder (right) made of Surrey borderware pottery. Dating to around AD 1500, it could have been used for a candlelit dinner in a medieval household. It is astounding that this fragile candlestick laid at the bottom of the River Thames for over 500 years, and it's still complete.

As I was wading through the shallow water in front of large historic houses along the Thames in West London in 2020, I spotted an unusual object (below right) submerged under the water. As I picked it up, I couldn't believe it was a candle holder from the 16th–17th centuries. It is made of green-glazed borderware which was typical in Tudor times. I wonder what books were read by its candlelight, and what games were enthusiastically played beside it after dark.

Bottom left: Medieval pewter candle holder (PAS). Middle right: Medieval candlestick (Jason Sandy). Bottom right: 16th–17th-century candlestick (Jason Sandy).

Shortly after a winter storm ripped through London in February 2022, I spotted a knife handle protruding from the surface of the exposed riverbed. I slowly dislodged and wiggled it loose. It was a satisfying experience as the long blade (above) slithered out of the mud. It is very rare to find a complete, old knife. Normally, the iron blade has rusted away years ago. According to knife expert Graham duHeaume, it is a table knife dating to 1750–1775. You can just imagine someone using this knife while cutting a delicious slab of beef carved from a Sunday roast. Based on the maker's mark on the blade, Graham was able identify the maker of the knife. According to historic records, Phillip Tyas from Sheffield made this knife around 1774.

Between 1970 and 1986, Graham assembled an impressive collection of over 860 knives, which were all recovered from the Thames foreshore. Some of Graham's most beautifully preserved knives (bottom left) are from the late 15th and 16th centuries. Five knives are scale tang, and the bottom two are whittle tang knives. They all have single-sided blades, and their handles were carved from wood or bone. The ends of the knives have decorative finials and knops. I especially like the horse hoof knop and finials in the shape of a crown and fleur-de-lis. All of these knives were produced for domestic use.

Some of Graham's 17th-century knives (bottom center) have beautifully decorated brass and bone handles carved with a diamond-shaped pattern, incised spirals, and circular rings. Each of these knives has a cutler's mark on the blade which can help identify the maker of the knife. The most common marks are in the shape of a star, crescent, fleur-de-lis, crown, rose, and sword.

In 2020, Graham generously donated his knife collection to the Worshipful Company of Cutlers, which is an ancient livery company in the City of London that received its Royal Charter from King Henry V in 1416. This is the ultimate goal of mudlarking—to donate an outstanding collection of historical artifacts to an institution which will permanently display the collection for educational purposes and preserve it for future generations.

Along with his unparalleled collection of knives, Graham has also found some exquisite, post-medieval forks (bottom right) in the Thames.

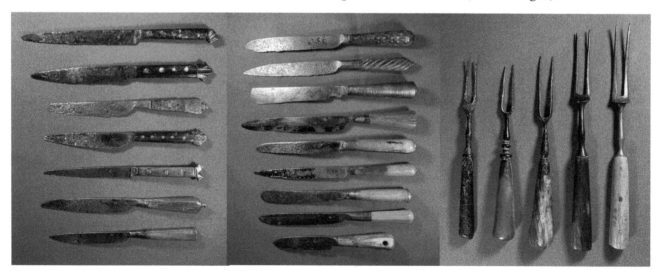

Top left: Georgian knife (Jason Sandy). Bottom left: Medieval knives (Jason Sandy). Bottom center: Post-medieval knives (Jason Sandy). Bottom right: Post-medieval forks found by Graham duHeaume (Jason Sandy).

It is believed that the Romans originally invented the first fork, but it wasn't until the 18th century that it became commonplace to use a fork when eating. On land, the bone and timber handles of the forks normally don't survive. But, in the water-logged conditions of the Thames, these delicate handles have been perfectly preserved.

Graham has also discovered several complete spoons (above) while mudlarking. Four of the pewter spoons are from the 16th century and are decorated with a ball knop, baluster knop, seal knop, and diamond knop. A 17th-century slip top spoon and a brass trifid Cromwellian spoon from circa 1680 are also part of Graham's collection. You can imagine a sailor eating his morning porridge with one of these spoons as he watched the sun rise over the Thames. Distracted by the passing ships and buzzing activity along the riverfront, he possibly dropped the spoon in the river accidentally.

Portrait spoons have also been retrieved by mudlarks from the river. A beautiful, complete example (left) dates to the early 18th century. The top of the trifid-formed spoon portrays Queen Anne, who ruled Britain and Ireland from 1702–1714. On either side of her portrait, two amorini (chubby cupids) hold a crown which is now missing above her head. Below Anne's portrait, scroll and vine decoration appear on the handle of the spoon along with the initials, "T*P," which is possibly the maker's mark. The back of the elongated spoon bowl is decorated with an ornate lacework of coiled vines with leaves. With over 30 types known, Queen Anne was the most popular monarch depicted on royal portrait spoons.

As Steve Brooker was mudlarking, he looked down and spotted a head popping out of the sand. To his surprise, it was an apostle spoon made of pewter. On the spoon terminal, a saint is depicted within an architectural frame. A column on either side of the saint supports a tiled roof structure with a cockerel perched on top. The bearded saint has articulated facial features and is wearing a loose robe. Beginning in the 16th-century, apostle spoons gained popularity, and different types of these spoons were made up until the early 20th century.

One of Mark Paros' favorite finds in his collection is a nearly complete 15th-century German stoneware jug (right). This vessel has a pale brown buff fabric and would have been used as a drinking jug. Frozen in time, the fingerprints of the German potter are still visible in the thumbed base of the jug. It's quite exhilarating to think that the potter pressed his fingers into the wet clay over 500 years ago and left delicate fingerprints which would travel in time for us to see today. It is quite literally a tangible connection with history!

Top left: 16th–17th-century spoons (Graham duHeaume). Bottom left: Queen Anne portrait spoon (PAS). Bottom right: 15th-century drinking jug (Jason Sandy).

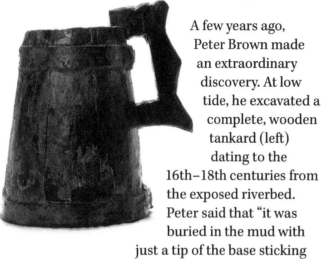

A few years ago, Peter Brown made an extraordinary discovery. At low tide, he excavated a complete, wooden tankard (left) dating to the 16th–18th centuries from the exposed riverbed. Peter said that "it was buried in the mud with just a tip of the base sticking out. I don't really know what made me investigate further as I had walked past it. I went back, and it was a bit of a surprise when I dug it out." The next day he took it to the Museum of London for conservation. The tankard is made of an oak stave construction and held together with two iron bands which are riveted. Made of beech, the large handle has been shaped to create a decorative profile. On the base of the tankard, the letters "R H" have been carved into the wood. They could be the initials of the former owner. According to the Museum of London, "objects of this type and date are exceptionally rare, and this vessel is in a very good state of preservation. So far it is the only one of its kind from London soil."

When Mark Paros discovered a 15th-century green glazed bowl (right), it was an unrecorded type of medieval pottery. He found it submerged below the water and resting against a timber where he had recovered two other pots. Using his years of experience, Mark was able to carefully restore the medieval bowl. The outside of the bowl is not glazed and has a brown buff surface. Inside the bowl and around the rim, a thick green glaze has been applied.

Over the years, mudlarks have found many handles from 17th-century tin-glazed porringers. Their curvilinear, openwork patterns are simply beautiful. However, it is very rare to find a complete porringer. Astoundingly, Nick Stevens discovered a ceramic porringer in two pieces and was able to carefully put it back together seamlessly. In the 17th-century, porringers were used as an all-purpose bowl for eating hearty soups, stews, and porridge.

Every day, mudlarks find broken pieces of pottery on the foreshore. One of the most common types of pottery is called Staffordshire combed slipware. Against the dark grey and brown tones of the foreshore environment, it is relatively easy to spot these bright yellow sherds of pottery. Some of the pieces I have found (above) are very large. Throughout the 17th and 18th centuries, this type of pottery was made of coarse earthenware to which a yellow "slip" (thin layer of liquid clay) was applied before being dipped into a clear lead glaze and fired. The unique decoration was achieved by trailing thin lines of a brown slip onto the yellow slip. Before the slips dried, a special combed tool was pulled perpendicularly to the lines to create the zigzag effect which resembles a feather-topped Bakewell tart. The rims of the

Top left: 16th–18th-century wooden tankard (PAS). Bottom left: Medieval bowl (Jason Sandy).
Above right: 17th–18th-century Staffordshire combed slipware (Jason Sandy).

plates were further embellished with a "piecrust" or crenelated edge which was made by hand or impressed with a mold. This type of pottery was used for baking, food preparation, and serving food at the table.

Because of the strong currents of the Thames, it is very rare to find complete plates in the river. While I was nightlarking in September 2021, I spotted an unbroken plate (right) that washed up on shore.

Queen Elizabeth II and the Duke of Edinburgh are depicted together below the dates 1952 and 1977. Representing a relatively recent moment in British history, this special plate had been made to commemorate the Silver Jubilee (25th anniversary) of the Queen's reign in 1977. It's amazing the plate didn't break when it was dropped in the river.

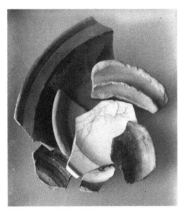

Mudlark and artist Mark Sowden has collected many large pieces of broken plates and bowls (left). He has developed an innovative and creative way of "reassembling" broken pieces of pottery so they are complete again. By rotating broken sherds on a turntable and using a long exposure setting on his camera, Mark produces photographs (right) of the complete dishes and bowls.

"I only use pottery pieces that have a whole profile (from base to rim) for this process, as this gives a sense of the original form in its entirety. They are fragments of plates and bowls that were originally made on a potter's wheel. I wanted to find out if I could re-form them photographically by turning them again on another wheel. The results

are more evocations than reconstructions. Detail other than concentric lines disappear," explains Mark. It is an ingenious way to bring history alive and make something broken appear complete. Mark has entitled his project, "Turnings."

Whether it's broken pieces of pottery or complete spoons, forks, knives, and other kitchen utensils, these domestic objects provide a wonderfully authentic insight into the daily lives of Londoners throughout the ages. A few years ago, I took my family to enjoy a medieval dinner in a crypt near the Tower of London. We dressed up in historic costumes and were entertained by musicians and actors who took us back in time in an immersive experience. During the delicious feast by candlelight, we used forks, knives, spoons, and tankards which were similar to those found in the river by mudlarks. Since we unfortunately cannot time travel, the medieval dinner and entertainment were the next best thing.

Top left: Queen's Silver Jubilee commemorative plate (Jason Sandy). Middle left: Roman, medieval, and post-medieval pottery sherds (Mark Sowden). Middle right: Roman bowl turning (Mark Sowden). Bottom right: Pancheon bowl turning (Mark Sowden).

GRAHAM DUHEAUME

My history lessons at school were not at all exciting. As with most young children in the 1950s, learning about the Corn Laws and Acts of Parliament held no magic for me. However, I was an avid listener to the "Children's Hour" on the radio in those days. During one particular broadcast, a gentleman recalled how he wandered along the north bank of the Thames in the City of London, picking up small reminders of life on the river hundreds of years ago. He found clay pipes, pot sherds, pins, coins, buttons, thimbles, and many other objects. I believe his name was Ivor Noël Hume, the former director of the Guildhall Museum, London Museum, and Colonial Williamsburg in USA. It wasn't until a good few years later, while I was working at the Natural History Museum in London, that I was reminded of this broadcast which prompted me to try my luck on the river.

Early one Sunday morning in 1970, I arrived at Queenhithe Dock full of expectations, just as the tide was receding. I wasn't disappointed! Of course, Ivor was right. Like he mentioned in the early radio broadcast, I came home with pipe stems and bowls, pins, pot sherds, and also a knife from the 17th century. The blade was broken, but it had a cutler's mark. I was heady with excitement and wanted more. That was the start of what I call "Collectomania Thame-sitis"—a pleasant malady of which there is no cure.

I started mudlarking with a shovel. I didn't have a metal detector in the early days—I got one later. I used to work in tandem with a friend, Martin Brendell, who also worked at the museum. I often went during lunchtime for a quick eyeball. I remember with pleasure my lunchtime forays with Simon Moore. There were many other folk on the foreshore who contributed in some way or another to the advancement of knowledge relating to life on the river. My mudlarking experiences in those days certainly enhanced my appreciation of history, especially that of London.

I don't really have a favorite find. To me, all the objects are exciting reminders of bygone ages. Having worked at a museum which is one large collection, it's not surprising that the environment I was in encouraged my desire to be a collector. As I always say, most folk don't actually start to collect a particular item. It's only when you realize you've got more of one item than the others, you think oh! I've got a collection. During my time on the foreshore, I found that as I was increasing my collection, I noticed I had more knives than other pieces.

It eventually led me in 2020 to donate my collection of over 860 knives, ranging from the medieval period to the 18th century, to the Worshipful Company of Cutlers in London. They are now on permanent display within the historic Cutler's Hall. In 2021, I became an "Honorary Freeman" of this exclusive organization, which is a true honor. It pleases me to think I have added an appreciable amount, especially to the world of cutlery. I think that the knives I have donated will improve the understanding of Cutlers' marks in general.

Portraits by Tom Harrison.

COINS,
TOKENS, AND
FORGERIES

While I was mudlarking one morning in April 2018, I spotted a stunning 17th-century trader's token along the water's edge. I wanted to photograph it in situ so I could post the token on Instagram. As I pulled out my smartphone to take a photo, a Thames Clipper boat roared past me, creating a large wave. I was so focused on taking the photo that I didn't realize the wave was headed my way. With my back to the river, I snapped one photo before the wall of water unexpectedly hit me from behind, knocking me over. I was stunned and shocked as the water quickly retreated, sweeping my trader's token into the river. I scrambled to find it, but the tide was coming in too quickly.

I was absolutely devastated! Determined to find the lost token, I decided to return to the spot at the next low tide around 11 PM even though I had to go to work the next morning. I tucked my kids into bed and read them a bedtime story before kissing my wife goodbye and leaving the house. I had to travel almost an hour from home to continue my search.

When I arrived back on the deserted foreshore, it was pitch black and eerily quiet. I was alone and unnerved. Strange sounds in the darkness startled me. I just wanted to find the token and return home as soon as possible. Unfortunately, I had forgotten to charge my head lamp because I hadn't plan to go night-

larking. So, I was crawling on my hands and knees searching the exposed riverbed with the dim light from my smartphone. The situation seemed hopeless as I carefully combed the area where I had lost the coin. As I turned over a rock, I couldn't believe my eyes.

I struck gold! After six years of mudlarking, I finally found my first gold coin (top). I was shaking with excitement as I held the precious coin in my hand. It's a gold 1/3 Guinea coin from King George III (left) dated 1803. I still can't believe it. Fortunately, I was in the right place at the right time. I would not have gone mudlarking that night if I had not lost the trader's token hours earlier. It's a real story of serendipity.

Facing page: Coin collection from the Thames (Jason Sandy). Top: Gold coin found while nightlarking (Jason Sandy). Bottom: King George III gold 1/3 guinea dated 1803 (Jason Sandy).

Although gold coins are extremely rare, some veteran mudlarks have found several of them in the Thames. In 2001, Tim Miller discovered a Roman gold coin (above) in mint condition. It is an aureus coin with the bust of Roman emperor Diocletian, who reigned from AD 284–305. On the back of the coin, Jupiter is depicted holding a thunderbolt in one hand and a scepter in the other. In the 3rd century AD, this coin was worth 25 silver denarii. Whoever dropped this coin in the Thames must have been absolutely horrified to have lost such a valuable coin.

Several years ago, Tim found a stunning 16th-century gold hammered coin (above) from the French king, Francis I, who reigned from 1515 until his death in 1547. This extraordinary coin is made of 24 carat gold and is called a "Ecu d'or au soleil du Dauphiné." On the front of the coin, dolphins and groups of fleur-de-lis are shown within a circle subdivided into quadrants (the arms of the Dauphiné) beneath a radiant sun. On the back, a cross is formed with a quatrefoil in the center and fleur-de-lis at the ends. The Latin inscription declares: "Christ conquers, Christ reigns, Christ commands."

Tim also found a gold "crown" coin (top right) from King James I dating to 1615–1616. James is shown wearing a crown on the front of the coin

that was minted at the Tower of London. The British royal coat of arms is illustrated on the back, along with the Latin inscription which proclaims: "Henry united the roses, but James unites the kingdoms." This refers to Henry Tudor, who united the House of Lancaster (red rose) with the House of York (white rose) at the end of the Wars of the Roses in 15th century. Born in Scotland and raised by his mother Mary, Queen of Scots, James united the kingdoms of England, Scotland, and Ireland when he became king in 1603 after the death of Queen Elizabeth I.

Because gold coins were so valuable, their weight was checked to ensure they had not been clipped or were underweight. The coins were literally "worth their weight in gold." To verify that gold coins were not below their legal weight limit, square pieces of brass were produced in the 16th century to weigh the same as the gold coin equivalent. On a small scale, the gold coin was weighed in comparison to the brass coin weight.

A few years ago, Simon Bourne discovered a square coin weight (below) dated 1576, which depicts a horse and rider who is holding a sword above his head, charging into battle. A cross and four pellets appear on his breastplate. On the back of the coin weight, an upright hand symbolizing the city of Antwerp is illustrated with the numbers and letters

Top left: Diocletian gold aureus coin (Tim Miller). Middle left: King Francis I gold medieval coin (Tim Miller). Top right: King James I gold crown coin, Tim Miller. Bottom left: 16th-century coin weight (PAS).

"7 K" and "6 I" on either side of the hand. "K I" are the initials of the maker, and the six-pointed star under the hand indicates that he was appointed by the king. This coin weight was used in the 16th century to weigh a "Gouden Rijder" (Golden Rider) coin from the Low Countries.

Special wooden cases were made to carry coin weights along with small scales. Over a period of a few months, John Mills unearthed several brass coin weights in a small area of the exposed riverbed. Perhaps someone dropped their coin weight case in the Thames. The wood disintegrated over time, leaving a cluster of coin weights on the riverbed. Most of the weights were made in either Britain or Antwerp. One of the finest examples John found (above) shows King Henry VIII seated on a throne and holding an orb and scepter. On the back of the coin weight, a crown is depicted above the letters "XX / S." It was used to measure the weight of a gold sovereign coin from Henry VIII that was worth 20 shillings.

Over the years, mudlarks have found a wide variety of fascinating coins ranging from Celtic to modern times. Although several Potin coins from the Iron Age have been recovered from the river, only a few gold staters have been discovered in the Thames. Oliver Muranyi-Clark unearthed a rare gold quarter stater (above) from King Cunobelin of the Catuvellauni tribe. Between the letters CA and MV, an ear of wheat is depicted on the front of the coin. A rearing horse, long leaf, and the letters CVN appear on the back.

One of the oldest Roman coins from the River Thames (below) was discovered by Nicole Lanoue. It is a silver denarius from Caecilia Metellus dating to 130 BC. On the front, the helmeted head of Roma is facing right with a star beneath her chin. Jupiter is shown holding a branch and thunderbolt while driving a quadriga (chariot pulled by four horses) on the back of this ancient coin. The word "ROMA" appears in the exergue.

Top left: King Henry VIII coin weight (John Mills). Top right: King Cunobelin gold quarter stater (PAS). Bottom: Caecilia Metellus silver denarius (Nicole Lanoue).

Counterfeit nummus of Diocletian (Jon Attenborough).

During the past ten years, I have found many Roman coins in the Thames. On Father's Day in 2014, my kids took me mudlarking as a special treat. To my surprise, I discovered a large Roman coin (facing page) lying on the surface of the exposed riverbed. Produced in the 3rd century AD, the bust of Emperor Diocletian is depicted on the front, and a "genius" (a guardian angel in Roman religion) with a cornucopia in the left hand and patera in the right hand appears on the back of the coin. Although it looks like an officially minted coin, it is a contemporary copy of a bronze nummus coin. Counterfeiting and forging coins were rife in Roman times.

One of the most interesting artifacts I ever found in the river is a forger's mold (above) for making counterfeit Roman coins. The clay mold was used to produce Severus Alexander denarii coins when he reigned between AD 222–235. It is a double-sided, disc-shaped mold which was produced by pressing both sides of an authentic coin into a wet clay disc, leaving a concave imprint on the front and back. After creating several of these impressions in separate round discs and air drying them, the discs were stacked, and molten metal was poured into the concave voids between the molds. Once cooled, the molds were broken apart to retrieve the freshly, copied coins. I can imagine that a forger tossed this mold into the Thames to destroy the evidence and escape prosecution for counterfeiting coins.

By the 5th century AD, London had been abandoned by the Romans, and the Anglo-Saxons began arriving in the 7th century. They established a small village called Lundenwic, which became one of the greatest international trading centers of the Anglo-Saxons in Europe.

To facilitate commerce, Anglo-Saxons began producing silver pennies in the 8th century by hammering a blank disc of silver between two dies to impress a design into the coin. While mudlarking one afternoon in 2012 with her husband John and friends, Stephanie Mills discovered a Saxon penny (above) in extraordinary condition. John describes their experience: "I saw her look at something in her hand. In a flash, she stood upright and started walking hurriedly towards us. A certain smile on her face told me she had found something nice. I was stunned with what I saw as she placed a small silver disc in the palm of my hand. When flipping it over, I found myself staring at a beautiful, diademed bust. I turned the air blue with jubilation at the realization we had found our first Saxon penny!" Produced around AD 1009–1017, it is a small cross penny of Aethelred II and is the first coin ever to be recorded in the UK from the moneyer Osgar in Bedford.

Anglo-Saxons also developed silver coinage called "sceattas." Often decorated with abstract animals and shapes, these small coins were beautiful works of art. Although sceattas are very rare, some mudlarks have found wonderful examples in the Thames. In 2021, Mark Vasco Iglesias picked up a Saxon sceat (right) from King Eadberht of Northumbria. Produced in the 8th century, the king is depicted facing right

towards a long cross pommeé. On the back of the coin, there is a figure standing in a crescent boat wearing a cynehelm and pelleted robe, holding a long cross pommeé in his right hand and a bird of prey in his left hand.

Top left: Roman forger's coin mold (Jason Sandy). Top right: Saxon silver penny from Aethelred II (John Mills). Bottom right: King Eadberht silver sceat (Mark Vasco Iglesias).

In 2019, Kevin James Dyer found a stunning Saxon silver sceat (top left) dating to AD 680–710. On the front, a diademed head is facing right within a pelleted, circular border. An abstract dove is shown above a cross with two annulets on either side.

A few years ago, Tobias Neto found a very unusual Iranian coin (second from top left) in the River Thames. Dating to AD 590–628, it is a silver drachm of Khosrow II, the Sasanian king in Iran. The crowned bust of Khosrow II is surrounded by Zoroastrian astrological symbols, stars, and crescents around perimeter of the coin. Within a series of concentric circles, a holy fire-altar is flanked by two attendants on the back of the coin. It is possible that Anglo-Saxons or Vikings brought this coin to London before it was lost in the river. They had a vast network of trade routes around Europe extending to the Middle East.

Over the past forty years, mudlarks have found hundreds of medieval silver hammered coins, including shillings, groats (third from top left), sixpence, pennies, half pennies, and farthings. Many of the coins were produced in the Royal Mint, which was located in the Tower of London castle along the River Thames. Several silver hammered coins have been recovered from the river in mint condition.

Because the silver coins were very valuable, they were sometimes forged illegally. During the weekend of February 9–10, 1980, three mudlarks discovered the largest hoard ever found in the River Thames. Ian Smith, Roger Smith, and Paul Woods recovered 495 medieval pennies (bottom left) from a small area of the Thames foreshore. No evidence of a container was found. As the coins were recorded and studied by the British Museum, it was established that they were all forgeries struck from false dies. They look like clipped coins because the forgers used silver discs which were too small for the larger size of the dies. The forgeries were made to imitate silver pennies of Edward IV from 1465–1483. However, they were likely struck in York around 1490–1500. The coins were made mostly of silver mixed with some copper. In the 15th century, the punishment for forgery was death, but the forgers still took the risk because of the huge profits they could make. Since the coins were found together on the riverbed, it is highly likely that the forger discarded them in the river to avoid being caught with the incriminating evidence.

In the medieval period, there was a lack of small denomination coinage. To make small change, silver pennies were sometimes cut into halves and quarters. Even these cut silver coins were often too valuable to make small purchases. Therefore, local communities created an unofficial currency using

Top row: Saxon sceat with abstract dove (Kevin James Dyer). Second row: 7th-century silver drachm from Iran (PAS). Third row: 15th-century silver groat of Henry VI (PAS). Bottom: 15th-century penny forgeries (PAS).

simple, decorated lead discs. These tokens were circulated in Britain from approximately the late 13th century to the mid-19th century.

The earliest tokens were small, thin discs of pewter decorated with very fine motifs of ecclesiastical origin. Over the centuries, lead tokens became more popular and increasingly larger in diameter and thickness. In comparison with medieval pewter tokens, the lead tokens from the 17th and 18th centuries were very crude and appear to have been hastily produced. Lead tokens (top) were decorated with repetitive motifs such as a flower of six petals, cartwheels, fleur-de-lis, and anchors.

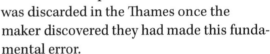

Not only have mudlarks found hundreds of lead tokens over the years, they have also discovered the stone molds which were used to make the tokens. In 2015, I spotted a rectangular stone (below), which had been carved to produce tokens with three different designs. The tokens are decorated with a 4x3 grid, two parallel lines intersected by a perpendicular line, and a crude star. A central, V-shaped groove was used as a casting channel to connect the three circular shapes. Molten lead was poured into the channel to create the single-sided lead seals. After the lead cooled, the tokens could be removed from the mold.

Mark Paros discovered a lead token mold (below right) made of stone which was used to produce six tokens of the same design. The initials "I E" of the token maker or business owner have been carved into each circular recess. The round shapes are connected by a shallow channel to allow the molten lead to run from one disc to the other. The person who made this mold forgot one thing—the initials should have been carved in reverse so that the letters would have been legible when the tokens were removed from the mold. Perhaps this mold was discarded in the Thames once the maker discovered they had made this fundamental error.

One of the best molds ever recovered from the Thames (right) is carved with four identical tokens. Within a circular recess, a shield has been carved with a central chevron and sets of dividers. This is the coat of arms of the Worshipful Company of Carpenters, which received its royal charter in 1477. From the top of the mold, a central funnel connects to the four discs. Two holes on either side of the mold would have been used to fix a flat stone against the mold with pegs. Lead was melted and poured into the gap between the two molds to create the simple lead tokens. This mold is possibly from the 17th century.

Unfortunately, no official records survive which document who produced the lead tokens, what they were worth, or where they were circulated. Based on the hundreds of lead tokens found each year in the River Thames, we know they were widely used throughout London. Hopefully, further research will reveal more about these mysterious lead tokens.

Top: Jason's collection of lead tokens (Jason Sandy). Bottom left: Stone mold for three lead tokens (Hannah Smiles). Top right: Lead token mold carved in stone (Jason Sandy). Bottom right: Mold for producing tokens for the Worshipful Company of Carpenters (PAS).

PAMELA AND TIM MILLER

I vividly recall a "sliding doors" moment when I was eight years old which was to have a profound effect on the rest of my life. It was to influence my education, my career, and to provide me with a pastime which has sustained over four decades—from primary school to middle age.

It was 1978, and my competitive, older brother was berating me for not having any hobbies. So, I triumphantly and somewhat randomly announced that I now collected coins. Fast forward a year, and I was wandering along the Southbank and spotted a man on the foreshore digging a hole. In his outstretched palm were a number of coins. Once he had gone, I sat in his hole and squeezed chunks of gooey mud through my fingers. This was my first "mudlark," and beginner's luck was to bestow on me a quarter fragment of a battered, grey coin. It was a Victorian florin dating to the 1890s, but it lacked a silvery gloss because it was a contemporary forgery and partially made of lead. I had discovered not just a coin, but a historical crime.

Hooked doesn't come close. I was on the fore-shore every weekend—sometimes on my own, sometimes my mum would join me. Thereafter followed school projects about London Bridge and Roman London, an A level in medieval history, and a degree in archaeology. My interest in the past was fueled by the intriguing arti-facts I was unearthing and the mysteries I was unraveling of what they might be. I was drawn in by the thrill of the "chase" and also by the fact that I never quite knew what I was chasing. The river constantly throws up surprises, and the unending possibilities of what you might discover provide an enduring lure.

I was adept at spotting the tiniest finds, and my mum specialized in the larger discoveries such as an 18th-century pewter tankard. For a period in the late 1980s and early 1990s, my mum and I paired up as "diggers"—going down six feet to unearth items in much better condition. I would smash through the rock-hard barge beds but hand over the shovel to her when we got to the 17th-century layer when the silt turned soft. She's tone deaf, so she struggled with the metal detector which meant the diminutive lady in her 60s was dispatched down the hole for the heavy lifting, while the 20-something luxuriated on the surface detecting over the spoil. Her digging days are now over, and I've reverted to the surface where I've benefited from the rampant erosion caused by the Thames Clippers boats.

My best find was a hoard of 12 medieval groats which I discovered over a period of two years. The location was only exposed when the tide was extra low in the spring, which limited my opportunities to return to my hotspot but extended my lucky streak for months. In the early 2000s, I discovered a mint condition gold Roman aureus lying on the surface of the foreshore. My favorite finds are two of the items I donated to the Museum of London. I found part of a 16th-century leather jerkin, and I also unearthed an inauspicious disc of lead with strange markings dotted across it. The inscrip-tions turned out to be that of a spoon maker who had been refining the mold for his stamp and trialing it on the lead disc. It's not just a historical artifact, but a moment in history.

Portraits by Tom Harrison.

LOVE, SEX,
AND
EQUALITY

Have you ever thrown a coin into a fountain for good luck? This is an age-old tradition which still continues today. Over the years, mudlarks have found hundreds of 18th-century copper pennies (below) and halfpennies on the bottom of the River Thames which sailors possibly threw into the river to "buy the wind" and gain good fortune on their journey.

In the 18th century, ocean-going ships did not have motors or steam engines, so they depended solely on the power of the wind in their massive sails to propel them to their destinations around the globe. The fastest ships were the most lucrative and profitable, so sailors needed fast winds and good luck to increase their earnings. Brits love their tea, so there were huge rewards for the fastest ships (top) who could sail from China to England in record time to deliver the freshly clipped tea leaves. In the 19th century, the ships—appropriately called "tea clippers"—would compete

in famous races to be first ship to dock in London with the new tea leaves of the season. During the Great Tea Race of 1866, three ships (Taeping, Ariel, Serica) sailed over 14,000 miles from China to London in 99 days. They completed the journey with an extremely close finish, arriving with 1 ½ hours of each other on the same tide. In 1870 on her maiden voyage, the fastest tea clipper ship called the *Cutty Sark* brought back 600,000 kg of tea, enough to make more than 200 million cups of tea. The *Cutty Sark* ship is now a tourist attraction in Greenwich (southeast London).

Top: Painting of 19th-century tea clipper ship called Taunton, 1884 (W.S. Alfred).
Bottom: Georgian penny dated 1742 (Jason Sandy).

During their long voyages to distant lands, sailors had a lot of time to kill. They were often separated from their girlfriends and wives for many months. To pass the time, I can imagine that sailors took the coins in their pockets and engraved them with unique designs as they dreamed of their sweethearts back home. Several years ago, Graham duHeaume unearthed a George II halfpenny (top right) which was inscribed by hand with the words, "Mary Coombs—Sept 2, 1729." In the center of the 18th-century coin, a beautifully detailed flower has also been skillfully engraved. Did a sailor customize this coin as he was longing to return to London to see Mary again? I wonder if the date is the day they met, got engaged, or married?

In the 17th–19th centuries, people would engrave common coins with the names of their lovers and messages of love. There are many theories why they did this. Maybe the coins were lovingly personalized to give as presents to their love interests in hope of starting a relationship. Possibly they were thrown into the river while whispering a prayer to the river gods for a blessing or for good luck in the relationship. Some of the customized coins are beautiful works of art. It must have taken hours or even days to carefully engrave the names and ornate designs into the surface of the coins. The painstakingly long process of producing these personalized coins demonstrates the strong desire and emotions of the admirers.

In Allison Barker's collection of mudlarking finds, she has two beautiful examples of engraved love tokens from the 19th century. They are both made from young Victoria silver sixpences. Queen Victoria is still visible on the front, but the coin has been worn smooth on the back and engraved with personal messages of love. Around the perimeter of one sixpence (middle right), the poem reads: "WHEN THIS YOU SEE, REMEMBER ME." A heart pierced by two arrows is depicted in the center surrounded by undulating vines with small leaves.

On the second sixpence (bottom right), the words: "My heart is fixt, I cannot range, I like my choice too well to change" have been inscribed on the back of the coin. A circular border with two furls surrounds the central text. Because these customized coins were recovered from the bottom of the River Thames, it could possibly indicate that the love ended and the love tokens were discarded.

Top right: 18th-century love token for Mary Coombs (Graham duHeaume). Middle right: Victorian silver sixpence engraved with the words: "WHEN THIS YOU SEE, REMEMBER ME." (Graham duHeaume). Bottom right: Victorian sixpence repurposed as a love token (Graham duHeaume).

Prostitution is considered to be one of the oldest professions in the world, and it has existed in London for thousands of years. In 2010, the first known Roman brothel token (above) in Britain was discovered along the Thames foreshore in West London by Regis Cursan. Similar tokens have been found elsewhere in the Roman Empire, but none had been previously found in the UK.

On one side of the token or spintria, a naked man and woman are depicted having sex. The female lies on her front beneath the male who straddles her on a bed or couch decorated with a swag. The Roman numeral XIIII appears on the back of the token which could indicate the value of the token or price of the service. Some historians believe the token could have been worth 14 assarius coins. In the first century AD, this amount of money would have been the equivalent to one day's wages for a laborer. The token could have been handed to a sex slave in one of the many Londinium brothels in exchange for the act depicted on the coin.

Caroline McDonald, the Museum of London's former Senior Curator of Prehistory and Roman London, says: "This is the perfect archaeological object. It's sexy and provocative in the best sense of the word. When we realized it was a saucy picture, we had a bit of a giggle, but there's also a sad story behind it because these prostitutes were slaves. It has resonance with modern-day London because people are still being sold into the sex trade. The lot of a Roman sex slave was not a happy one."

Top left: Roman brothel token (PAS). Bottom: Theaters located along the Southbank around 1630, *(anonymous Dutch School painter).*

In Tudor times, prostitution was not permitted within the City of London, so the red-light district flourished on the south side of the river. Looking for a great night out, men and women would cross the river in ferries to the Southbank. All types of entertainment were on offer. Bear and bull baiting, cock fighting, gambling, and visiting the theater were some of the most popular forms of entertainment in the 16th and 17th centuries. In the earliest known oil painting of London (facing page), many theater buildings are shown along the south side of the river. Flags proudly fly over the Swan, the Hope, the Rose, and the Globe theaters, which indicate that a performance was happening that evening. William Shakespeare's well-known plays were featured on their stages.

In 2020, I discovered a beautiful 16th-century token (top) in stunning condition. Dating to 1575–1590, a similar token was found during the excavations of the Rose theater along the Southbank. Built in 1587, it was the first purpose-built

playhouse to stage a production of Shakespeare's plays in the 16th century.

According to the Museum of London Archaeology who excavated the Rose Theatre in 1989–1990, the type of token I found would have been used by those who could afford the more expensive gallery seating in the playhouse. These pewter tokens, also known as "Lyon counters," had other uses too.

The Southbank was a lawless and raucous part of London where prostitution was rife. The ladies of the night were called "Winchester Geese" because the land on which they operated was owned by the Bishop of Winchester. The dark alleyways of Southwark provided the perfect place to perform their services. Named after the medieval term for a brothel, Stew Lane was a narrow, pedestrian path leading down to the Thames on the north side of the river. From here, watermen ferried passengers across the river to Southwark in the pursuit of pleasure. Directly on the other

Top: 16th-century Lyon token (Jason Sandy).

side of the river, there is a discreet alleyway called Cardinal Cap Alley which led to a popular brothel named "The Cardinal's Cap." It was owned by Henry Cardinal Beaufort, the Bishop of Winchester, who wore a red cap during a parade in celebration of his appointment as a cardinal by the Pope in 1426.

Sadly, many of the prostitutes died from mistreatment, ill health, and sexually transmitted diseases contracted from the men they served. Because of their "immoral" profession, they were not allowed to be buried in the local churchyards. Since medieval times, they were laid to rest in the unconsecrated "Cross Bones Graveyard" (below) in Southwark. Today there is a small memorial to the hundreds of prostitutes who lived, worked, and died in the red-light district centuries ago. This desolate plot of land has an iron gate decorated with colorful ribbons and hand-written, personal messages remembering the "Outcast Dead" who were buried here.

A few years ago, as I was mudlarking along the river in Southwark, I found a modern token (above) with a steamy, erotic scene. On the front of the sex token, it says, "CONNECT WITH A PISCES, FEB 19–MAR 20." On the back, it says, "PROVIDER," and the service being "provided" is graphically illustrated. A naked woman is shown in the "missionary position" with a man on top of her. The woman has her arms and legs wrapped around him in a passionate embrace. This modern token is evidence of the continuing association of Southwark with sex.

Steve Brooker found a similar token depicting a naked man and woman in the "69" position. Above them is the word "CREATIVE" which describes their non-conventional way of love making. The token has been counter stamped with the abbreviation "NFM" which is slang for "Not for Me." I can just imagine the person receiving this token, engraving their response, and returning the token, or in this case, throwing it in the river.

A German sex token was also recovered from the Thames by Steve. A naked man and woman are shown having sex "doggy style." Above them are the words in German, "Unity and Sex and Freedom, F***ed in Germany 1993." The back of the coin looks almost identical to a real German 5 Mark coin, but it has the number 6 and words "Sex Mark."

Top left: Plaque outside Cross Bones Graveyard (ProfDEH). Bottom left: Cross Bones Graveyard entrance (Matt Brown). Top right: "Provider" sex token (Jason Sandy).

For millennia, women have not been treated with equality. In Britain and most countries around the world, women were not given the same chance for a good education, the right to vote, equal job opportunities, and equal pay in comparison to men. At the turn of the 20th century, the suffragette movement was founded to raise awareness for this inequality and fight for women's right to vote in public elections. In 1903, Emmeline Pankhurst established the Women's Social and Political Union (WSPU) in Britain (right). The activist group used civil disobedience to make their voices heard through deeds, not words. They organized marches, carried out a nationwide arson and bombing campaign, went on hunger strike, destroyed government property, and heckled politicians. In 1907, hundreds of women stormed the Houses of Parliament along the River Thames. They smashed windows and chained themselves to railings to protest against inequality.

To spread their message to the general public, the suffragettes defaced government coins with their slogan. The coins remained in circulation and exchanged hands many times, conveying their motto to a wider audience. In 2021, Florrie Evans spotted an unusual coin (above) as she was nightlarking. As she plucked the coin out of the black mud, Florrie could see the words, "VOTES FOR WOMEN" stamped into the surface of the Victorian halfpenny dated 1899. On the back of the coin, the suffragette union's initials "WSPU" have been engraved. Florrie explains the special photos above: "I've displayed my coin on illustrations by Max Beerbohm of his eponymous heroine *Zuleika Dobson*, a novel published by my great-grand-father in 1911 (a patriarchal lineage). Zuleika's super-power was charming young men to mass suicide in the name of unrequited love. Even in jest, women were regarded as a danger to—or the cause of—male fragility! Plus ça change?"

Although some women were given the right to vote in 1918, it took ten more years before every woman over age 21 could vote in public elections in Britain. Ultimately, the suffragettes achieved their goal through their activism and sheer determination. Although the equality gap between men and women is slowly closing, there is still a lot of work to do. Hopefully true equality will be achieved in the near future.

Top: Victorian penny stamped with slogan "Votes for Women" (Florrie Evans).
Bottom: Suffragettes holding placard with campaign slogan.

ALESSIO CHECCONI

My name is Alessio, and I am an Italian "madlark." I have been fascinated by our past since I was a child, mesmerized by pictures of majestic creatures like dinosaurs. This passion continued, and I became a micropalaeontologist and geologist, working as a researcher in academia. The day I co-discovered and named a new species of fossil micro-organism was one of the most unforgettable days of my life! It was an honor to be the first person to observe an organism that lived more than 300 million years ago.

When I moved to London over 12 years ago, I changed my career, but I missed the excitement of unearthing history and the thrill of a discovery. I live next to the River Thames, and at the beginning of the first Covid lockdown, I discovered steps to the foreshore just opposite my house. A walk on the riverbank became my daily routine. It was a place to rest my body and mind.

During my first-ever walk there, I spotted small, white, clay cylinders. I had no idea what they were, so I collected a couple and did some research. I couldn't believe when I found out they were century-old clay pipes. I was hooked! I immediately got a permit from the PLA, and I have been mudlarking ever since.

Mudlarking is an addictive hobby because you never know what the river will offer you next. It could be a plastic button from a Primark shirt or a gold Roman ring. Although the goal is not to find something precious, the real excitement is to find something "interesting." While talking to many other fellow mudlarks, I have learned that "interesting" is a very subjective concept.

My favorite finds are hand-made, daily used objects such as a Roman bone hairpin, a Tudor wooden hand-carved spoon, an Iron Age bone bobbin, a hand-engraved love token, and a pinner's bone. Those finds are direct evidence of the lives of common people who lived before us. Even if history books don't record their names, their existence and actions have played an important role in building the world as it exists today.

Each find allows me to meet someone who lived centuries ago—an individual who lived, loved, cried, regretted, forgave, hoped, dreamed, and eventually died. It was a person who most likely lived an ordinary life, but whose existence has survived the centuries through an object that they used and left for the River Thames.

The Thames democratizes history. It preserves whatever you throw in it—whether it's a king's brooch or a peasant' broken shoe. These objects reveal the real history of the whole demographic of the city of London.

For me, sharing these finds with others and finding out about their backstories represents an homage and a gesture of reverence to those that came before us. They made history in their own way, regardless of whether they were kings, butlers, prisoners, children, farmers, or prostitutes. Each life linked to an object we find becomes important and noteworthy. The artifacts open our eyes and remind us of the people who lived here centuries ago.

Portraits by Tom Harrison.

BUCKLE UP

18th-century painting of John Montagu, 4th Earl of Sandwich (Thomas Gainsborough).

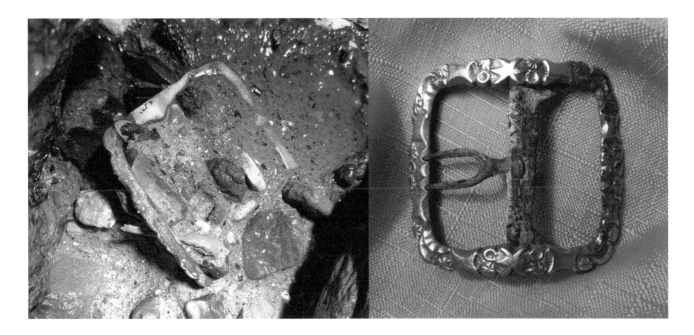

It was a cold, wintry morning, but I was determined to go mudlarking. After my alarm rang at 5 AM, I reluctantly dragged myself out of my warm bed. Still exhausted from the night before, I slept during the hour-long journey on the London Underground to East London. When I arrived on the foreshore, it was ominously dark, raining, and unnervingly silent.

As I was mudlarking alone in the darkness, I caught a glimpse of something golden illuminated by my headlamp (top left), and my heart started racing with excitement. As I slowly lifted the object out of the black mud, I couldn't believe my eyes! A complete, highly decorated 18th-century shoe buckle appeared. When I returned home, I carefully cleaned it. Made of solid brass, the ornate shoe buckle (top right) is decorated with six-pointed stars and abstract, curvilinear shapes around the perimeter. It definitely is an eye-catching design. The Georgians loved their bling, and this buckle is evidence of the ostentatious and exuberant styles of the 18th century.

For millennia, buckles have been worn for practical and functional reasons, but they were also highly valued fashion accessories which indicated one's wealth and social status. Although buckles were used primarily by the military in Roman and early medieval times, they came into more widespread use among the civilian population in the 13th century. This reflected changes in fashion and a general increase in the wealth and prosperity of society at that time.

By the 1680s, shoe buckles were virtually in universal use among all social classes. In the 18th century, buckles became more and more extravagant and were worn to catch attention, especially of the opposite sex. Portraits and paintings (facing page) of wealthy noblemen illustrate how shoe buckles were a prominent feature in men's attire in the 18th century.

Mudlarks in London have recovered a wide range of buckles of all ages, shapes, and sizes from the river. These highly ornate, beautiful works of art tell the story of fashion and culture throughout the centuries. Several years ago Tom Main discovered an unusually shaped buckle (left). Dating to 1400–1450, the kidney-shaped frame and integral buckle plate are made of pewter. A series

Top left: Georgian buckle stuck in the mud (Jason Sandy). Top right: Highly ornate, 18th-century brass buckle (Jason Sandy). Bottom: Medieval, kidney-shaped buckle (PAS).

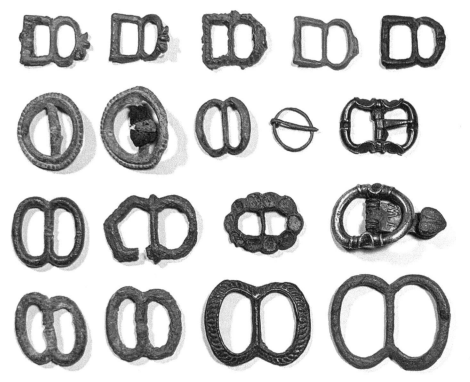

of undulating, parallel lines adorn the frame. The plate has been cast with a geometric pattern inside a circular, openwork feature beside a row of triangular shapes containing a three-pointed foliate design. The pivoting pin of the buckle is still attached.

Mark Paros found an exquisite medieval buckle (below) with a champlevé enamel buckle plate and intact pin. Dating to the 13th century, a lion is portrayed with its head up, chest out, and long tail extended upwards. Champlevé is a technique of etching the design into the surface of the metal and filling it with vitreous enamel.

In 2010, Mark Jennings discovered an ultra-rare buckle (top right) made of bone. It has been designated by the Museum of London as an object of national importance on the Portable Antiquities Scheme. Dating to the 12th century, the buckle frame is D-shaped and carved from one piece from animal bone. Engraved with decorative V-shaped lines around the perimeter, the bone pin pivots on an iron dowel and rests in a notched slot on the buckle. A leather belt or strap would have been fastened to the buckle with rivets through the two holes in the integral bone plates. Over the centuries, buckles were primarily made of metal, so it is highly unusual to find a medieval buckle made of bone.

In the 17th century, buckle shapes became more creative and elaborate. Dating to 1620–1680, a superb example (right) was found in the Thames which is made of silver in a double loop, openwork shape. The outer edge of the buckle is decorated with five scallop shells articulated with three radiating rows of incised lines. The shells are cast

Top left: Jason's collection of buckles (Jason Sandy). Bottom left: Medieval buckle depicting a lion (Jason Sandy). Top right: Medieval bone buckle (PAS). Bottom right: Post-medieval buckle with scallop shells (PAS).

onto a semi-circular frame. The integral pin tapers to a point and rests against the curved frame. A circular terminal decorated with a stylized flower is fixed to the thin, flat plate where the leather belt or strap would have been attached.

Although mudlarks have recovered many buckles from the river, it is very rare to find a leather belt. Leather is an organic material which normally decomposes and disintegrates over time. Miraculously, Mark Paros unearthed part of a medieval leather belt (below) that has been beautifully preserved by the anaerobic Thames mud. The leatherwork from the 15th century has been stamped with the Gothic letters "IHS" in a repeating pattern. Representing Jesus Christ, the symbol IHS was a popular Christogram in the Middle Ages.

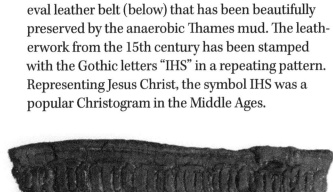

Buckles were not only used on belts and shoes. One of the most intriguing finds from the Thames is an archer's wrist guard (below center), which is made of leather and fastened with a buckle. Astonishingly, the medieval leatherwork is in excellent condition, and the buckle is still securely fixed to the leather straps. The holes in the strap are decorated with pewter studs in the shape of flowers. An archer wore this thick leather guard to protect his wrist from injury caused by the powerful snap of the bow's string when an arrow was fired.

During the medieval and post-medieval periods, horses were an important means of transportation. People traveled long distances on horseback and also rode horses for pleasure. Riders wore boots with spurs to prod a horse to move

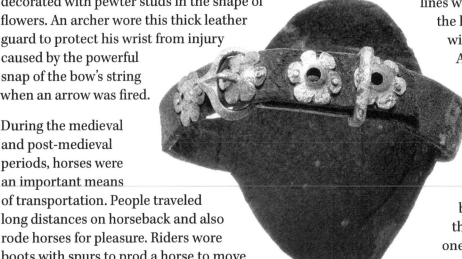

forward or run faster. By the 16th and 17th centuries, it was fashionable to wear spurs as part of your normal attire.

Over the past ten years, I have found several 16th– and 17th-century buckles that had once been attached to a spur. In 2007, a mudlark found a buckle still mounted in its original position on a spur (top right). Dating to 1600–1700, the U-shaped spur would have been attached to the heel of a horse rider's boot with leather straps. The neck and rowel box are cast in the form of a beast's head. Its neck has flowing, incised lines which look like a mane, and the head has been engraved with eyes, ears, and a mouth. Although it is missing now, the circular rowel had been fixed inside an open slot within the head, and an iron pin secured it in place and allowed the disc to spin freely. Originally, four buckles were mounted on the sides of the spur, but only one remains.

During the golden age of decadence and flamboyance in the 18th century, Georgian gentlemen were dressed to impress from head to toe. Some of the most extraordinary Georgian shoe buckles were inlaid with real gemstones or glass paste stones. Each buckle was highly ornate and designed to glisten and sparkle. Developments in glass paste stone production and cutting methods during the late 17th and early 18th centuries gradually increased the luminosity and brilliance of the glass stones. However, a major improvement came in the 1760s when a silver foil was placed behind the glass stones. The reflective foil acted as a mirror, making the glass paste stones appear larger than they actually were, greatly enhancing their faceted sparkle. The cut glass stones were arranged to complement the geometry of the buckle frame.

Worn as a flashy display of their wealth and social status (below), buckles encrusted in paste stones would glisten, dazzle, and create an eye-catching appearance in the sunlight. Mudlark Alex Rushe found one of these buckles in Amsterdam. (above) Several elaborate 18th-century shoe buckles set with glass stones were found by Steve Brooker in the Thames.

Top: 18th-century buckle with glass paste stones (Alex Rusche).
Bottom: Georgian shoe with gem-encrusted buckles (Los Angeles County Museum of Art).

Throughout history, leather straps have been used for a multitude of purposes. They have been utilized as belts to secure clothing and to suspend purses, bags, swords, and daggers. To protect the ends of the vulnerable leather and to prevent it from fraying, pieces of metal were fixed to the tips of the straps. In medieval and post-medieval times, strap ends became very decorative and ornate. Brass was the preferred material, and it was often engraved with various motifs.

When I first spotted a folded piece of brass (above) on the foreshore, I didn't know what it was, but I could see some engraving on the surface. Dating to 1300–1500, it is a medieval strap end (right) made from a single sheet of brass which was folded in half. It had been riveted to the end of a leather strap, and the rivet holes are still visible. The Lombardic letter "N" is inscribed into the surface, surrounded by a hatch pattern comprised of diagonal, incised lines. I wonder if it is the first initial of the previous owner who lived 700 years ago?

Strap ends were also produced with creative shapes and designs. For instance, Mark Paros found an elongated strap end (below) with the two plates tapered to a rounded finial in the shape of an acorn. To decorate the brass plates, linear rows of dots have been gently hammered into the surface. Within the central band, a series of diamond shapes are depicted.

One of the most historically significant strap ends found by a mudlark (right) is from the 16th century. According to Hazel Forsyth, Senior Curator at the Museum of London, it is an "inscribed silver-gilt chape from the Vintry belonging to Ralph Felmingham, who was Sergeant-at-Arms to Henry VIII; probably associated with the ceremonial sword worn as a badge of office. Felmingham officiated at the trials of Lord Dacre in 1534 and Anne Boleyn and Lord Rocheford in 1536." According to the Museum of London, "This silver-gilt chape bears a cast-relief figure of St. Barbara and incised motifs of a rose and pomegranate, the royal badges of Henry VIII and Katherine of Aragon. The chape has an inverse inscription, RAF+FEL+MIGAM, an abbreviation of the name Ralph Felmingham." It is now on permanent display in Medieval London gallery of the Museum of London.

Buckles and strap ends may seem like mundane, utilitarian objects, but the artifacts featured in this chapter demonstrate that they can also be beautiful works of art and craftsmanship. They give us intriguing insights into the popular fashions, styles, and material culture throughout the ages. Mudlarks have recovered thousands of buckles and strap ends from the river, which have helped historians research and understand more about past Londoners. Geoff Egan, former Small Finds Specialist at the British Museum, wrote a book called *Dress Accessories,* which features many buckles and strap ends, as well as mounts, brooches, buttons, lace chapes, hair accessories, pins, beads, chains, pendants, finger rings, combs, cosmetic sets, needle cases, and other artifacts primarily found on the Thames foreshore or waterlogged sites along the River Thames. If you want to read more about these interesting artifacts, I would highly recommend this book.

Top left: Medieval brass strap end (Jason Sandy). Middle left: Gothic letter "N" engraved on strap end (Jason Sandy). Bottom left: Medieval strap end with acorn finial (Jason Sandy). Top right: Silver-gilt Tudor chape from Ralph Felmingham (Jason Sandy).

LIZ ANDERSON

History has been my passion since childhood. I studied the subject at university and taught it for many years. Thames archaeology and learning about the use of the river in the past, its wharves, jetties, and other features, has added a new dimension to my knowledge. Mudlarking has shown me how much the two are deeply connected.

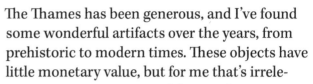

I began mudlarking in 2015 after walking along the South Bank one grey winter's day and noticing someone on the foreshore below, head down, searching for something. I was intrigued and went down to see what was going on. I must have seen this activity before, but for some reason it hadn't registered until that moment. I then spotted a large sherd of tin-glazed pottery from the 17th-century, hand-painted with blue ferns and foliage in a gloriously unrestrained freestyle manner on a white background. After picking it up, I was instantly hooked.

The thrill of mudlarking for me is to be able to hold history in my hands, to be the curator of my own finds, and to share that love of the river with others. The artifacts we find form an instant connection to the past, because they tell the story of ordinary people whose names we'll never know.

There is something liminal about being on the Thames Foreshore—that sense of a barely perceptible space where you're on the threshold of past and present. We're living in difficult times, and mudlarking can provide a temporary respite. It helps still anxious thoughts. The river is balm for the soul, a precious open space where I can grab a few hours of peace and solitude. It's this that keeps me coming back.

Portraits by Tom Harrison.

The Thames has been generous, and I've found some wonderful artifacts over the years, from prehistoric to modern times. These objects have little monetary value, but for me that's irrelevant. My most important find is a pilgrim badge from the medieval period. Small, made of pewter, and fashioned in the shape of a Lombardic "M" for Maria, it speaks of long, tiring journeys made by pilgrims hundreds of years ago to Canterbury, Walsingham, or Santiago de Compostela, asking for Our Lady's intercession.

I also have a small, 17th-century hawking or hunting bell in my collection. Cast from copper alloy, its clay pip remains intact. The bell still rings after centuries immersed in river mud, and it was spine-tingling hearing this for the first time since it was lost in the Thames. It's literally the sound of the past.

Just before lockdown, I found a lead bale seal showing the crest of Riga, capital of Latvia, an important Baltic port for centuries. The seal would have been attached to goods such as salt, flax, hemp, wood, fur, or amber. I'm London born and bred, but my heritage is Polish. My parents settled here after the Second World War. I've recently discovered that I also share ancestry with people in the Baltic States, and knowing this has really connected me to this bale seal. It's a tangible reminder that for millennia the Thames has been at the heart of trade from Europe and around the world, contributing to the growth of the city. Mudlarking is a constant reminder of the long history and diversity of London.

Can you believe that the birth of the United States of America began on the River Thames in London? In 1606, English colonists departed in three ships on the Thames in Blackwall, London, to start a new colony in Jamestown, Virginia, which became the first permanent British settlement in North America. Several years later in 1620, the *Mayflower* set sail on the Thames in Rotherhithe, London, on its voyage to the New World. These two events established colonies, which would eventually grow to become one of the most influential nations in the world.

As an American living in London, I am enthralled and captivated by the *Mayflower*'s connection to London. The ship's crew and 65 Pilgrims boarded the *Mayflower* in London and sailed to Southampton to join the Pilgrims on the *Speedwell* from Holland. The *Mayflower* crossed the Atlantic Ocean

SEARCHING FOR EVIDENCE OF THE MAYFLOWER

to the New World with 102 passengers, arriving in November 1620 (below).

During the first winter, half of the Pilgrims died in the cold, harsh conditions in New England. Fortunately, the friendly Wampanoag Indians taught the colonists how to survive and live off the land. Following the first harvest in 1621, the Pilgrims and Wampanoag Indians celebrated together with a large feast, which is considered the "First Thanksgiving."

Painting of the Pilgrims arriving on the Mayflower *in the New World by W. J. Aylward (Pictorial Press Ltd/Alamy Stock Photo).*

Christopher Jones, the captain and co-owner of the *Mayflower*, lived in Rotherhithe and was buried in St. Mary's church. Across from the church, the popular "Mayflower" pub stands on the original site of the 16th-century "The Shippe" pub, which Christopher Jones and his crew often frequented.

Hoping to find clues and evidence of the *Mayflower*, several mudlarks and I have searched at low tide along the exposed bed of the River Thames in Rotherhithe, and we have made some amazing discoveries. We have found ships' timbers, shipbuilding tools, cannonballs, musket balls, padlocks, clay pipes, buttons, buckles, leather shoes, glass bottles, tokens, coins, children's toys, and other artifacts that reveal the maritime history of the area.

Some of most prominent features on the riverbed here are large, solid oak ship timbers from the ship-breaking yards that used to be located along the river. Some of the timbers were ships' windlasses, and have been reused for mooring. Rudders from warships now form a barge bed. Some histo-rians believe that the *Mayflower* was dismantled in Rotherhithe and its timbers sold to a farmer in Buckinghamshire, England and reused in a barn, now called the "Mayflower Barn."

Alan Murphy is a mudlark who lives in Rotherhithe and has been combing the riverbed for over 30 years. One of his favorite finds is a French coin called a "Double Tournois" dated 1619 (below). Before the *Mayflower* took Pilgrims to the New World, it traveled to France many times, taking English wool products to French ports and returning to London with wine. Could this French coin have been dropped by one of the *Mayflower's* crew after returning from France?

French Double Tournois coin dated 1619 (Alan Murphy).

Nautical dividers carved with a flower motif (Pete Wakeman).

On a particularly low tide, mudlark Pete Wakeman spotted the tip of a pair of nautical dividers (above) sticking out of the mud in Rotherhithe. The circular terminal of the dividers was engraved with a stylized flower, which could be associated with the *Mayflower*. The Museum of London has dated the nautical dividers to AD 1500–1700, which is approximately the time period when the *Mayflower* was active in Rotherhithe.

The *Mayflower* was a merchant ship equipped with cannons to defend itself when carrying cargo. Alan Murphy found a hollow cannonball (below) on the foreshore in Rotherhithe that dates from the 17th century. According to Alan, "the cannonball would have been packed with iron shot and gunpowder with a lime fuse. It would have been fired at ships' hulls."

Clay tobacco pipe from ca. 1620 (Jason Sandy).

17th-century cannonball (Alan Murphy).

Nestled between the rocks on the riverbed in Rotherhithe, I found a small clay tobacco pipe (above) from circa 1620. Sir Walter Raleigh is claimed to have introduced tobacco to England after his return from expeditions in America in the 16th century, and smoking became popular in London. Tobacco was expensive, so pipe bowls were made very small and nicknamed "nose warmers." I can imagine one of the *Mayflower's* crew members smoking one of these clay pipes and tossing it overboard before traveling with the smoke-sensitive, pious Pilgrims.

James I hammered silver penny (Jason Sandy).

James I copper farthing (Jason Sandy).

On the exposed riverbed in Rotherhithe, I have recovered several 400-year-old coins (above) near the location where the *Mayflower* was often docked. A hammered silver penny and hammered copper farthing from the reign of King James I (1603–1625) are two of my personal favorite finds from this time period.

During the long, three-month journey to America, I can imagine that the passengers and crew members played games to pass the time. While I was mudlarking in Rotherhithe, I found a 17th-century hand-carved die (right) made of bone.

A few years ago, mudlarks Philly Gumbo and Judy Hazell discovered a 17th-century glass bottle seal (below) in Rotherhithe. With remarkable similarities to the Mayflower, a three-masted galleon ship is depicted on the seal which could have been attached to a bottle from The Shippe pub. The letters "I T" on the bottle seal are possibly the initials of the pub landlord back in the 17th century.

17th-century glass bottle seal (Philly Gumbo and Judy Hazell).

Although these intriguing 17th-century arti-facts were found in Rotherhithe near the location where the *Mayflower* set sail, it is not possible to confirm that these objects are directly associated with the *Mayflower* or its crew and passengers. However, as a descendent of an American colonist, I am thrilled to have found coins, clay pipes, and other artifacts from the same time period and place where the *Mayflower* sailed from London to start a new colony in America.

17th-century hand-carved bone die (Jason Sandy).

Now, when I celebrate Thanks-giving in London every November, it has a new meaning and significance. For my British friends, I prepare a traditional American Thanksgiving feast with all the trimmings. After everyone has stuffed themselves, I enjoy telling the story of the *Mayflower* and showing them the interesting artifacts I have found from this time period.

ALAN MURPHY

As I was growing up, my father was a Thames mudlark. Seeing all the artifacts he found really interested me, so I always knew about mudlarking from a very early age, as did most of my friends. When playing on the foreshore, I would often bump into my dad and his friends digging away on the foreshore—back when you didn't need permits to be there.

I remember my dad coming home with a metal bucket filled with clay pipes, which all had long stems and looked brand new, as if they had just been made that day. Later I found out that he and his friends found a big, wooden box full of pipes that had been wrapped in hessian sacks and hidden behind a panel on one of the old boats. The next day, I searched every boat I could get onto, looking for anything I could take back home. I never found any more pipes, but I did find lots of brass that had been saved in an old tea chest.

I played on the river as a child, climbing over the corrugated iron fences through the derelict buildings and warehouses to get onto the foreshore and explore the abandoned boats. This was the early 1970s, when children used to go out early in the morning and come home late at night covered in mud. I would also fish from the old wooden pier on the foreshore below Tower Bridge next to where City Hall stands now.

This was where I found two knives wrapped in newspaper in an old biscuit box as I was climbing down the ladder that had been hidden on one of the wooden beams and held on by some old rope. One of the knives was a small military dagger without the original handle. I still have them today and imagine that they once belonged to a docker who worked on the river. I wonder what work they would have been used for.

I started mudlarking in my teenage years while out fishing for eels underneath Tower Bridge by Horselydown Old Stairs. I would search the foreshore looking for pieces of lead to use as fishing weights, and pick up clay pipes, bottles, and coins. I always found plenty of things to bring home, and then would sell my small eels known as "bootlaces" to Bob the Eel Man.

For me, mudlarking is an escape from life's daily problems. A way to relax and help my wellbeing. I live in two worlds—the mudlarking world and the real world. The mudlarking world keeps my mind active. I can travel to different time periods within seconds by discovering items I come across, washed out from the Thames and preserved by the anaerobic mud.

My favorite finds are Stone Age flint tools. I have found so many different tools over the years, including barb and tanged arrowheads, Paleolithic blade cores, Mesolithic adze, and a Mesolithic tranchet axe known as a "Thames Pick." This is what keeps me going back to the river most days.

As a Bermondsey boy born and bred, the river runs deep in my veins. I will continue to mudlark for as long as I can, and share my knowledge with new mudlarks. I've been a member of the Society of Thames Mudlarks since 2017.

Portraits by Tom Harrison.

LOST FOR WORDS

It was midnight as T.J. Cobden-Sanderson stepped out into the dark, summer night in West London in August 1916. He struggled to remain inconspicuous as he carried a heavy wooden box down the small passageway, his face concealed under his large beret. It was an arduous task for a 76-year-old man, but he was on a mission to destroy the very thing he loved so much: his life's work.

After a ten-minute walk along the River Thames, Cobden-Sanderson arrived at Hammersmith Bridge, a beautiful suspension bridge gracefully supported by towering green turrets and decorated with ornate, golden features. Concealed by the darkness of night, Cobden-Sanderson went to a discreet spot on the bridge where he quietly dumped trays of

metal typeface into the River Thames. The sound of passing buses and traffic on the timber-decked bridge drowned out the splash of the heavy type in the river below. Between 1916 and 1917, Cobden-Sanderson made around 170 trips to Hammersmith Bridge to condemn his precious masterpiece to the depths of the River Thames, hoping it would never be seen again.

So why did he dispose of his life's work? T.J. Cobden-Sanderson was a printer and book binder who established the Doves Bindery in 1893, which he named after The Dove pub located next to his house along the River Thames. Cobden-Sanderson was part of the Arts and Crafts movement and was friends with Emery Walker and William Morris, who ran Kelmscott Press in Hammersmith near Cobden-Sanderson's house. After Morris died in 1896, Cobden-Sanderson convinced Walker to set up their own printing press. In 1900, the Doves Press was established by the two men who became partners in the joint venture.

Critical of the quality of recently mechanized printing technology, Cobden-Sanderson and Walker decided to create their own bespoke typeface

Top: Hammersmith Bridge, West London (David Iliff).
Bottom: T.J. Cobden-Sanderson in 1902, (Bonhams). Doves Press Bible (Sockenkind).

inspired by Nicholas Jenson, a Venetian printer in the 15th century. Cobden-Sanderson commissioned the production of the Doves typeface, and Emery Walker oversaw the design of the unique type used to print all of their books which were bound at the Doves Bindery. They created many extraordinary books, but the Doves Bible is considered to be their greatest masterpiece. The first page of Genesis is one of the most iconic pages in printing.

Despite their success, Cobden-Sanderson and Walker were entangled in a bitter dispute. Walker was distracted by his many other business ventures, and Cobden-Sanderson did the lion's share of the work, managing the printing and binding operations with meticulous attention to detail. By 1906, Cobden-Sanderson had grown increasingly unhappy with the arrangement and wanted to terminate their partnership. He was able to negotiate a deal, whereby he would run the printing press on his own, retaining sole use of the type until his death, at which point it would pass to Walker. Cobden-Sanderson wrote to a friend proclaiming, "nothing on earth will now induce me to part with the type." In July 1909, the deal was agreed, and their partnership came to an end.

Cobden-Sanderson continued to print with the Doves Type until his retirement in 1917. Because of his long-standing feud with Walker, he wanted to destroy the typeface to prevent Walker from obtaining it after his death. He could not imagine the typeface being used in books other than those he had so carefully and passionately crafted. To prevent anyone else printing with his beloved type, Cobden-Sanderson dumped the entire font off of Hammersmith Bridge into the Thames between

1916 and 1917, only five years before his death in 1922. He also threw its punches and matrices into the Thames to ensure that Walker could never recreate the typeface.

In 1917, Cobden-Sanderson announced publicly that the Doves Press would close, and he admitted that the typeface had been "bequeathed" and "consecrated" to the Thames. Over the following 100 years, the typeface laid in its watery grave at the bottom of the Thames, concealed in the gravel and mud. Many attempts were made to find the discarded typeface, but no one succeeded. Cobden-Sanderson had been very successful in hiding the typeface at the bottom of the river.

While studying graphic design at the University of the Arts London (Central Saint Martins) and the Royal College of Art in the 1990s, Robert Green was introduced to the Doves typeface. "I remember being blown away by the typesetting and layout of the first page of Genesis in the Doves Bible, after seeing it in a typography book," explains Robert. Slowly, he became obsessed with the typeface because it is so unique and extraordinary. "It's incredibly elegant and was thought by some to be the most beautiful type in use at the time," describes Robert.

Fueled by his passion for the Doves typeface, Robert decided to create a digital facsimile of the font. Over the course of five years, he slavishly digitized the original typeface. Although he released the first version of his facsimile in 2013, he was dissatisfied with the result. "I wasn't happy with it for various reasons and wanted to partially redraw it. One of my former tutors had said to me that the only way I could be sure it was as accurate as

Facing page: Doves Type discovered by Jason Sandy. Boat and diver from Port of London Authority (Toby Amies/Ali Tollervey). Doves typeface in a sieve shortly after its retrieval from the Thames, (Toby Amies/Ali Tollervey).

possible was by referencing the metal (the original type). I knew where it was, pretty much, so off I went," explains Robert.

Determined to retrieve the typeface from the riverbed, Robert conducted endless hours of research and detective work over several years to ascertain where Cobden-Sanderson had dumped the Doves typeface in the Thames. "The exact location was gleaned by a combination of reading some entries in Cobden-Sanderson's journals and fieldwork—visiting the bridge and guessing what I'd do if I were him. Turns out, I guessed right," states Robert.

In 2014, Robert contacted the Port of London Authority in order to commission divers to retrieve the typeface from the thick, black mud. "They were quite concerned I might be wasting my money, searching for tiny artifacts disposed of so long ago. So, they advised me to get a mudlarking license and go to the foreshore at low tide, have a look for myself before commissioning them just to see if I thought it was feasible to salvage some," explains Robert.

Searching along the exposed foreshore at low tide, Robert found three pieces of the typeface, which had been washed up from the depths of the Thames. This confirmed his theories about the location where Cobden-Sanderson had dumped the typeface between 1916–1917. Robert went back to the officers at the Port of London Authority to show them his discovery and convince them to send a diver down to excavate more of the typeface. "A boat arrived from Gravesend with a full crew onboard including three divers (top left). They wore full scuba gear, diving down and dredging the riverbed with a bucket, which they took over to the abutment and sorted through a household sieve. It was all pretty low-tech apart from the boat and the scuba gear, relying on the skill and experience of the divers," describes Robert.

His in-depth research and persistence paid off. "As the divers got closer to the spot after around 90 minutes, small amounts of type (bottom left)

began appearing in the sieve. The spot where the type was dumped is never fully exposed at low tide. It's probably just over chest height when the tide is lowest, so scuba gear was still necessary to execute a thorough search of the riverbed," explains Robert. During the two dives over a week, 147 pieces were recovered by the divers. From the metal typeface retrieved from the river, Robert was able to digitally recreate an accurate facsimile which was released in 2015. The digital version is available to buy from Type Spec at typespec.co.uk.

Several years ago, I heard the story about the famous Doves typeface for the first time. As I live close to Hammersmith Bridge in West London, I searched for many years but was not able to find the elusive Doves Type. On a cold February evening in 2019, I arranged to meet Robert at The Dove pub next to Cobden-Sanderson's house and former site of the Doves Press. As I enjoyed a chilled pint of locally crafted lager next to a crackling fireplace in the cheerfully small pub, Robert showed me some of the original Doves typeface he had found.

Inspired by his detective work, I followed some of the clues left behind from his search. I have now found twelve pieces of the original Doves Type. Astonishingly, fellow mudlark Lukasz Orlinski has recovered over 500 letters (facing page, bottom) from the discarded type. As a local Hammersmith resident, I am thrilled to have found pieces of this incredible history concealed in the River Thames for over 100 years.

Cobden-Sanderson's former house is still lived in, but it is not open to the public. However, Emery Walker's House has been converted into a museum located along the River Thames and operated by the Emery Walker Trust. The house has been

beautifully and lovingly restored and still contains many of its original contents. In 2020, I decided to donate my pieces of Doves Type to the museum. I'm sure Cobden-Sanderson would be rolling in his grave! He discarded the type in the river to prevent Walker from ever obtaining them. Now, I have retrieved some of the type and returned them to Walker's house.

Mallory Horrill, senior curator at Emery Walker's House, was delighted with the donation and wrote, "This is such a generous and most welcome offer of donation! You may be aware that we do not have a piece of Doves Type in our collection but have always remained hopeful that one day we might."

Lucinda MacPherson, spokesman for Emery Walker's House, thanked me for my donation stating, "It really is so kind of you to give this gift—especially as the house does not have so much evidence of Emery's publishing as they had to sell his books to pay for setting up the Trust to care for the house in the first place."

My Doves Type is now on permanent display in Emery Walker's House. This story began with a disgruntled Cobden-Sanderson stealthily dumping the type in the river, and the story ends over 100 years later with the recovered type displayed proudly in Walker's house. It's definitely not the "happy ending" Cobden-Sanderson was hoping for!

Top: Upper and lowercase letters of Doves Type discovered in the Thames (Karl Donovan). Facing page: Doves Type found by Lukasz Orlinski. Left: Interior of Emery Walker's House (Emery Walker Trust).

JASON SANDY

I was born in the USA and have always been interested in history because of my family heritage. In 1638, my English ancestors immigrated to America and started a new colony on Long Island with several other families. My uncle and I have researched our family genealogy extensively, and I have visited Southold, New York, which my ancestors founded in 1640. I am the first generation of my family to immigrate back to England after over 360 years in the United States.

When I moved to London in 2007, I was fascinated by the historical sites and stories of British colonization. I first heard about mudlarking in 2012 when I watched TV shows called *Thames Treasure Hunters* on the National Geographic Channel and *Mud Men* on the History Channel. I simply couldn't believe that mudlarks were finding incredible, historic artifacts on the foreshore when the tide receded. I went mudlarking for the first time in April 2012 and was instantly addicted.

Since watching the *Indiana Jones* films as a kid, I have been fascinated with archaeology and lost treasures. When the farmers plowed the fields behind our house in Indiana, I would go searching for freshly unearthed flint arrowheads left behind by Native Americans hundreds of years ago. I also liked collecting coins, and my parents were truly embarrassed when I would search for lost coins under vending machines and in telephone booths.

Although I'm an architect working on luxury projects around London for a high-profile property developer, I love getting muddy on the weekends. Because of my fascination with Colonial America, I especially enjoy mudlarking in Rotherhithe,

where the famous *Mayflower* ship departed en route to America in 1620. To find and hold artifacts from the early 17th century—and to think that my forefathers could have held these objects in their hands—is absolutely mind-blowing. It's a tangible connection to my ancestors!

I live in a historic, riverside community along the Thames in West London. Our lives revolve around the river, and my family has spent countless hours exploring the river and its surroundings. I often wander down to the river to escape reality and clear my head. I love sitting on the river wall and watching the sun set over the Thames.

Since I started mudlarking, I have luckily found some unique, historically important artifacts. Some of my favorite finds include a carved Roman hairpin with the bust of a woman, a medieval knight's knuckle guard, a boar badge from infamous King Richard III, a complete medieval leather children's shoe with shoestrings still attached, and a complete World War II helmet which would have been worn by a member of the Fire Guard. I have donated some of my best finds to the Museum of London, Natural History Museum, Victoria and Albert Museum, London's Roman Amphitheatre in the Guildhall Art Gallery, Stone Museum, Emery Walker House, and King Richard III Visitor Centre in Leicester.

I think the thrill of mudlarking is not only finding the history but sharing it with a captive audience. I love giving talks to school children and seeing their eyes light up each time they hold a unique artifact in their hands. You can just see their young minds absorbing the history and developing the same fascination that I discovered along the river.

Portraits by Tom Harrison.

WORKING
RIVER

*19th-century painting of the Port of London
(John Gendall).*

Since the Romans established Londinium in AD 43, the River Thames has served as a vital port for vessels importing and exporting goods. Without the port, London would not have become one of the most important cities in the world. The Romans imported wine, olives, olive oil, salted fish, garum (fish sauce), pottery, glassware, and other goods from around their empire, and they exported raw materials from Britain such as wheat, cloth, timber, silver, lead, tin, and iron.

Over the centuries, the maritime trade and importance of the port steadily increased. In AD 731, the medieval monk and writer Venerable Bede described the Anglo-Saxon settlement as "an emporium (market) of many peoples coming by land and sea." Lundenwic was one of the largest Anglo-Saxon trading centers in Europe, and merchant ships from foreign lands imported exotic goods such as silks, precious stones, gold, wine, olive oil, ivory, bronze, glass, and other luxuries to the city.

In the Middle Ages and Tudor period, maritime trade continued to flourish, and London merchants became very wealthy. Between the beginning and end of the 17th century, the

amount of shipping passing through the Port of London increased five-fold. Because of its monopoly on trading with the Far East, London (facing page) became the busiest port in the world in the 18th century. The port was handling 80% of Britain's imports and 69% of the country's exports. During the course of the 19th century, London became the world's largest and wealthiest city, serving as the capital, global hub, and financial center of the vast British empire.

Connected to this global trade network, the River Thames provided an ideal location for businesses and trades of all types. Fish markets, slaughterhouses, ship builders, ship breakers, pottery factories, whaling industries, tanneries, skinners, weavers, dyers, breweries, and other industries were densely packed together along the river. Based on the evidence found on the foreshore, you can tell where the trades were once located. Over the years, mudlarks have recovered many different types of tools from the river. Some of the most common finds are iron tools from the heyday of the port in the 18th–early 20th centuries. They are a testament to the "working river" and the tradesmen who plied their trade along the Thames. Some of the tools have been personalized and stamped with the owner's name or initials.

At the beginning of the 18th century, around 7,000 ships were entering the port each year, importing goods and fresh produce from around the globe. Between 1794 and 1824, the number of ships entering London increased from around 14,000 annually to nearly 24,000. In 1700, about 435,000 tons of shipping were recorded in London. By 1830, approximately 3,500,000 tons of cargo were

Top left: Ships docked by the Tower of London painting (Samuel Scott).
Bottom left: Engraved illustration of the Port of London in 1845 (S.C. Smyth).

THAMES LIGHTERMEN.

handled each year. To handle this huge volume of cargo, an army of workmen was required.

When large ships arrived in London from overseas, they entered the enclosed docks or cast anchor in the center of the river. Flat-bottomed boats called "Lighters" were used by Lightermen (above left) to transfer cargo from the large ships to the wharves and warehouses along the river. When the tide receded, the flat-bottomed boats rested on the exposed foreshore without tipping over, as cranes and men transferred the cargo into the warehouses. The river was often overcrowded and congested with ships and boats of all sizes. Lightermen were highly skilled at navigating the river, and they used boat hooks which were attached to wooden poles to maneuver (push and pull) between boats. Over the years, I have found numerous iron boat hooks from the 19th century (below) in the Thames.

Quayside workers such as stevedores and lumpers moved the cargo from the boats into the warehouses. They used essential tools made of iron (left) to manually carry the goods. Double bag hooks were the most common tool used for handling smaller sacks such as coffee beans. Drum hooks were used by dockers to transport drums and barrels. At the tip of the hook, a small plate was used to grip the rim of the container, making it easier to carry. Double sack hooks were formed with two hooks to handle large bales of commodities such as wool.

At the heart of the global shipping industry, London was known as the "warehouse of the world." The vast network of warehouses and storage facilities along the riverfront contained valuable commodities from around the globe, and security was paramount to deter river pirates, thieves, smugglers, and even desperate mudlarks. Tall gates would have been secured with sturdy padlocks. They were also used to lock barges which were floating on the river. Padlocks were made by fastening plates of thick iron together with brass rivets. Over the years, Alan Murphy has recovered many types of iron padlocks (below) from the 18th–19th centuries.

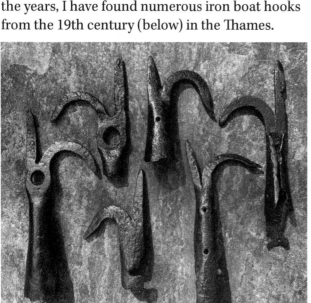

Top left: 19th-century illustration of Thames Lightermen, London Labour and the London Poor, *1861 (Henry Mayhew). Top right: Various iron sack hooks found by Monika Buttling-Smith (Jason Sandy). Bottom left: Jason's collection of 19th-century boat hooks (Jason Sandy). Bottom right: 18th–19th-century padlocks (Alan Murphy).*

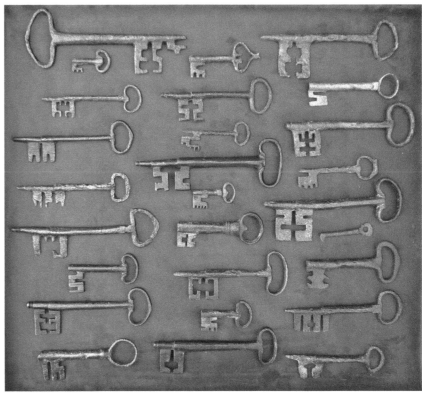

Some of them have very unique shapes such as a spherical padlock (top left) dating to AD 1450–1700. It has a circular locking arm which is D-shaped in cross-section. In the center of the sphere, there is a keyhole still present.

Many of the padlocks which Alan has found have a name and address stamped into the iron surface. "G. CARR, 108 & 110 ROTHERHITHE STREET" appears on two of the 19th-century padlocks (above left). George Carr was a barge builder, anchor smith, and engineer whose business was located on Rotherhithe Street. Although George's business disappeared a long time ago, this padlock is a reminder of his important trade.

For every lock, a key is required. Graham duHeaume has found hundreds of medieval and post-medieval keys (top right) in the Thames. The creative designs and unique shapes of these keys are absolutely beautiful. Just imagine what doors and locks these keys opened in London centuries ago!

Top left: Spherical padlock from 1450–1700 (Alan Murphy). Middle left: 19th-century padlocks from George Carr's business (Alan Murphy). Top right: 15th–16th-century keys (Graham duHeaume).

Since Romans times, the Port of London has been a place where ships and boats were built and repaired. Some of the largest and most successful docks for shipbuilding were located along the river in Deptford, Woolwich, Blackwall, and Millwall in East London. The famous naval dockyard in Deptford was established by Henry VIII in 1513. In operation for over 300 years, the docks produced impressive warships that fought under Horatio Nelson in the Battle of Trafalgar. The Deptford docks were also associated with the great Tudor explorers Sir Frances Drake and Sir Walter Raleigh. The largest ship ever launched from the Thames foreshore was the steamship SS *Great Eastern*, which was designed by Isambard Kingdom Brunel and built by J. Scott Russell & Co. in Millwall. After some difficulty, the ship was successfully launched in 1858, and could carry 4,000 passengers from Britain to Australia without refueling.

Until the 19th century, most ships were made of timber. Axes, saws, chisels, and files were used to cut, shape, and finish the timber. Over the years, mudlarks have found a wide variety of these ship building tools on the foreshore.

Tony Pilson discovered a complete 17th-century carpenter's axe head (left) made of cast iron. It has an integral socket where the wooden handle had been fixed. The triangular blade is decorated with a band of incised cross-hatching within two curved lines. Two marker's marks in the shape of conjoined letters "OC" have been stamped on the blade.

Iron hammers were an important tool for ship building. Brian Pitkin found a beautiful hammer (left) from the 17th century. The head is made of cast iron. A large, iron tang is securely wedged into the socket of the hammer head. The tang flattens and tapers to a point, and a wooden handle would have been fastened to the iron tang with the two rivets which are still visible.

Located near the East India Docks, the Thames Ironworks and Shipbuilding Company constructed iron-hulled steamships. Dock workers from the company started a football team in 1895 called the Thames Ironworks Football Club, which later became West Ham United in 1900. The Premier League football team still has two diagonally crossed hammers in their logo (left), which are a reminder of the dockworkers who used hammers to build the large ships along the Thames. The football club is still referred to as "The Hammers."

To ensure that the joints between the timber planks on a ship's hull were watertight, shipbuilders would use a caulking tool (left) to wedge caulk into the gaps. The iron tool has a flat head and cylindrical handle which flattens and widens to a narrow edge that is slightly rounded to push the caulk into narrow gaps.

Rope was an important part of a ship's rigging. It had a variety of functions, but its primary role was to secure the ship's sails. A simple bone tool called a "marlin spike" or "fid" was used to splice and mend the ropes and keep them in good working order. Formed from a sheep's metapodial bone, the proximal end of the bone was sliced in half to create a simple scoop (left). Dating to the 15th–18th centuries, these simple, lightweight tools were portable, and some were drilled with a suspension hole so

Top to bottom: 17th-century carpenter's axe head (PAS). 17th-century iron hammer (Brian Pitkin). Logo of West Ham United football club (West Ham United). Iron caulking tool (PAS). Carved bone marlin spikes or fids (PAS).

The Fighting Temeraire, tugged to her last berth to be broken up, *1838 (J.M.W. Turner).*

it could be carried around the neck on a leather cord, ready for use whenever needed. Others were embellished and carved with criss-cross designs, rings and dots, and patterns of incised lines which indicates that they were beloved, personalized tools. It is thought that these tools may have also been used as apple corers, cheese scoops, or bone marrow scoops.

Ship breaking was a lucrative business along the Thames. The famous English artist J. M. W. Turner immortalized London's ship breaking industry in his painting, *The Fighting Temeraire* (above). The 98-gun ship played a distinguished role in the Battle of Trafalgar in 1805. The painting depicts the HMS *Temeraire*

Rusting ironwork visible on the exposed riverbed (Jason Sandy).

being towed by a paddle-wheel steam tug towards to the yards of shipbreaker John Beatson in Rotherhithe in September 1838 to be broken up for scrap.

To this day, the Thames foreshore is littered with traces of the ship breaking industry. Especially in Rotherhithe, there is a vast amount of rusting metalwork (below) lying on the foreshore. Heavy timbers, ship building and breaking tools, copper and brass nails, large ropes, and chains demarcate where some of the largest ship building and breaking companies were situated along the river. Because of the weight of the metal tools and ironwork, they have not moved from the location where they were dropped hundreds of years ago.

Billingsgate Fish Market token from F. Jary (Jason Sandy).

Over the centuries, there have been numerous markets located along the Thames. One of the oldest and most famous is Billingsgate Fish Market in Central London, which dates back to the 16th century. During the 19th century, the fish market was the largest in the world. It was famous for its foul-mouthed fishmongers and so-called "oyster-wives" who shouted the offers of the day in their own special dialect.

While mudlarking along the foreshore below Old Billingsgate fish market, I have found many remnants of the original market, such as scallop shells, oyster shells, bag seals, fishing weights, and fishing hooks. In 2019, I found a 19th-century market token (above). The fish salesman's name "F. Jary" and "Billingsgate" are stamped on the front. The value of the token "One Shilling" is stamped on the back. Although it has been relocated, Billingsgate Fish Market still exists.

The banks of the River Thames were also used as open marketplaces to sell fresh fruit, vegetables, and other commodities. I have discovered several brass jetons (below) on the foreshore where the marketplaces once stood. Jetons were coin-like counters produced across Europe from the 13th–17th centuries. They were used as reckoning counters for financial calculations on a lined board similar to an abacus.

Jason's collection of 16th–17th-century jetons (Jason Sandy).

Jeton production increased after the Protestant Reformation in the 16th century, and the famous Nuremburg jeton makers often stamped religious proverbs and messages in German on their counters. One of my favorite inscriptions is "Gottes Segen macht reich" which means "God's blessing makes you rich." As merchants were conducting their accounting with jetons, I'm sure they were hoping for God's blessing to increase their wealth and prosperity.

One of the most famous groups of workers along the river were the Thames Watermen. For centuries, the Watermen transported people across the river in their wherries. For over 600 years, there was only one bridge across the river in London. If you didn't live near Old London Bridge, you had to hop into a wherry if you wanted to cross the river.

Wapping Old Stairs was a popular crossing point in East London. In a painting entitled *Miseries of London* (left) produced by Thomas Rowlandson in 1804, he illustrated a woman being assailed by a group of Watermen, begging her to step into their boats to cross to the south side of the river. At Wapping Old Stairs and other river crossings, I have found many rose farthings (below) which are very small, copper coins produced in the 17th century. It is believed that these small coins could have been used to pay the Waterman's fare to cross the river.

In 2020, Guy Phillips recovered a 17th-century trade token (above) from a riverside tavern called the "Waterman's Arms" at Wapping Dock. Within a shield, a wherry and crossed oars are illustrated on the token. The tavern was owned by Edward Willdee and named after the Watermen who lived locally. You can imagine the raucous tavern, overcrowded with sweaty Watermen after a hard day's work on the river.

For centuries, London was the largest and most important port city in the world. Thousands of people lived and worked along the docks, and the tools and artifacts which they dropped in the river are a salient reminder of their hard work and contribution to the success of the port. To find out more about the history of the Port of London, I would highly recommend a visit to the Museum of London Docklands. Located in an original brick warehouse built in 1802 to store rum, sugar, molasses, coffee, and cotton imported from the West Indies, the museum tells the story of the Docklands and its people throughout the ages. Within the original timber structure of the warehouse, they have recreated a "Sailortown" (below) to provide an immersive, time-traveling experience back to the heyday of the port city in the 19th century.

Above left: Watermen at Old Wapping Stairs *(Thomas Rowlandson). Bottom left: Jason's collection of 17th-century rose farthings (Jason Sandy). Top right: 17th-century token from the Waterman's Arms tavern (PAS). Bottom right: Museum of London Docklands (Jason Sandy).*

JACK AND STEVE ENGEHAM

Jack and Steve (Dad) go mudlarking together, day or night and in all weather! Right from the start, Jack has been the driving force behind our interest in mudlarking. When he was a child, Jack carried out mock archaeological digs in his Gran and Granddad's garden—typically in the middle of the lawn—much to his Gran's despair. The first item Jack found was a 1926 halfpenny in a flowerbed. We went mudlarking for the first time as part of an organized session suggested by Jack's former primary school Head Mistress. Well, Jack's attitude about history changed overnight!

Now Jack is over six foot tall and would like to study archaeology at a university. Steve finds it amusing when people ask him for help identifying their own finds and typically says, "You're better off asking Jack."

Steve grew up in a 15th-century house, where visitors bumped their heads on the low ceilings and "witch's marks" had been carved in timber beams long before. Steve's passion for history came from his own father who loved that old house and enjoyed researching the local history.

The enjoyment of mudlarking for us goes beyond the discovery and involves the preservation and research of the stories behind the finds. It is always a treat to have items recorded by the Museum of London for the Portable Antiquities Scheme.

Despite our competitive nature and wanting to discover the best artifact, when either of us finds something special, it always spurs the other one on. A good day is when both of us have found something cool, but bragging rights are typically in favor of Jack. The time when both of us found complete torpedo bottles was really special.

Over the last five years of mudlarking, we have collected anything from silver hammered coins to decorated clay pipes to Roman pottery, but we treasure personal items the most. Hand-carved bone knife handles, a Tudor bone comb, and a Georgian miniature toy plate are some of the personal items that we love. From discarded machetes to live ordnance or gold rings, you just never know what the Thames will gift.

However, our favorite item has to be a 17th-century trader's token from John Standbrooke, a Lymeman at St Mary Ouer Stairs (next to Southwark Cathedral). The research really made this find special. It connected us to a time when many people suffered during the Great Plague of 1665 and the Great Fire of London in 1666, but others such as John Standbrooke probably benefited from increased business.

A Lymeman is someone who produces or supplies lime, a fine powder made by crushing and pulverizing limestone or chalk. It had several uses during the period between 1648–1672, when traders' tokens were in circulation. Usually, lime was used in mortar for building, but it was also spread on graves in the false expectation that it aided the decomposition of bodies (which it didn't, but it did help counter the smell).

Portraits by Tom Harrison.

BACK IN TIME

Big Ben and Westminster bridge in London (S.Borisov/Shutterstock).

Time is money. Time waits for no man. Time is on my side. Save time. Keep time. Time after time. Time flies. Turn back time. Wasting time. Killing time. On time. Do time. Against the clock. Beat the clock. The clock is ticking. These idioms and well-known phrases in the English language stress the importance and value of time in our culture.

Throughout history, mankind has kept track of time—from observing sun and star positions in ancient times to checking the digital clock on a smartphone today. For centuries, London has been associated with time. Located along the River Thames, Greenwich has a special location in time and space. Greenwich Mean Time (GMT) is the local clock time in this Royal Borough of London.

In 1767, astronomer Nevil Maskelyne published a Nautical Almanac, which contained tables of lunar distances based on astronomical data collected at the Royal Observatory in Greenwich and using GMT as the standard time. By utilizing these tables, British mariners were able to pinpoint their positions at sea by calculating their longitude from the Greenwich meridian (0° longitude). In 1880, Greenwich Mean Time was officially recognized as Britain's legal standard time. Installed in 1852, the Shepherd Gate Clock (right) is the first clock to display GMT time to the public, and it is still ticking today in the outer wall of the Royal Observatory in Greenwich.

During the International Meridian Conference in Washington, D.C., in 1884, "Greenwich was selected as the Prime Meridian of the world because of the observatory's long-standing reputation for producing good-quality data for navigation," explains Emily Akkermans, Curator of Time at Royal Museums Greenwich. "Seventy percent of the world's shipping companies were already using charts and data tables based on the Greenwich meridian." Therefore, the Prime Meridian (0° longitude) in Greenwich became the center of world time and the basis for the global system of time zones.

Keeping track of time in London has always been important. One of the most famous clocks along

the River Thames is located at the top of "Big Ben," the neo-Gothic clock tower at the Houses of Parliament in Westminster (facing page). Standing at 96 meters (316 feet) tall and completed in 1859, the four-faced clock in Big Ben was once the largest and most accurate clock in the world. With dials measuring 6.9 meters (22.5 feet) in diameter, the clock tower is one of the most iconic and prominent British symbols renowned around the globe. When the clock strikes midnight on December 31st, it is televised throughout Britain and signals the beginning of the New Year, followed by a breathtaking fireworks display along the River Thames.

Centuries before public clocks were readily available throughout London, people kept track of time by using portable devices. In Tudor and Stuart times, small sundials which could fit in your pocket became a popular way of keeping time when you were out and about.

Several years ago, mudlark Peter Olivant discovered a portable, diptych sundial (below right) dating to 1580–1620. It is carved from ivory and was possibly produced in Nuremberg, Germany. Radiating lines and Arabic numbers 4–12 and 1–8 are inscribed on the surface to mark the hours of daylight. Measuring 32.1mm (1.26 inches) in length, the sundial is calibrated for use in the Northern Hemisphere. In the center, the circular recess would have been fitted with a brass ring and sheet of glass, which are now missing. To cast a shadow and indicate the time, a gnomon was fixed in the small hole at the junction of the radiating lines. Providing an ingenious

Above center: Shepherd Gate Clock in Greenwich (Alvesgaspar).
Bottom right: Post-medieval ivory pocket sundial (PAS).

way to tell time anywhere, the small sundial fit comfortably in the palm of your hand.

On a different day, Peter also found a brass sundial (left) from 1580–1620. Inside the tiny, circular frame, which is 15.9mm (0.63 inches) in diameter, there are two projecting tags with lugs to secure a triangular fin which functioned as the gnomon. To fit in one's pocket, the fin could be folded over and laid flat on the face of the sundial. Engraved around the perimeter of the sundial are the numbers 5–12 and 1–7 which represent the hours of the day.

A similar pocket sundial (left) was found by another mudlark. Dating to 1570–1650, the brass sundial also has a circular frame with an ornate, scrolled bar in the center. Used to cast a shadow and tell time, the gnomon is formed by a triangular fin with a decorative, fimbriated profile along one edge. It is fixed with lugs to the central bar and outer circle. Measuring 25.3mm (1 inch) in diameter, the sundial is collapsible so it could lay flat and compact. Around the edge of the circular frame, the Roman numerals 4–12 and 1–8 are engraved. The adjacent, calibrated ring is scored with simple lines which represent the quarter hours. Inscribed at the top of the sundial, the maker's initials "I S" are visible.

Several years ago, Ian Smith unearthed an unusual, ring-shaped pocket sundial (below) from the 17th century. Considered a luxury

Top left: 16th–17th-century brass pocket sundial (PAS).
Left: Collapsible, brass pocket sundial (PAS).
Above: 17th-century brass ring sundial (Ian Smith).

item, this sundial was imported from Nuremberg and would have been a cherished possession and well maintained. Therefore, it is very unusual to find one of these types of sundials in the Thames.

Consisting of two brass rings with a 38.8mm (1.5 inches) diameter, a sliding ring made of sheet metal fits into a central groove between the upper and lower rings. A square clasp is pierced with a pinhole and acts as a handle to rotate the sliding ring. The inner surface of the ring functions as the clock face and is subdivided into three rows, one for each season: S (summer), H (harvest), and W (winter). Slanted to the sun angles entering the dial, the hours are marked with incised lines. Punched dots denote the half hours.

On the outer surface, the initials (I F M A M I) of the months from January to June are indicated on the upper half of the sundial. Upside down on the lower half, the months July through December (I A S O N D) appear. When turned over, you can tell the time during these months. After 400 years at the bottom of the river, the individual parts of the sundial are still movable and fully functional. By rotating the pinhole of the sliding ring to the correct day of the year, the time can be told from the sunlight shining through the pinhole onto the markings of the inner clockface.

All of these compact, portable sundials demonstrate the ingenuity and creativity of the craftsmen in the 16th and 17th centuries. But, there's only one problem. In London, it's often cloudy and overcast, so a sundial is of little use without direct sunlight to cast a shadow.

At the beginning of the 16th century, the famous German watchmaker, Peter Henlein, developed a timepiece that wasn't dependent on the sun. Produced using recent advancements in main-

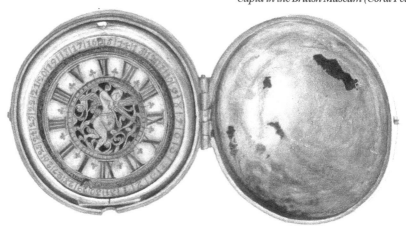

Illustration of a 17th-century pocket watch depicting Cupid in the British Museum (Coral Pearce).

springs, Peter created a portable watch, which was worn as a pendant around the neck. In the 17th century, the design was further refined, and King Charles II made watches fashionable by wearing a waistcoat and placing the watch inside a pocket. The popularity of pocket watches skyrocketed, and every esteemed gentleman wore a pocket watch as a status symbol to display his wealth. This luxury item was embellished with ornate designs and sometimes encrusted with diamonds and other jewels.

In 1993, one of the most extraordinary pocket watches (above) was unearthed from the Thames foreshore by Tony Pilson with its cover, chain, and winder. Miraculously, it is completely intact except for the glass dome which has disintegrated over time.

Produced by John Cooke in London between 1670–1675, it is a pre-balance spring verge watch within a silver case. The dial of the pocket watch consists of an outer ring engraved with the numbers 1–31 for the days of the month, and the exact day is indicated by a steel pointer attached to a revolving, gilt-brass ring. Infilled with black wax, the Roman numerals I–XII are engraved on the circular, silver chapter ring. Small, red fleur-de-lis between the numerals mark the half hours. In the center of the pocket watch, Cupid is beautifully engraved on a revolving gilt-brass disc with an openwork, foliate decoration. Ingeniously, Cupid's arrow indicates the time. This exquisite pocket watch is now in the permanent collection of the British Museum.

18th–19th-century watch winders (Collage by Jason Sandy).

18th-century watch winder with galleon ship (Jason Sandy)

Before batteries were invented, watches had to be wound on a regular basis to ensure they kept time accurately. The hollow, tubular end of a watch winder was inserted into the pocket watch or clock, and the head was rotated 360 degrees around a central pivot point to wind the watch. The winders had a loop or hole at the top to suspend it from the pocket watch chain.

Watch winders were not only a practical tool, but they were also worn as a fashion accessory. Because they were suspended from the watch chain, they were very visible, unlike the watch, which was concealed in a pocket. Therefore, watch winders were highly decorated to attract attention and indicate the high value of the hidden pocket watch.

The heads and shanks of the 18th– and 19th-century watch winders were cast in brass with a wide variety of creative and imaginative designs. Foliate and floral patterns, flowerpots, roses, thistles, vines with leaves, furls, crowns, chubby cherubs,

banners, scrolls, shells, cartouches, and inscriptions appear on the different watch winders. They are little works of art and were made in all shapes and sizes.

As watch winders are relatively small, they easily slipped out of people's hands and fell into the Thames. Kevin James Dyer, Mike Walker, Florrie Evans, Mark Vosper, Mark Paros, and I have found a wonderful array of watch winders (facing page) from the 18th and 19th centuries.

One of the nicest watch winders I found in the river (above) is highly decorated with a lovely maritime theme. One side depicts a galleon ship in full sail, equipped with four cannons. On the other side, a helmeted knight's head is surrounded by cannons, spears, poles with flags, and a trumpet at the top. I can imagine a highly respected admiral or naval commander used this watch winder before arriving in London and accidentally dropping it in the river.

As pocket watches became popular among adults in the 17th and 18th centuries, children were also fascinated by the portable time pieces owned by their parents. As gifts, parents would buy miniature watches made of inexpensive pewter for their children to play with. Kids would proudly wear them and pretend they were real pocket watches.

Over the years, I have found two toy pocket watches from the 17th and 18th centuries. Other mudlarks have also discovered some exquisite examples. For instance, Matthew Goode found a stunning, complete toy watch (above) with an openwork pattern. It was cast in pewter in a single mold between 1625–1800.

Post-medieval toy pocket watch (PAS).

At the top of the clock face, there is a loop where it would have been suspended similarly to an adult pocket watch. In the center, the hours on the chapter ring are depicted with Roman numerals from I–XII. The hour and minute hands are subtly suggested by a central cross and three pellets surrounded by openwork scrolls in each quadrant. Around the perimeter, the clock is decorated with a beaded border and openwork pattern of repetitive scrolls, circles, and lozenges.

Several years ago, Ian Smith discovered a complete Hux toy pocket watch (below) from the 18th century. It was carefully restored by Iain McIntyre at the British Museum. Ian states

18th-century Hux pocket watch (Ian Smith).

Mariners' Time Ball at Flamsteed House, Greenwich (Originalpickaxe).

emphatically that, "it now clicks, and the hand turns!" For a toy, the pocket watch is very sophisticated comprised of several movable components made of pewter. The hours are indicated by the Roman numerals I–XII, and the hand is attached to a central rod so it can be rotated from the back of the watch via a winder hole, creating a ticking noise.

In the book, *Toys, Trifles & Trinkets*, author Hazel Forsyth explains that, "these circular watches are the only known type with moving parts and a simple mechanism. They are a very good imitation of English or French pair-case watches dating from about 1700 to the mid-18th century."

Sharks are incredibly rare in the River Thames, but a surprised fisherman caught one in Poplar (East London) in 1787. When he dissected the shark measuring 2.8 meters (9 feet 3 inches), the fisherman made a startling discovery—a silver pocket watch was found in the shark's belly. It was inscribed with the words: Henry Warson, London. Once the bizarre story hit the London newspapers, Henry came forward and said he had sold the watch to Ephraim Thompson of Whitechapel who

gave the watch to his son as a present before his first voyage on a merchant ship. During a violent storm off the coast of Falmouth, Ephraim's son fell overboard and was never seen again. Since the watch was found in the shark's belly, it was assumed the son was eaten. To provide closure and symbolically lay his son to rest, Ephraim bought the dead shark from the fisherman to preserve it as a memorial to his son. Although the details of this story are disputed, it has to be one of the more bizarre stories from the Thames if it is true.

On a hill overlooking the river, a bright red "time ball" is mounted on a post on top of the Royal Observatory in Greenwich (above). Since 1833, it has been used as a time-signaling device, and the ball drops at exactly 1 PM every day. Once the largest port in the world, it was essential that seagoing ships docked in London knew the time. Clearly visible from the ships on the river, captains could set their marine chronometers to Greenwich Mean Time (GMT) indicated by the time ball. Accurate timekeeping was essential to navigate and establish a ship's longitude on the open sea. Still to this day, the red ball drops at 1 PM above the River Thames, keeping London "on time."

IAN SMITH

During the school holidays in 1973, I was the typical, bored 10-year-old boy. But, I had just seen a program on TV about a man who searched the Bristol Channel for clay pipes. He had converted his shed into a mini museum and made some very impressive displays. That was it! My elder brother and I headed down to the foreshore. I lived in Battersea then, so it was only a 15-minute walk. For the next few weeks, we rummaged about down there, picking up a few broken stems until finally...a whole clay pipe bowl! It was a Victorian example, shaped like an acorn. Over the coming weeks, we slowly headed further east, but to be honest, our pipe collection wasn't growing that quickly. It was all housed in one of those mini sets of plastic drawers.

Eventually we reached Blackfriars Bridge, and we could see in the distance on the north foreshore a small group of people digging. We headed over to see what they were doing and were amazed to see the foreshore around their digs strewn with clay pipes. They were clearly looking for something else. That day we went home with a carrier bag full of pipes. Although a little cagey at first, the mudlarks gradually opened up to us and started showing us their finds, mainly small, metal artifacts and coins. Nobody used a metal detector back then, and no permit was required.

The people involved were those slightly eccentric, loner types. The technique was to dig a hole, sieve the earth at the waterline, and then methodically flick through the stones with a kitchen knife. I vividly remember one of these first mudlarks, Eric the Bookbinder, a man in his 50s. He would turn up in a white shirt and smart trousers, tie a knotted handkerchief to his head, and don a pair of marigold gloves before he started digging. He always had a pack of "Refreshers" which he frequently offered around. The biggest miracle was that he would leave the foreshore as clean as when he went down.

You never forget your first metal find. Mine was a Tudor brass jeton which I spotted while digging in a hole, perfectly preserved and still shiny. Once the tide was in, we would often meet up in the Samuel Pepys pub along the river. Out would come re-used tobacco tins containing the day's finds, which we would all eagerly pore over. There was always that bit of competition as to who had made the most interesting find!

After the initial "buzz" of making a find had subsided, there was the second wave of excitement when you proudly took your finds to the Museum of London for their perusal. We were lucky that Brian Spencer was the Director and Head of the Medieval Department. A practical Yorkshireman, he instantly realized that there was a treasure trove of finds that could soon be lost, and he gave us his fulsome encouragement. I remember waiting for the post to arrive with a letter from Brian, containing the latest batch of finds photocopied, a fascinating description accompanying each item. When I see how much of the foreshore has eroded in the last 50 years it fills me with pride to think I have played even a small part in saving London's history.

Portraits by Hannah Smiles

LIQUID
LEGACY

Sunrise over the Thames (Antoine Buchet).

River wall in the Museum of London (Jason Sandy).

Much of what we know about the early inhabitants who lived along the River Thames has been ascertained from the objects which they deposited in the river. As there are no written records from these time periods, archaeology is the primary source of knowledge about early humans in the Thames Valley. In the Museum of London, many of the artifacts on display in the "London before London" gallery (above) were discovered and recovered from the Thames. By studying these objects, historians have learned a lot about these ancient cultures.

Through the long-term collaboration between the mudlarks and Museum of London, a vast amount of artifacts have been found and recorded. "Over the last 40 years, the mudlarks have made a really important contribution to the study of London's history through the sheer volume and variety of finds that they have recovered from the Thames foreshore," explains Meriel Jeater, a Curator at the Museum

Roman artifacts found by Ed Bucknall (Jason Sandy).

of London. Dr. Michael Lewis, Head of Portable Antiquities and Treasure at the British Museum, says that mudlarks' finds can "alter our picture of the past. Many of the finds are very small pieces. They are like little pieces in a jigsaw puzzle that help us create a picture of the past. By putting them together, we get an idea of what's going on. They can actually rewrite history."

"The Society of Thames Mudlarks has a long and

Infant WOOLLY Mammoth Tooth Mammuthus primigenius Around 2 million years old

Adult Woolly Mammoth Tooth Mammut Mammuthus Primigenius around 2 million Years old

Bone Ice Skate used on the river Thames during the frost fairs 1600s - 1800s

Bronze age red deer antler axe mattock 3,000-1,000 BC

proud history of making a unique contribution to the story of London. For more than 40 years, its members have used their special privileges, not only to swell the shelves of the Museum of London, but also to further our understanding of the capital's heritage," explains Ian Smith, former chairman of the Society.

"Mudlarks have played a unique role in expanding our understanding of history by uncovering the everyday items that were part and parcel of life in London, such as children's toys, cutlery, trading tokens, and buttons worn by paupers as well as princes. Our view of history is skewed by what's written down, and the chroniclers tend to concentrate on 'High Society.' The mudlarks have redressed the balance and shone a light on the capital's every folk," proclaims Tim Miller, current chairman of the Society of Thames Mudlarks. "The Society has made an extraordinary contribution to the historical record. The scale of the discoveries—over many decades—has led to historians rethinking some of what they thought they knew about life for ordinary Londoners. This information would have been lost had it not been gleaned from the riverbank by a dedicated band of searchers committed to salvaging vital evidence."

Veteran mudlarks have also made important contributions and donations to local museums. For instance, Tony Pilson donated thousands of medieval and post-medieval toys and buttons to the Museum of London. In 2012, Peter Elkins donated around 5,000 marked clay pipes to the National Pipe Archive. In 2020, Graham duHeaume donated over 860 knives to the Worshipful Company of Cutlers.

Following the acquisition and research of mudlarks' discoveries, many books have been written about the unique artifacts found on riverside sites and on the Thames foreshore in London. For instance, Michael Mitchener, Brian Spencer, and Dr. Michael Lewis have all written books about the Museum of London's extensive collection of medieval pilgrim and secular badges. Brian Spencer, former Keeper in Charge of the Museum of London, worked very closely with the mudlarks for several decades, identifying and recording their finds. In his book, *Pilgrim Souvenirs and Secular Badges*, Spencer expressed his gratitude to the mudlarks saying, "I am greatly indebted to past and present members of the Society of Thames Mudlarks. Their boundless enthusiasm and their skill in the use of metal detectors have vastly increased the number and variety of medieval small finds found at London. I gratefully acknowledge the promptness with which most of their finds have been submitted to the museum so that they could be identified, recorded, photographed and, where appropriate, published."

Some people claim that the "golden age" of mudlarking is over, and others complain that the amount of finds are far fewer than in previous years. However, that is not necessarily true. "Interesting artifacts are constantly being discovered by mudlarks and brought to the museum. Finds from the Thames are still giving us new information and adding to the collective knowledge. These objects are continuing to enhance our understanding of London's history and the lives of Londoners who inhabited the city over the last two millennia," explains Stuart Wyatt (below), Finds Liaison Officer at the Museum of London.

It is vital that these discoveries be recorded on the Portable Antiquities Scheme, so that they can be researched and help us form a deeper understanding of the historical context. The Portable Antiquities Scheme was established by the British Museum in 1997 in order to record the incredible amount of artifacts found by the general public.

"These tell us about past landscapes, the people who were once there, and how they lived and worked. Many of the finds are interesting in their own right, but collectively, they are helping to transform our understanding of Britain's past," according to the Portable Antiquities Scheme. At the publication date of this book, over 1.6 million artifacts have been recorded on the PAS online database (www.finds.org.uk). According to Hartwig Fischer, Director of the British Museum, "there have been major advancements in our knowledge of the past through archaeological finds discovered by the public and recorded with the Portable Antiquities Scheme." The PAS annual report in 2020 states that there were 49,045 artifacts recorded on the database that year. The online records have been used in 823 research projects, including 57 pieces of large-scale research and 168 PhDs. When mudlarks have their artifacts recorded on the PAS database, they are adding to the material being researched and interpreted by historians globally, who are transforming our understanding of the past. Mudlarks play an important part in recording our history for future generations.

In 2022, a British documentary series on Channel 4 called "Great British History Hunters" showcased

Stuart Wyatt educating exhibition visitors (Jason Sandy).

Part of Jason's mudlarking collection (Jason Sandy).

some of the most historically significant and interesting finds which have been recorded recently on the Portable Antiquities Scheme. The TV show attracted national interest in the wide range of artifacts found by members of the public. A few mudlarks and I were featured in the TV series, along with some of our best artifacts from the Thames.

After decades of searching, many mudlarks have amassed extensive collections (above) of artifacts. Since the Museum of London returns most artifacts to the finder once they have been recorded, mudlarks are allowed to

keep them. The majority of these historic objects are in personal collections and are unfortunately not on public display. In the future, the Thames Museum (below) will provide a place to display these collections and tell the story of London through mudlarking finds. The new museum will be specifically dedicated to the archaeology of the River Thames, and academics, visitors, and school children can research and learn from these extraordinary finds.

Since the River Thames and its foreshore are a living museum, guided mudlarking tours will be offered to give visitors the

Architect's illustration of Thames Museum interior (Flanagan Lawrence Architects).

chance to discover and engage with history for themselves in a tangible way. By experiencing "hands-on history," it will bring the past to life and inspire people to learn more about the objects they find. With new discoveries being made every day, the museum's collections will grow and evolve with something new to see during every visit. The Thames Museum Trust is a registered charity (1163381) that was founded by Steve Brooker and Nick Stevens.

As the Thames Museum is being developed, we are taking the museum to the people. Through pop-up exhibitions in historic venues around London, the mudlarking collections can now be enjoyed by a larger audience. As part of the Totally Thames Festival in 2019, 2021, and 2022, mudlarking exhibitions were held in the Bargehouse at OXO Tower, St. Paul's Cathedral, Cutler's Hall, National Maritime Museum, Roman Amphitheatre in Guildhall Art Gallery, Chiswick Pier Trust, and Watermen's Hall. These venues created a dramatic and historic backdrop for the displays of mudlarks' personal collections. A series of educational mudlarking talks and guided foreshore tours accompanied the exhibitions. The events have attracted large crowds.

Mudlarking exhibition in Roman amphitheater (Jason Sandy).

Mudlarking exhibition in Guildhall Art Gallery (Jason Sandy).

Mudlarking exhibition at Chiswick Pier Trust (Jason Sandy).

Left: Medieval children's shoe freshly extracted from the mud (Jason Sandy).

Within the last ten years, mudlarking has quickly gained popularity, as more and more mudlarks post their discoveries on various social media channels such as Instagram, Facebook, Twitter, YouTube, and TikTok. Social media has provided a great platform for mudlarks to share their finds with the global community and get people interested in history. Some mudlarks go to great lengths to research their finds and share their knowledge by posting photos along with intriguing backstories. People love the thrill of seeing artifacts (above) plucked fresh from the mud. Many "armchair mudlarks" live vicariously by watching mudlarks' videos on YouTube and following their muddy adventures. The TV show, *Mud Men*, which aired on the History Channel for three seasons from 2011–2013, was the network's most watched and most popular UK-produced show at that time. Steve Brooker and Nick Stevens starred alongside Johnny Vaughan in discovering London's past along the Thames foreshore.

Mudlarks have found historical treasures with truly amazing stories which have attracted widespread media interest over the years. The Roman brothel token, King Richard III boar mount, 17th-century ball and chain, and the Victoria Cross medal are examples of recent artifacts found in the Thames that captured international attention. The stories behind these important finds have been reported to a wide audience through major newspapers, magazines, and books.

Because of TV shows, social media, and international press coverage, people around the world have discovered mudlarking. "Mudlark tourists" travel to London to go search and discover London's history for themselves. Since mudlarks became active on social media, there has been an exponential increase in the amount of people applying for permits from the Port of London Authority (PLA). When mudlarking licenses became a legal requirement in 2017, the PLA handed out 751 licenses. In 2021, the PLA issued 1,750 mudlarking licenses,

which is more than double the number of licenses given to new mudlarks (right) four years earlier. The Museum of London has also seen an increase in the number of new people reporting their finds. Although the PLA issues day permits to foreigners, it is illegal to take any historic objects out of Britain, unless an export license has been obtained from the Arts Council England.

The artifacts featured in this book are just the tip of the iceberg. They represent a selection of the wide range of finds from several millennia of London's history which have been discovered in the river. Each object reveals a unique story about London's illustrious history and give us a tangible connection to the people who lived here. For years to come, mudlarks will continue to make significant discoveries and write new chapters in the capital's history. The long legacy of the eternal river is still being uncovered with each new tide.

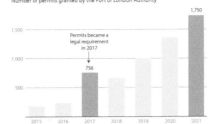

Number of permits granted by the Port of London Authority

Permits became a legal requirement in 2017

756

1,750

2015 2016 2017 2018 2019 2020 2021

Chart illustrating increase of mudlark license applications (Tom Nunan).

Jason mudlarking near Tower Bridge (Jon Attenborough).

RECOMMENDATIONS

RECOMMENDED MUSEUMS

Museum of London, 150 London Wall, Barbican, London EC2Y 5HN. museumoflondon.org.uk. Phone: +44 20 7001 9844.

Museum of London Docklands, No1 Warehouse, West India Quay, London E14 4AL. museumoflondon.org.uk. Phone: +44 20 7001 9844.

British Museum, Great Russell St, Bloomsbury, London WC1B 3DG. britishmuseum.org. Phone: +44 20 7323 8000.

Thames Museum (pop-up museum with temporary exhibitions in various venues), thamesmuseum.org.

National Maritime Museum, Park Row, Greenwich Peninsula, London SE10 9NF. rmg.co.uk/national-maritime-museum. Phone: +44 20 8312 6565.

Discover Greenwich Visitor Centre, Pepys House, 2 Cutty Sark Gardens, London SE10 9LW. ornc.org/visit/attractions/discover-greenwich-visitor-centre. Phone: +44 20 8269 4799.

Victoria and Albert Museum, Cromwell Rd, Knightsbridge, London SW7 2RL. vam.ac.uk Phone: +44 20 7942 2000.

Natural History Museum, Cromwell Rd, South Kensington, London SW7 5BD. nhm.ac.uk. Phone: +44 20 7942 5000.

London's Roman Amphitheatre, Guildhall Art Gallery, Guildhall Yard, London EC2V 5AE. cityoflondon.gov.uk/things-to-do/attractions-museums-entertainment/londons-roman-amphitheatre. Phone: +44 020 7332 3700.

Tower of London, St Katharine's & Wapping, London EC3N 4AB. hrp.org.uk/tower-of-london. Phone: +44 33 3320 6000.

Imperial War Museum, Lambeth Rd, London SE1 6HZ. iwm.org.uk/visits/iwm-london. Phone: +44 20 7416 5000.

National Army Museum, Royal Hospital Rd, Chelsea, London SW3 4HT. nam.ac.uk. Phone: 020 7730 0717.

Gunnersbury Park Museum, Gunnersbury Park House, Popes Ln, London W5 4NH. visitgunnersbury.org. Phone: +44 20 3961 0280.

Hampton Court Palace, Hampton Ct Way, Molesey, East Molesey KT8 9AU. hrp.org.uk/hampton-court-palace. Phone: +44 20 3166 6000.

Cutty Sark Visitors Center, King William Walk, Greenwich, London, SE10 9HT. rmg.co.uk/cutty-sark. Phone: +44 20 8312 6565.

Mary Rose Museum, Main Rd, Portsmouth PO1 3PY. maryrose.org. Phone: +44 23 9281 2931.

Ashmolean Museum, Beaumont St, Oxford OX1 2PH. ashmolean.org. Phone: +44 1865 278000.

The Fitzwilliam Museum, Trumpington St, Cambridge CB2 1RB. fitzmuseum.cam.ac.uk. Phone: +44 1223 332900.

Jorvik Viking Center, 19 Coppergate, York YO1 9WT. jorvikvikingcentre.co.uk. Phone: +44 1904 615505.

The Roman Baths, Abbey Churchyard, Bath BA1 1LZ. romanbaths.co.uk. Phone: +44 1225 477785.

The Box, Tavistock Place, Plymouth, Devon PL4 8AX. theboxplymouth.com. Phone: +44 1752 304774.

Mayflower Museum, 3-5 The Barbican, Plymouth, Devon, PL1 2LR. visitplymouth.co.uk/things-to-do/mayflower-museum-p928703. Phone: 01752 306330.

National Museum of Scotland, Chambers St, Edinburgh EH1 1JF. nms.ac.uk/national-museum-of-scotland. Phone: +44 300 123 6789.

RECOMMENDED BOOKS

Ackroyd, Peter. *London: The Biography.* Chatto & Windus, London, 2000.

Ackroyd, Peter. *Thames: Sacred River.* Vintage, London, 2008.

Ayto, Eric G. *Clay Tobacco Pipes.* Shire Library, Oxford, 2012.

Berry, George. *Seventeeth Century England: Traders and Their Tokens.* Seaby, London, 1988.

Chivers, Tom. *London Clay: Journeys in the Deep City.* Doubleday, London, 2021.

Cohen, Nathalie and Wragg, Eliott. *The River's Tale: Archaeology on the Thames Foreshore in Greater London.* Museum of London Archaeology, London, 2017.

Crampton, Caroline. *The Way to the Sea: The Forgotten Histories of the Thames Estuary.* Granta Books, London, 2019

Croad, Stephen. *Liquid History: The Thames Through Time.* B T Batford, London, 2003.

Egan, Geoff and Pritchard, Francis. *Dress Accessories, 1150-1450.* Boydell Press, Woodbridge, 2002.

Ellmers, Chris and Werner, Alex. *Dockland Life: A Pictorial History of London's Docks 1860-1970.* Mainstream Publishing Company, Edinburgh, 1991.

Ellmers, Chris and Werner, Alex. *London's Lost Riverscape: A Photographic Panorama.* Guild Publishing London, 1988.

Elton, Stuart F. *Cloth Seals: An Illustrated Reference Guide to the Identification of Lead Seals Attached to Cloth.* Archaeopress Archaeology, Oxford, 2017.

Forsyth, Hazel and Egan, Geoff. *Toys, Trifles & Trinkets.* Unicorn Press, London, 2005.

Hume, Ivor Noël. *Treasure in the Thames.* Frederick Muller, London, 1956.

Laing, Lloyd. *Pottery in Britain.* Greenlight Publishing, Witham, 2014.

Leahy, Kevin and Lewis, Michael. *Finds Identified: An Illustrated Guide to Metal Detecting and Archaeological Finds.* Greenlight Publishing, Witham, 2018.

Lewis, Michael. *Saints and their Badges.* Greenlight Publishing Company, Witham, 2016.

Milne, Gustav. *The Port of Roman London.* B T Batford, London, 1993.

Milne, Gustav. *The Port of Medieval London.* Tempus, Stroud, 2003.

Ross, Cathy and Clark, John. *London: The Illustrated History.* Penguin Books, London, 2011.

Russell, Malcolm. *Mudlark'd: Hidden Histories from the River Thames.* Thames & Hudson, London, 2022.

Sandling, Ted. *A Mudlark's Treasures.* Aurum, London, 2021.

Sandy, Jason and Stevens, Nick. *Thames Mudlarking: Searching for London's Lost Treasures.* Shire, London, 2021.

Spencer, Brian. *Pilgrim Souvenirs and Secular Badges.* Boydell Press, Woodbridge, 2010.

Spragg, Iain. *London's Strangest Tales: The Thames.* Portico Books, London, 2014.

Thomas, Chris. *London's Archaeological Secrets: A World City Revealed.* Yale University Press, London, 2003.

Whitehead, Ross. *Buckles, 1250-1800.* Greenlight Publishing, Witham, 2003.

Winn, Christopher. *I Never Knew That About the River Thames.* Random House, London, 2010.

ACKNOWLEDGMENTS

First and foremost, I would like to thank Kirsti Scott. This book would not exist without her tireless enthusiasm, vision, and hard work over the past four years. Kirsti single-handedly produced this book while working full-time as publisher and editor-in-chief of *Beachcombing* magazine. I am forever grateful for her colorful, creative layouts and skillful editing. Throughout the process, she has been a mentor, motivator, encourager, and close friend, although we live on different continents.

I have thoroughly enjoyed working with Tom Harrison, who has beautifully photographed the mudlarks in the foreshore environment. It was no small feat to contact the elusive mudlarks and arrange the photoshoots over many months. He spent countless hours—in all weathers—carrying his expensive equipment through the mud to capture these images. I am grateful for his patience, determination, and professionalism. Tom's portraits are a time capsule and record of currently active mudlarks for future generations.

Over 90 mudlarks have passionately shared their finds, photos, and stories, and I am greatly appreciative of their willingness to contribute to this book. Their names appear throughout the book, which is a testament to the friendliness, kindness, strength, and overwhelming generosity of the mudlarking community in London.

I would like to thank Coral Pearce for her amazing talent in bringing artifacts to life through her stunning illustrations. She spent numerous hours over many months creating the hand-painted artwork that is featured this book.

Professional photographers Hannah Smiles, Julia Fullerton-Batten, Antoine Buchet, Jon Attenborough, Broni Lloyd-Edwards, and Neil Hall kindly gave me permission to use their beautiful photos. I am grateful for their contribution. The technical descriptions and high-resolution photos on the British Museum's Portable Antiquities Scheme have been an invaluable resource. I thank Stuart Wyatt, Kate Sumnall, and other Finds Liaison Officers at the Museum of London who dutifully recorded the mudlarks' artifacts.

Throughout the creation of the book, my gorgeous wife, Rose Sandy, has been a great motivator and adviser. She has guided me along the way and has tolerated the long hours as I focused on the book.

I would also like to thank Monika Buttling-Smith, Cheryl Sandy, Ben Scott, Matt Scott, and Anne Scott, who proofread the book before publication.

www.silvergravitypublishing.com

INDEX

Ambrogi, Stefano 139
Anderson, Liz 254, 255
Anglo-Saxon 45, 79, 80, 85, 174, 176, 194, 271
Annand, Vicky 106
Anne, Queen 122, 207, 225
Attenborough, Jon 9, 234, 297, 299
axe 127, 183, 221, 261, 274
badge 9, 116, 129, 147, 191, 211, 253, 255, 269
Bagshaw, Anthony 99
ball and chain 59, 296
bead 63, 64, 65, 66, 67, 69, 147, 188, 189
Becket, Thomas 115, 128, 129, 131, 191
bell 23, 73, 112, 115, 116, 150, 151, 152, 255
Bellarmine Museum 51, 52, 53
Beverlo, Mark 88
Billingsgate Fish Market 276
Bland, Tom 26, 27, 64
boat hooks 272
bodkin 191, 195, 196
bomb 171, 180, 181
bone 64, 70, 113, 131, 147, 155, 187, 189, 193, 195, 197, 215, 217, 218, 219, 224, 225, 247, 250, 259, 274, 275, 279, 292
Borzello, Anna 35, 36, 38, 39, 45, 46, 133, 136, 137, 192
bottle 43, 53, 95, 97, 98, 99, 101, 103, 104, 105, 106, 119, 162, 163, 180, 216, 259
Bourne, Simon 23, 32, 33, 89, 157, 158, 184, 185, 188, 232
British Museum 10, 128, 160, 176, 236, 253, 283, 286, 291, 293, 298, 299
brooch 5, 45, 79, 80, 83, 85, 89, 247
Brooker, Steve 33, 58, 59, 77, 81, 157, 165, 187, 211, 225, 244, 252, 295, 296
Brown, Peter 226
Buchet, Antoine 117, 290, 299
buckle 5, 7, 88, 249, 248, 250, 251, 252
Bucknall, Ed 22, 24, 103, 257, 291
Buddin, Dean 50
Bushell, Martin 187
Buttling-Smith, Monika 14, 24, 25, 170, 171, 178, 179, 182, 183, 195, 204, 272, 299
button 43, 119, 165, 167, 168, 169, 170, 171, 203, 211, 247
Caethoven, Sam 138, 139, 140, 141, 142, 143, 146, 147
candlestick 5, 7, 148, 150, 151, 223
Cannizzaro, Sara 13
cannon 59, 73, 177, 185, 258
Canterbury 115, 126, 128, 129, 178, 191, 255
Casati, Kit 46, 47
Celtic 63, 79, 127, 128, 129, 174, 187, 203, 212, 213, 233
chainmail 177, 178
Charles II, King 111, 167, 283
chatelaine 49, 205
Checconi, Alessio 15, 98, 246, 247
clay pipe 5, 7, 13, 14, 15, 16, 17, 18, 19, 85, 98, 119, 137, 173, 289
clock 11, 149, 152, 281, 283, 285, 286
cloth seal 199
Cobden-Sanderson, T.J. 262, 263, 264, 265, 266, 267
coin 21, 43, 57, 58, 61, 83, 109, 125, 131, 155, 157, 159, 161, 165, 211, 231, 232, 233, 235, 236, 239, 240, 241, 242, 244, 245, 257, 276
comb 131, 155, 197, 215, 216, 279
Cook, Jo 28, 29, 42, 43
cufflink 137, 206, 207, 208, 209
Cursan, Regis 242
Davey, Jason 79, 159, 203, 215
Deadman's Island 185, 187, 188
death 5, 7, 56, 58, 67, 75, 88, 116, 151, 152, 153, 167, 173, 174, 184, 185, 186, 188, 189, 209, 211, 232, 236, 264
Dixon, Charlie 192, 200, 201
Docklands 174, 277, 298

Donnellan, Tommy 129
Doré, Gustave 57
Doves Type 264, 265, 266, 267
Duff, Malcolm 54, 55, 64, 88, 194
duHeaume, Graham 8, 178, 179, 204, 205, 224, 225, 228, 229, 241, 273, 292
Dunford, John 129, 130, 131, 197
Dyer, Kevin James 236, 285
ear scoop 195, 196, 205, 218
East India Company 45, 169
Egan, Geoff 55, 253
Elizabeth I, Queen 13, 81, 169, 193, 232
Elkins, Peter 8, 292
Elton, Stuart 199
Engeham, Jack 278, 279
Engeham, Steve 278, 279
Evans, Adrian 3
Evans, Florrie 11, 31, 35, 45, 46, 48, 49, 63, 64, 66, 67, 90, 115, 122, 167, 192, 193, 195, 196, 205, 245, 285
Execution Dock 57, 58, 59
Farge, Julian 14
Fernbank, Christine 89, 102, 105, 106, 108, 109
First World War 158, 159, 162
Flanagan Lawrence Architects 294
Forlino, Giovanni 195, 196
Forsyth, Hazel 45, 72, 112, 253, 287
fossil 43, 85, 140, 141, 142, 143, 147, 201, 247
French, Francis Arthur 159
Frost Fair 144
Frozen Charlotte 74, 75
Fullerton-Batten, Julia 8, 144, 186, 299
garnets 5, 7, 44, 45, 46, 47, 87
Goode, Matthew 286
Great Fire of London 88, 149, 152, 153, 168, 279
Green, Robert 264, 265, 266
Greenwich 21, 33, 53, 58, 81, 181, 186, 240, 281, 287, 298
Guildhall Art Gallery 131, 221, 269, 295, 298
Gumbo, Philly 58, 84, 85, 259
hairpin 147, 214, 215, 247, 269
Hall, Neil 95, 299
Harrison, Tom 3, 4, 11, 21, 33, 43, 49, 55, 61, 69, 77, 85, 93, 101, 109, 119, 125, 131, 137, 147, 155, 165, 173, 183, 191, 201, 211, 221, 229, 239, 247, 255, 261, 269, 279, 299
Hazell, Judy 80, 84, 85, 259
helmet 128, 129, 181, 269
Hemery, Richard 24
Henry VIII, King 81, 167, 204, 216, 233
Hiddleston, Dave 199
Higginbotham, John 63, 73, 82, 89, 90, 151, 218, 223
Hines, Johnny 121
Hodgson, David 15, 122, 175, 216, 217, 220, 221
Horrill, Mallory 267
Hume, Ivor Noël 8, 229
Iglesias, Mark Vasco 178, 235
intaglio 43, 69, 121, 122, 123
James, King I 17, 232, 259
Jennings, Mark 202, 206, 207, 250
jeton 277, 289
jewelry 5, 7, 21, 45, 46, 47, 78, 79, 80, 83, 87, 89, 90, 91, 135, 155
John, Duncan 26
Johnson, Stephen 188
Jones, Rick 59
Key, Rex 17, 18, 19
keys 44, 119, 205, 273
Knap, Michal 97, 98, 100, 101, 219
knife 8, 19, 131, 218, 224, 229, 279, 289
knight 72, 125, 129, 178, 269, 285
Kuss, Candace 217, 219
LaMotta, Casper James 159, 160
LaMotta, Frank 159, 160

Lanoue, Nicole 233
Layton, Thomas 175
Lewis, Dr. Michael 291, 292
Love, Rae 88, 92, 93, 165
love token 83, 137, 241, 247
Main, Tom 115, 151, 249
Mayhew, Henry 272
Mayflower 5, 7, 256, 257, 258, 259, 269, 298
McKibbin, Chelsea 187
medal 5, 6, 109, 125, 158, 159, 160, 296
Medieval 9, 26, 27, 64, 80, 113, 114, 115, 121, 129, 177, 178, 183, 196, 197, 213, 215, 218, 223, 224, 226, 249, 250, 251, 253, 289, 296, 298
Meister, Wendy 46, 47
Miller, Tim 232, 238, 239, 292
Mills, John 93, 165, 194, 233, 235
Mills, Stephanie 164, 165, 235
mirror 212, 213, 252
Mud Men 55, 77, 269, 296
Muranyi-Clark, Oliver 58, 64, 65, 81, 123, 180, 233
Murphy, Alan 45, 47, 73, 85, 113, 127, 139, 185, 257, 258, 260, 261, 272, 273, 292
Museum of London 2, 5, 9, 17, 23, 45, 59, 63, 64, 69, 72, 73, 88, 112, 121, 125, 127, 129, 131, 133, 135, 167, 171, 175, 187, 194, 207, 211, 212, 215, 218, 219, 221, 226, 239, 242, 243, 250, 253, 258, 269, 277, 279, 289, 291, 292, 293, 294, 297, 298, 299
musical instruments 5, 7, 112, 113, 116
National Army Museum 6, 125, 298
National Maritime Museum 33, 295, 298
Natural History Museum 45, 145, 229, 269, 298
needle 77, 195, 197, 253
Neto, Tobias 4, 5, 6, 90, 91, 124, 125, 180, 236
Newton, Sarah 75, 105, 216, 217
Nunneley, Caroline 79, 189, 190, 191, 218
oil lamp 25, 183, 222, 223
Olivant, Peter 205, 215, 281, 282
Orlinski, Lukasz 86, 87, 90, 176, 266, 267
padlock 183, 273
Parker, Nicolette 46
Paros, Mark 26, 27, 202, 204, 213, 223, 225, 226, 237, 250, 251, 253, 285
Pearce, Coral 23, 72, 73, 76, 77, 98, 112, 121, 127, 165, 175, 283, 299
Pew, Lynne 40, 41
Phillips, Guy 64, 277
pilgrim 9, 114, 115, 128, 129, 131, 191, 211, 213, 223, 255, 292, 298
Pilson, Tony 115, 171, 177, 274, 283, 292
pirates 5, 7, 19, 56, 57, 58, 59, 272
Pitkin, Brian 178, 274
Place, Alan 17
Plum, Marie-Louise 195, 207, 210, 211
Port of London Authority 2, 8, 9, 69, 77, 93, 125, 265, 296
Portable Antiquities Scheme 10, 93, 160, 250, 279, 293, 294, 299
Posener, Nathan 33, 157, 158
pottery 2, 3, 5, 7, 10, 21, 22, 23, 24, 26, 27, 28, 29, 31, 35, 36, 37, 39, 40, 41, 49, 52, 93, 107, 119, 125, 155, 173, 183, 191, 201, 223, 226, 227, 255, 271, 279, 298
ring 43, 46, 47, 55, 63, 80, 82, 85, 88, 90, 91, 93, 116, 119, 121, 157, 178, 188, 189, 194, 207, 218, 247, 281, 282, 283, 286
Roman 6, 22, 23, 24, 25, 26, 28, 33, 43, 63, 64, 69, 70, 79, 80, 85, 121, 122, 125, 131, 147, 173, 174, 176, 183, 187, 191, 194, 201, 204, 212, 213, 214, 215, 218, 221, 222, 223, 227, 232, 233, 235, 239, 242, 247, 249, 269, 279, 282, 283, 286, 287, 291, 295, 296, 298
Roman Amphitheatre 131, 221, 269, 295, 298
Ross, Alan 121
Rotherhithe 29, 170, 256, 257, 258, 259, 269, 273, 275
Russell, Malcolm 82, 171, 172, 173, 193, 216

Sandy, Jason 268, 269
Sandy, Jayden 154, 155
sceat 235, 236
Scott , Kirsti 1, 2, 299
seal matrix 120, 121, 123
Second World War 255
shark 69, 119, 140, 287
shield 26, 64, 82, 127, 128, 129, 177, 199, 237, 277
Sibthorpe, Fran 65, 68, 69
skull 67, 85, 88, 139, 185, 187, 188, 189, 211
Smiles, Hannah 16, 25, 49, 59, 64, 70, 237, 289, 299
Smith, Ian 9, 115, 236, 282, 286, 288, 289, 292
Society of Thames Mudlarks 8, 9, 85, 93, 109, 131, 165, 261, 291, 292
Southwark 185, 191, 243, 244, 279
Sowden, Mark 227
spear 24, 176
Spencer, Brian 289, 292
spoon 61, 225, 239, 247
St. Paul's Cathedral 4, 6, 152, 295
Stevens, Nick 58, 75, 77, 140, 208, 226, 295, 296
Sumnall, Kate 5, 59, 299
Suttie, Alan 82, 222, 223
sword 45, 72, 125, 129, 131, 176, 178, 224, 232, 253
tankard 55, 226, 239
teeth 55, 69, 109, 114, 139, 140, 187, 188, 215, 216, 217, 221
Thames Discovery Programme 69
Thames Festival Trust 3
Thames Museum 294, 295, 298
thimble 196, 197, 198, 205
Thira, Tony 17, 81, 114, 129, 199
tools 127, 158, 195, 218, 257, 261, 271, 272, 273, 274, 275, 277
toothpaste 217, 219
Totally Thames Festival 49, 69, 295
Tower of London 69, 131, 143, 155, 177, 179, 227, 232, 236, 271, 298
toy 71, 72, 73, 74, 213, 279, 286, 287
trade token 58, 69, 101, 149, 150, 151, 152, 153, 277
Trim, Steve 23, 188
Tudor 6, 13, 29, 43, 49, 73, 77, 79, 81, 83, 85, 125, 147, 155, 167, 173, 183, 191, 194, 203, 204, 205, 215, 216, 218, 223, 232, 243, 247, 253, 271, 273, 279, 281, 289
Upritchard, Hannah 46, 47
Victoria and Albert Museum 65, 80, 87, 269, 298
Victoria Cross 5, 6, 125, 296
Victorian 5, 7, 3, 8, 13, 14, 15, 17, 18, 19, 35, 36, 37, 46, 55, 61, 66, 71, 74, 89, 102, 104, 113, 137, 144, 161, 167, 171, 173, 179, 192, 193, 206, 212, 216, 217, 219, 221, 239, 241, 245, 289
Viking 176, 298
Virgo, Matthew 159
Wakeman, Pete 258
Walker, Emery 263, 264, 267, 269
Walker, Mike 57, 60, 61, 81, 122, 180, 202, 208, 285
Walker, Paige 118, 119
Wapping 56, 150, 165, 170, 277, 298
watch winder 122, 285
Watermen 243, 277, 295
weapons 5, 7, 73, 127, 174, 175, 176, 177, 181, 183
whistle 114, 115
White, Nicola 14, 15, 20, 21, 98, 103, 104, 106, 107, 113, 114, 145, 158, 162, 163, 181
wig curler 216
Wise, Jacqui 34, 35, 36, 39, 41
Worshipful Company of Cutlers 224, 229, 292
Wright, Alex 51, 52, 53
Wyatt, Stuart 194, 202, 222, 293, 299